KNOW YOUR
PFAFF

KNOW YOUR PFAFF

JACKIE DODSON
with AUDREY GRIESE

CHILTON TRADE BOOK PUBLISHING

RADNOR, PENNSYLVANIA

Published in Radnor, Pennsylvania 19089,
by Chilton Trade Book Publishing
No part of this book may be reproduced, transmitted or stored
in any form or by any means, electronic or mechanical,
without prior written permission from the publisher

Designed by William E. Lickfield
Manufactured in the United States of America

Library of Congress Cataloging in Publication Data
    Know your pfaff.
    (Creative machine arts)
    Bibliography: p. 193
    Includes index.
    1. Machine sewing.   2. Sewing machines.   I. Title.
II. Series: Creative machine arts series.
TT713.D636   1988   646.2'044   87-48013
ISBN 0-8019-7869-6 (pbk.)

2 3 4 5 6 7 8 9 0   7 6 5 4 3 2 1 0 9

Contents

Foreword

In 1987, we published a book by Jackie Dodson called Know Your Bernina. *Jackie and I had met more than ten years ago on a tour bus in Chicago. Since then, she has showered me with wacky, inspiring letters. This is a woman who is brimming with laughter and ideas, sharing both freely. Most of the letters arrived with swatches of machine-embroidered fabric pinned to them. "Have you tried this?" she'd ask, again and again.*

When it came time to revise my machine-embroidery book, I knew who to ask for help as a designer and critic: Jackie. Next I asked her to write a book about her teaching methods; the result was the Bernina book.

The Chilton editors and I knew Know Your Bernina *was a good book, but even we were surprised at the enthusiastic response: we had to reprint it four times in the first six months. We also received letters and calls from storeowners and home sewers saying, "I bought the book, even though I don't have a Bernina—but I wish you'd publish one for my brand."*

So we did. In April, 1988, we published a generic version called Know Your Sewing Machine. *Having taught on all major brands of sewing machine, Jackie adapted her techniques to include all of them. She kept the same lesson format, but changed all the tote bag squares and some of the projects, added a chapter on using decorative stitches, and showed some of the projects on color pages, along with inspiring artists' work.*

But as the second book developed, Jackie and I realized we could barely touch on the unique features of each brand. Like cars or computers, sewing machines are not all alike. They each have special features, stitches, feet, capabilities: that's why Jackie and I own so many machines. (We've been known to buy a brand-new computer sewing-machine that does everything but your income taxes . . .and to hold onto four old machines "because I love the feather stitch on this one and the buttonhole on this one and I'm keeping this one in case my daughter wants it and this one in case all the others fail."

So Know Your Pfaff *was born. I contacted Audrey Griese, whose work I had admired for years. In Champlin, Minnesota, Audrey and her husband*

Walt own A-1 Sew Craft Sewing Center. Audrey wrote an excellent column on machine embroidery for "Stitch and Sew." Through the years, she has shared some wonderfully inventive ideas that she teaches in her store.

Audrey stitched her way through the entire manuscript, making changes appropriate to Pfaff machines. Again, Jackie changed all the tote bag squares and many of the project designs. Then Audrey wrote two special sections— "Why I Love My Pfaff" in Chapter 1 and Chapter 11 on using Pfaff's unique decorative stitches. Meanwhile, we canvassed the country, looking for creative work done on the Pfaff, which we've shown on the color pages (and it is only the tip of the iceberg—we wish we could have included much more).

We are also publishing versions for other brands—Elna, New Home, Singer, Viking, and a revised Bernina book, so far—in which knowledgable co-authors have adapted the book to their brand and have contributed a unique chapter on decorative stitches. Each Chapter 11 is completely different, as are all of the tote bag squares, so even if you don't own that brand, be sure to read the book. Your head will be filled with enough ideas to make clever gifts, garments, and accessories for many years to come.

And best of all, after stitching your way through the book, you will truly know your Pfaff.

Robbie Fanning

Series Editor, Creative Machine Arts, and co-author
The Complete Book of Machine Embroidery

Are you interested in a quarterly magazine about creative uses of the sewing machine? Robbie Fanning and Jackie Dodson are planning to start one. For more information, write:
The Creative Machine
PO Box 2634, Ste. 2
Menlo Park, CA 94026

Preface

When our children were small, we took long car trips. I remember one that took longer than planned. We all grumbled about being lost, but one of our boys said, "It's just one of Dad's long-cuts."

We loved that new word, so we came up with dictionary meanings.

Long-cut (noun): When it takes longer, but Dad convinces everyone he wanted it that way. A "little something extra." An adventure. An educational side-trip. You are happier when you finally reach your destination. And so on.

What does this have to do with the sewing machine? This book contains long-cuts, those adventurous techniques that help you and your sewing machine create something special, something out of the ordinary.

Most of us learned basic techniques of sewing when we bought our machines—how to thread it, wind a bobbin, make a buttonhole, sew a straight seam. We were shown each presser foot and how to use it. . . and, I'll bet, except for the zipper and buttonhole feet, you haven't looked at those other feet again.

But there's so much more to learn. Join me on an educational side-trip. By the time you're done with this book, you'll truly know your machine.

Let's begin by exploring how we can change a piece of fabric: we can add texture to it, appliqué it, quilt it, stitch across holes in it, draw thread out of it, gather it up and decorate it. We can stitch in space with our sewing machines, make cording–but, more importantly, once we understand the machine, it makes all our stitching easier.

As we explore all these effects, which are presented in 40 lessons, we'll make small samples for a notebook; make finished 6" squares to fit on a totebag, displaying what we've learned; and make more than 25 other projects. In the process of stitching the samples and projects in the book, you'll take an educational side-trip as well. You'll learn to adjust and manipulate your sewing machine until you can use it to its full potential.

This workbook of ideas does not take the place of your basic manuals. Instead, it is to be used as a reinforcement and supplement to what you already know. By working through the lessons, you will come to know your machine better.

Yes, there is much more to sewing than straight stitching. And wouldn't you rather go that long-cut route–to make your stitching more interesting and original?

In my classes I often hear this progression: "I can't do that" to "Can I really do that?" to "I can do that!" I hope this book is the next best thing to having me prompting, prodding, patting you on the back in person.

Jackie Dodson
LaGrange Park, Illinois

Acknowledgments

Thank you:

To Debbie Evans and Elvi Tarien, especially; to Jackie Toole, Glenna Good, Ranier Moser, Herb Wild and all of the wonderful people at Pfaff. They have been a joy for me to work with, both as a dealer and as an author.

To my husband Walter, and my good friend Darlene Tollison, for their help and support while this was being written.

To Theta Happ, who shared ideas when I called her out of the blue and she didn't know me from Adam.

To my students, whose classes got put on hold while *Know Your Pfaff* was underway, for constant encouragement and for asking "When will the book be ready?"

To Robbie Fanning, who got me into this in the first place, and who was always supportive.

To my co-author, Jackie, for her support and encouragement, and especially for her endless sense of humor in the face of all calamities.

A.G.

Thank You:

To all the friends who answered questions when I needed help. To Elvi Tarien and Jacquelin Toole at Pfaff American Sales Corp., who supplied me with information and help when I needed it.

And to Deborah Evans, also at Pfaff, who opened up a new world of computer-assisted creativity for me.

To Caryl Rae Hancock, Nora Lou Kampe, Gail Kibiger, Pat Pasquini and Marcia Strickland for sharing ideas; Ladi Tisol who helped me before I had to ask; and Marilyn Tisol, critic, sounding-board, and special friend.

To Chuck, who took the photos, and to the rest of my family.

To Robbie Fanning, for her optimism, encouragement, and endless support.

And to Audrey, whose hard work makes this book special, whose dry humor made my work fun.

J.D.

KNOW YOUR
PFAFF

CHAPTER 1

Getting Started

by AUDREY GRIESE

This book is organized by the changes you can make to a piece of fabric – add stitches, add texture, subtract threads, and so on. Following this introductory chapter, each chapter consists of several lessons, and some projects. Each lesson asks you to stitch up practice samples for a notebook or for finished projects. The largest project in the book is the tote bag (directions for making it are in Chapter 12). It was designed to show off interchangeable decorative squares, which you'll make as you proceed through the lessons.

For the practice samples, you will want to set up a three-ring notebook – the kind with the largest rings – to keep track of your stitching (Fig. 1.1). Buy plastic pockets and blank notebook paper (both available at office supply stores). Write the settings you've used directly on the stitched samples and slip them into the plastic pockets for future reference.

Clip pictures from magazines that trigger ideas. Ask yourself: Could I get that effect if I loosened the bobbin? Which presser foot would I use for that? Which thread

Fig. 1.1 A reference notebook, open to a page of stitch samples. Notations on the stitchery will help you reset the machine.

would produce loops like that? Write notes to yourself with ideas to try and add these to the notebook along with the magazine pictures.

Why I love my Pfaff Creative

When I bought my first Pfaff back in the early 1970s, I had had ample experience with sewing machines and knew the good points and bad features of every make, because I was in that line of business. I firmly believe in knowing my competition, as well as the lines of machines I sell. I might add that, at that time, I wasn't selling Pfaffs, but was concentrating on two other major European brands.

All of the European machines were of good quality and offered good warranties. However, there were some major differences among the features offered. Most had numerous decorative stitches in addition to the utility stitches, either through the addition of cams or through a built-in automatic mechanism.

I liked working with the automatic stitches. In many respects they were more challenging than doing the free machining that I had been taught years ago on my old straight-stitch machine. While I found it boring to stitch these automatic decorative stitches in a straight line, I truly enjoyed finding novel ways of using them for special effects.

One thing that impressed me then was that Pfaff allowed me to combine the automatic decorative and utility stitches to create more stitches, and that the decorative satin stitches could be elongated for different uses without losing the density of the satin stitch.

From a practical viewpoint, however, Pfaff had a feature that made it stand out over every other machine on the market: the dual-feeding system with built-in walking foot. On the Pfaff, this system is an integral part of the machine; on other brands, it's a jury-rigged afterthought that

all too often does not do the job and creates more problems than it solves. With the dual feed, I could sew any kind of fabric without slipping, shifting, sliding, or puckering. The stitches were perfect every time and I literally did not have to touch the fabric.

It was truly a pleasure to sew without having to stretch, tug, grease, powder, or line with paper whatever fabric I happened to be working on. Because sewing became easier and faster, I had more time for the "fun stuff"—automatic stitchery, free-machine stitchery, lacemaking, and all the other techniques that were possible.

The electronic control made precision stitching (for example, one stitch at a time for some of the lace techniques) so easy and, at the same time, gave the needle penetration power on any type of heavy fabric or leather.

The full rotary bobbin mechanism was smooth running, jam-proof and vibration free, unlike the old oscillating machines which, unless they weighed a ton, vibrated off the table. This made my machine portable, so I could take it with me wherever I wanted to go. The bobbin was easily wound (it could even be wound while sewing), easily changed, and the bobbin tension easily adjusted.

Because the top tension was calibrated, it could easily be changed and returned to its original setting. Threading the machine was also easy and because of the needle threader, I could use many different colors in my stitchery without wasting a lot of time trying to locate the eye of the needle. I was finding that, as I got older, either my arm had gotten shorter, or the eye of the needle smaller, so the needle threader was a real plus.

The machine accepted very large size needles for other projects. Experimentation showed that it would take a size 150, enabling me to sew with yarn as a needle thread.

When the first computerized machines came on the market, I wan't even tempted by them. My Pfaff was too good and too reliable to be traded for anything else. However, the Pfaff Creative 1471 was another story. This was not merely a computerized sewing machine, but a *sewing computer*. When the 1471 was introduced, it was love at first sight. Here at last was the machine that I had always dreamed of—one that combined all the good features of my old Pfaff and added many more. Finally, I could create the stitches I wanted and needed, and could leave them in the machine as long as necessary. I could treat these personally designed stitches the same as the ones already in the machine, in that they could be widened, narrowed, lengthened, shortened, balanced, and incorporated with everything else, including utility stitches, in the memory. It was truly an incredible sewing experience.

The bobbin sensor light told me when I was running low on bobbin thread, so I no longer ran out at a crucial point. The needle stopped up or down, and thread delivery was smooth from a horizontal spool pin, eliminating the hassle of using rayon threads. There were so many features, it would be impossible to list all that I love.

Computer technology made precise stitch lengths and widths a reality, and teaching customers to use these machines was unbelievably easy.

My old Pfaff started gathering dust, so I finally sold it to a lady who was looking for a good starter machine for her daughter. She has informed me that instead she uses it and that she gave her other machine to the girl. She is constantly amazed that even this well-used machine is still so solid and quiet running.

All of my friends have Pfaff Creatives. We meet regularly to exchange ideas and, needless to say, they are excited about *Know Your Pfaff* and about sharing sewing ideas with others.

Presser feet and attachments

Each Pfaff Creative 1471 comes with standard accessories and presser feet. Additional presser feet and accessories are available, relatively inexpensively, which means that everyone can easily afford them.

The Creative is a short-shank machine. You may be able to use some generic attachments if you remove the shank along with the foot itself, as long as they do not interfere with the dual-feed mechanism. When using other attachments the needle hole on the attachment foot must be wide enough to accommodate the Pfaff Creative's 6mm stitch width.

If you use only the attachments designed for the Pfaff Creative 1471, however, you won't be limited in any way. Most attachments have many uses and will cover every sewing operation you can devise.

Many people who sew do not use even the standard attachments that come with the machine because they do not know when to use them. Pfaff has solved this problem with the built-in visual readout key. Bring up whatever stitch program you desire, press the button to the right of the display, and you will see whether or not to use the dual feed with that stitch, where to set the tension, and what foot to use.

Chart 1.1 shows the presser feet and accessories provided with the Pfaff 1471 Creative, and Chart 1.2 shows the presser feet and accessories that are available as extra options. We'll briefly discuss these attachments and how they're used.

Foot #0

The ordinary sewing foot is numbered "0" in your attachment box, and is made of metal with a clear plastic center. This greatly increases visibility while you are sewing. It is cut out in back to accommodate the dual feed. The bottom is smooth and flat, so it will hold the fabric securely

Chart 1.1 Standard Feet and Accessories for Pfaff Creative

Number	Uses	Part Number
0	Ordinary sewing foot	98-694-816-00
1	Fancy-stitch foot with dual feed	98-694-814-00
2	Fancy-stitch foot without dual feed	98-694-897-00
3	Blindstitch and overlock foot	98-684-890-00
4	Zipper and edge stitching foot	98-694-884-00
5	Buttonhole foot	98-694-882-00
6	Darning foot	93-035-960-91
7	Hemming foot	98-694-818-00
8	Edge guide	98-802-422-00

while you are sewing. As the upper and lower feed dogs engage to move the fabric, the foot lifts slightly, thereby eliminating fabric shift and slippage and, in the case of fine fabrics, the "dog tracks" on the bottom layer.

Foot #1

Foot #1 is a fancy stitch foot that will accommodate the dual feed mechanism. It differs from foot "0" in that it has double grooves on the bottom, making it ideal for the keyhole buttonhole. I like to use it when I am doing decorative topstitching on problem fabrics, or using the satin stitch to quilt several layers of fabric.

The exact needle position is marked with red lines at right angles to the direction of stitching, making it simple to line up and start that first stitch when doing precision sewing.

Foot #2

A fancy stitch foot, #2 does not have the accommodation for dual feed. This foot is also raised on the bottom but does not have the double groove in front. It also has the red lines to aid alignment of patterns. You will note, as with the two previous feet, it has a clear plastic center.

Foot #3

The blindstitch and overlock foot is #3. It has a movable guide so that you can accurately blindstitch your hems, and the little wire to the right of the needle opening keeps the edge of the fabric flat when you are doing the overlock stitches or stretch blind hems.

This foot is cut out to accommodate the dual feed. I also use the adjustable guide as an aid when stitching in the ditch, edge stitching or topstitching.

Foot #4

Foot #4 is the zipper and edge stitching foot. The two prongs go to the back when you are snapping it on the shank, and are there to accommodate the dual feed, either in the right or left position. It is excellent for cording and piping seams, edge stitching of all kinds, as well as for zippers.

Foot #5

The sliding buttonhole foot is #5. This is used exclusively with program 86, the memory buttonhole. Because of the design of this foot, it is easy to make a corded buttonhole.

Chart 1.2 Optional Accessories for Pfaff Creative

Accessory	Sewing Operation	Part number
Appliqué foot	For appliqué work	93-042941-91
Binder	Binding edges with tape	98-053484-91
Cording foot (5-groove)	Cording work (needle size 80)	93-042950-91
Cording foot (7-groove)	Cording work (needle size 70)	93-042953-91
Cording blade (2 sizes)		93-035952-45
Fringe sewing foot	Sewing fringes, pattern marking, basting	93-042943-91
Straight stitch foot	Topstitching and sewing very delicate fabrics	98-694821-00
Needle plate (straight stitch)		98-694822-00
Felling foot, 4.5mm	Felled seams	93-042046-91
Felling foot, 6.5mm	Felled seams	93-042948-91
Shirring foot	Shirring	93-036998-91
Single-needle cording foot	Single needle cording	93-036915-91
Eyeletting plate	Making eyelets	93-036975-45
Knit-edge sewing foot	Sewing knitted fabrics	93-042957-91
Rolled hem foot, 4mm	Wider rolled hems	98-694823-00

Foot #6

Foot #6 is the darning foot, used for non-automatic darning. The feed dogs are lowered and the fabric moved manually. It can also be used for free stitchery techniques if use of a hoop is not feasible.

Foot #7

The rolled hem foot is #7, used for neatly turning up a narrow hem in fine- to medium-weight fabrics. It is possible to use decorative stitches with this foot.

Accessory #8

The edge guide, accessory #8, should be used if you have a problem following an even seam line. I use it for accurately spacing rows of decorative stitching, and for circular stitching by putting the fabric in a hoop and allowing the guide to follow around the inside of the hoop.

The optional attachments available from your dealer are shown in Chart 1.2, along with part numbers.

Appliqué foot

This small plastic foot will accommodate the 6mm needle width, and is cut out on the bottom with a groove to accommodate the satin stitching. This cutout is flared in back to make turning corners easier. The left front side is contoured underneath for ease in guiding the foot over the appliqué.

Bias binder

This foot accommodates many different widths of prefolded bias tape, in addition to flat, unfolded bias strips. The foot can be used with zigzag and decorative stitches. Use of this foot requires the removal of the presser foot shank, as it is not a snap-on attachment.

Cording feet and blades

The cording feet, 5-groove and 7-groove, along with the cording blades, are designed for use with double needles for straight lines of pintucks. Needle hole is a maximum of 4mm.

Fringe foot

The fringe sewing foot is used for decorative fringe stitches, as well as tailor tacking. It may also be used for basting and making thread shanks when sewing on buttons.

Straight stitch foot and plate

A straight stitch foot is available with back cut out to accommodate dual feed. It has a clear plastic center for visibility. A special needle plate with a small round hole is included.

Felling feet

The felling feet come in two sizes and are nice to use if you make a lot of flat-felled seams. The large size needle hole will enable you to use a decorative stitch on these seams.

Shirring foot

The shirring foot is designed primarily to shirr and attach a ruffle to the fabric at the same time.

Single-needle cording foot

The single-needle cording foot is used for couching decorative and heavy threads to fabric. Tiny slots on top will help guide threads in the right- and left-needle position, and one groove underneath will guide yarn or thread put through the hole in the needle plate.

The cutout on the back of the underside of the foot enables you to turn corners, still keeping the cords evenly spaced.

Eyelet plate

The eyeletting plate is plastic, snaps on easily, and is used for making both conventional and decorative eyelets.

Knit-edge foot

The knit-edge sewing foot is used for sewing bulky knit fabrics neatly. Because of the design, it is an excellent foot for sewing on bulky cords, yarn, and even strings of beads and sequins. The large needle hole will accommodate the full 6mm width.

"Unwinding collars"

I have added to my machine extra "unwinding collars," as they are called in the instruction book. The small ones serve to stabilize the tubes of thread and, as I sometimes forget to take them out of the ends of the tubes when I change thread, I've acquired a few spares. I especially like the large collars because they make it easy to use all kinds of different spools on my machine. Ask your dealer to order extras, if he does not have them in stock.

Circle maker

Older Pfaff machines from the 1950s had an expensive, complicated circular stitching attachment (no longer available). You can easily fashion a circle maker for your Pfaff Creative 1471, using transparent tape, a thumb tack and a hoop. Determine the radius of the circle you wish to stitch. Measure that distance from the needle to a place at the left of it on the machine bed. Place a tack there, point up. Hold the tack in place by pushing the tape over the point and sticking it onto the machine (Fig. 1.2).

Then stretch your fabric into the hoop and place the center of the circle over the tack. Push a small cork or eraser over the point. When you rotate the hoop and stitch, you'll create a perfect circle.

If your fabric is heavy enough, or if the diameter of the circle is larger than the

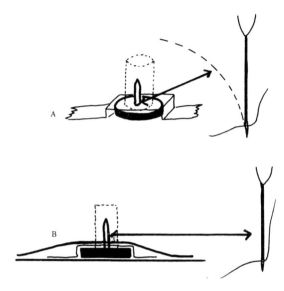

A

B

Fig. 1.2 A. Make your own circle maker by taping a thumbtack upside-down on the bed of the machine a radius away from the needle. Tape it in place. B. Place material in a hoop and stick the fabric onto the thumbtack wherever you want the center of the circle to be. Secure the fabric with a cork. Keep the fabric taut between the thumbtack and the needle as you sew a circular design.

hoop, you can use the dual feed with either the ordinary foot #0 or fancy stitch foot #1 and allow the machine to feed the fabric, keeping it taut between the needle and tack.

4mm rolled hem foot

This foot makes a wider rolled hem, making it practical to use on heavier fabrics. The foot has the back cut out to accommodate the dual feed, whereas foot #7 in the attachment box does not.

Supplies

In addition to your sewing machine and a good supply of threads, here's a shopping list of what you'll need for the lessons.

(Each lesson will give you a detailed materials list). You probably have many of the supplies in your sewing room.

1. Scissors and shears: sharp embroidery scissors, plus shears for cutting fabric and paper-cutting scissors
2. Water-erasable markers for light fabrics; white opaque permanent marker for water-soluble stabilizer; slivers of soap or light-colored chalk pencils for dark fabrics; vanishing markers
3. T square or 6″ × 24″ (15.2cm × 61.0cm) plastic ruler; 6″ (15.2cm) and 12″ (30.5cm) see-through rulers are also helpful; protractor for drawing perfect angles (available at stationery and art stores)
4. Wood and spring-type hoops in varied sizes, maximum 7″ (17.8cm) for ease
5. Rotary cutting wheel; extra blades; mat
6. Extra bobbin case (optional)
7. Graph paper and Programming sheets
8. Tweezers (optional)

Have fabric ready for stitching samples. A handy size is a 9″ (22.9cm) square. It will fit in the 7″ (17.8cm) hoop and can be trimmed slightly for your notebook. Cut up a variety of fabrics from extra-light-weight types like organdy, lightweights like calicos, and medium-weight poplins, to heavy-weight denim. Extra-heavy-weight canvas scraps will be left over from your tote bag and can be used for experiments.

In the projects, you'll also use felt, transparent fabrics, bridal veil, ⅛″ (3.2mm) and ½″ (12.7mm) satin double-faced ribbon, lace insertion, scalloped lace, lace beading, Battenberg tape, fleece, batting, stabilizers and fusibles. Now let's discuss your choices of threads needles, and other supplies.

Threads

One of the most useful charts I have in my notebook is a piece of doubled fabric with line after line of satin stitches on it.

Each row is stitched using a different type of thread. I recommend that you make one, too. More important than telling you which thread to use, your chart will graphically convince you that what is called machine-embroidery cotton is usually more lustrous and covers an area more quickly and more beautifully than regular sewing thread. It's easy to compare differences among threads.

Generally, sewing threads are not used for machine embroidery. Ordinary sewing threads are usually thicker, stretch more (if polyester), and do not cover as well as machine embroidery threads. However, for durability or when you need a certain color, try using a high quality sewing thread. I never use thread from the sale bin—the ones that are three spools for 88 cents. This thread does not hold up to heavy use; it breaks, shrinks, knots, and, after all the time spent stitching with it, looks sloppy. If I am going to take the time to sew or embroider anything, then it deserves quality thread.

Machine embroidery rayons and cottons are more lustrous and have a softer twist than ordinary sewing thread. Rayon embroidery threads are silky and loosely twisted, but if you use a #90 needle and sew evenly and at a moderate speed, they are easy to use. However, don't use rayons or any other machine embroidery threads for clothing construction because they aren't strong enough.

Besides regular sewing threads and those used for machine embroidery, there are others to become acquainted with. The fine nylon used for lingerie and woolly overlock used for serging are just a couple of them. Another is darning thread: It's often used on the bobbin for machine embroidery because it's lightweight and you can get so much more of it wound on. It comes in only a few colors, so it cannot always be used should you want the bobbin thread to be seen on the surface.

Monofilament, another popular thread,

comes in two shades. One blends into light-colored fabrics, the other darks. It is not the wild, fish-line type anymore, so don't be afraid of making it work.

If you use silk and silk buttonhole twists as well as fine pearl cottons, crochet and cordonnet, the needle must be large enough to keep the threads from fraying against the fabric and the eye large enough to enable the thread to go through smoothly. Sometimes top-stitching needles are called for. Or you may have to use a needle larger than you normally would embroider with.

Waxed or glacé finished quilting thread should never be used on your machine, as the finish wears off and does your machine no good.

Chart 1.3 is a handy guide, showing which needles and threads to use with which fabrics. More about where to purchase threads can be found in Sources of Supplies at the end of the book.

Needles

It is important to choose the right needle for the job. Match fabric weight, thread, and needle size, as well as type of material. The lighter the material, the smaller the needle and finer the thread should be. The heavier the fabric, the larger the needle should be.

Like presser feet, needles come in different sizes and shapes and produce different effects. I once had a student in quilting class who struggled to get a needle out of her machine—it was rusted in. "I don't do much sewing," she said. (Why didn't that surprise me?) No matter how mind-boggling this sounds, I know that few sewers change needles unless they break, even though a new needle keeps thread from fraying, fabric from being damaged, and your stitches from skipping. The correct size and shape enables you to stitch through the heaviest or the flimsiest materials with ease. Also, hemstitching and

8

Chart 1.3
Needle and Thread Chart

Fabric	Thread	Needles
Very heavy (upholstery, canvas, denim)	Heavy-duty cotton; polyester; buttonhole twist; cordonnet	18 (110)
Heavy (sailcloth, heavy coating)	Heavy-duty cotton; polyester	16 (100)
Medium weight (wool, poplin, velvet)	Ordinary sewing cotton and polyester; machine-embroidery cotton and rayon	12, 14 (80, 90)
Lightweight (shirt cotton, dress fabrics, silk)	Extra-fine to ordinary sewing cotton and polyester	9, 11 (65, 75)
Very lightweight (lace, net, organdy, batiste)	Extra-fine sewing cotton and polyester	8, 9 (60, 65)

double needles allow you to create unique, decorative work.

But all needles do not fit all machines. Your Pfaff uses the 130/705 H system made by Schmetz.

	Very Fine	Fine	Med.	Strong	Large	Very Large
U.S.	8, 9	10	11, 12	14	16	18
Europe.	60, 65	70	75, 80	90	100	110

Needles are available in pierce point, used for woven fabrics; and ball point, used for knits to minimize cutting threads and causing runs in the fabric. The universal-point needle is all-purpose and can be used for knits, as well as woven fabrics. Instead of cutting through the fabric, the slightly rounded point deflects off the threads and slips between them. Because of its versatility, it is the needle in greatest use today.

Following is a list of needles and their uses:

Universal Needles: All-purpose sewing.
Fine Ballpoint Needles: Fine fabrics, including knits and wovens.
Medium Ballpoint Needles: Heavier knitted fabrics.
Medium Ballpoint Stretch Needles: Special needles for problem stretch fabrics.
Extra-Fine Point Needles: Used to pierce closely woven fabrics such as canvas or denim; often called jeans needles.
Topstitching Needles: Equipped with an eye and thread groove larger than a regular needle of the same size. Use buttonhole twist or double thread when topstitching. Use them for embroidery, too.
"Freddie" Needles: Deborah Evans of Pfaff American Sales Corporation gave the nickname "Freddies" to the 103FR needle. This is a totally different needle system, used originally on the old Free-Westinghouse sewing machines manufactured in the 1920s. It is a shorter needle, although it does have the same diameter flat shank.

When this needle is put in the Pfaff

Creative, it produces a long basting stitch. The machine is set on the widest zigzag, and depending on the length of the zigzag stitch, you will get long straight stitches on the right swing, because it is skipping the stitches on the left swing. This is handy if you need to do really long basting stitches and the longest normal straight stitch will not suffice.

"Freddies" come in sizes 80, 90 and 100, which means that you can use a heavier thread or even a double thread for topstitching.

Experiment for yourself on other uses for "Freddies."

Double and Triple Needles: Used for sewing with more than one thread on top. Double needles come in six sizes (1.6mm, 1.8mm, 2mm, 2.5mm, 3mm, 4mm).

Hemstitching Needles: Double and single types.

Leather Needles: Often called wedge needles because of their cutting points. Use them on real suede and leather. Or use a regular #110 needle in place of a leather needle. Another needle which works particularly well on clingy deerskin or Ultrasuede is the #90/14 stretch needle.

To keep your machine running trouble-free, change the needle often. Be sure the needle is straight and has no burr on the point. Damaged needles damage fabric and machines.

If your machine is noisy and is skipping stitches, change the needle (assuming the machine is clean). Be sure you've used the correct needle system for your machine and be certain you've placed the needle in the machine correctly. Most of the time a damaged needle is the only problem—and an easy one to rectify.

To make it easier for you to prepare appropriate supplies before beginning the lessons, let's discuss items often called for and the terms I'll use.

Batting, fleece, and fiberfill

Batting, both cotton and polyester, is used between fabric layers for quilting. Different weights and sizes are available, as well as different qualities. For our use, most of the projects can be quilted with bonded batting, which holds together firmly, or with fleece, which is a filler that's thinner than bonded batting and about as thick as a heavy wool blanket. Alternative fillers can be flannel, when only a light garment is desired, or a wool blanket. Fiberfill is the shredded batting used to fill toys. Or stuff toys with batting.

Fusibles

Fusibles are used to hold appliqués to background fabrics so edges are held firmly for the final step of stitching them in place. Plastic sandwich bags or cleaner's garment bags can be used. Stitch Witchery, Fine Fuse, Magic Polyweb and Jiffy Fuse are commercial fusible webbings. To use, place them between two pieces of fabric and press with a hot iron until the webbing melts and holds the two fabrics together. Use a Teflon pressing sheet to protect your iron and also to allow you to press the fusible to one fabric at a time. The Applique Pressing Sheet or Teflon sheet has eliminated any problem with the fusible melting on your iron: it looks like opaque wax paper, is reusable, and comes in handy sizes.

A fusible webbing already backed by paper, which saves one step in application, is called Wonder-Under Transfer Fusing Web. Draw your design directly onto the paper and place it, rough side down, on the wrong side of the appliqué fabric. Press for a few seconds, which fuses the webbing to the fabric. Then cut out the pattern and pull the paper away from the webbing. Place the appliqué on the fabric, with a damp cloth over it, and press. Stitch the appliqué onto a background fabric.

Appliqué papers are paper-backed products that look very much like freezer wrap, but act like the transfer web. One side of the paper has a glue finish.

See Chapter 4 for more about fusibles.

Stabilizers

Stabilizers are used behind fabric to keep it from puckering when you embroider. At one time, we used typing paper, but today we have more choices of stabilizers, available at fabric and quilt shops and through mail-order (see Sources of Supplies).

The old standby, typing paper, still does the job. Or, use shelf paper when stitching large pictures and adding-machine tape for long strips of embroidery. A problem with paper is that it dulls machine needles faster than tear-away stabilizers do. It's also harder to remove from the back of the embroidery, although dampening the paper will help.

Another stabilizer you probably have in the cupboard is plastic-coated freezer wrap. I find I'm using it more and more. If I'm embroidering a fabric that could be damaged by the hoop, I back it instead with freezer wrap, which I iron to the back of the fabric. The freezer paper adheres to the fabric and stiffens it. When I finish my embroidery, I peel off the freezer paper. I like using it if I have a small piece of fabric to embroider. I iron the small piece to a larger, easier-to-manipulate piece of freezer paper.

Tear-away stabilizers come in crisp or soft finishes and some are iron-ons. When embroidering, place them between the fabric and machine. When the embroidery is completed, they tear away from the fabric easily.

Don't confuse stabilizers with interfacings. Interfacings are permanent and don't tear away. They can be used, of course, and so can fabrics like organdy, but they are usually used when you plan to leave the stabilizer on the back of the embroidery after it's completed.

One of the newest stabilizers is a thin film of plastic, available by the sheet or the yard, that will dissolve when wet. Clamp it into the hoop along with the fabric. It is transparent, and can be used on top of the embroidery, too. It can be marked on, but choose a water-erasable marker or permanent white opaque marker that will not leave ink on your embroidery when the plastic is dissolved. When your embroidery is completed, rinse out the stabilizer. It will become gooey, then disappear. I'll refer to it as water-soluble stabilizer.

Helpful hints for sewing

Before beginning to sew, check out the following general helpful hints:

1. Because settings on a computer machine are extremely accurate, you may have to change the suggested settings only due to fabric and thread differences, or if you prefer different ones.

2. Take your sewing machine in for regular check-ups whether you think it needs it or not. Between checkups, keep it clean and oil the hook occasionally. The mechanical parts of computer machines need different lubrication, but this is a job for your Certified Pfaff dealer. Take it easy. There are more problems with too much oil on the hook than with too little. You will need only one drop of oil, so it will be safe to oil *before* sewing rather than when your sewing is completed, without staining the fabric.

3. You must keep the inside free of lint and threads. Clean the bobbin area by first removing the bobbin, then wiping out all the lint. A Q-tip works well and so does canned air. It's used for cameras and is wonderful to blow out lint from hard-to-reach areas. I sometimes vacuum out lint from inside the machine. Remember to clean the feed dogs whenever you finish

sewing or during a long period of stitching nappy fabrics such as corduroy, fur, or velvets. This is especially important because of the bobbin thread sensor. It will not operate if the machine is dirty.

After the inside has been freed of lint, put a single drop of oil on the hook.

Now gather your supplies together and begin the adventure—to know your Pfaff.

I ♥ MY PFAFF CREATIVE

Tote Bag Squares: (upper left, clockwise) Chapter 11—Blackwork; Chapter 4, Lesson 19—Applique and Quilting; Chapter 4, Lesson 10—Straight Stitch Applique, Edge-Stitch Applique.

Chapter 2, Lesson 2 (opposite, top)—Pendants are a fast way to practice free machining and satin stitches.

Close-up of Duck Quilt (opposite, bottom) by Audrey Griese—machine applique, free-machine quilting, tufting.

Knitting needle work on a sweatshirt (above, with close-up) developed from a watch ad by Deb Evans of Pfaff American Sales Corp.

Cross-stitch on the Pfaff 1471 (left) by Edith Tanniru of DeWitt, NY.

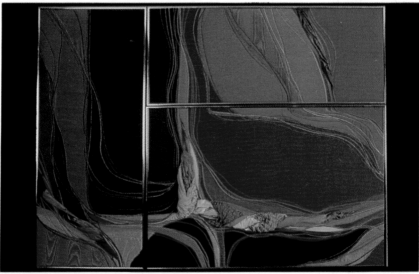

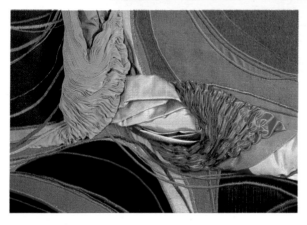

Close-up of quilt block by Margaret Rolfe of Curtin, ACT, Australia, author of Australian Patchwork—relatives and friends contributed fabric and lace scraps for this patchwork quilt. Margaret embroidered their names by machine. The quilt appeared in the Australian magazine "Women's Weekly."

"Kanso," three panels 41" × 55" of manipulated fabric and satin stitch by B.J. Adams of Washington, DC. Collection of Camilie and Alex Cook, Chicago, IL.

CHAPTER **2**

Adding Stitches to Your Fabric

- **Lesson 1. Using built-in stitches**
- **Lesson 2. Using free machining**

In this chapter you'll become acquainted with the range of stitches your Pfaff can produce. By the end of it, you'll easily switch back and forth from stitching with the feed dogs up to stitching with feed dogs down or covered. To demonstrate your new facility, you'll make beautiful small buttons and pendants.

Lesson 1. Using built-in stitches

The first thing I did when I bought my Pfaff was to try all the built-in stitches. I wanted a reference, so I sewed stitches in rows at different widths and lengths and put them in a notebook, along with notations from the Basic Manual. I was determined to know my sewing machine, and this has been so helpful to me that I've made it your first lesson too.

To save you time, practical and decorative stitches have been built into sewing machines: I classify them as "closed" and "open." "Closed" refers to those where the beauty is in stitching it close together (6.0 stitch width, stitch length 0.35) like the satin stitch or programs 60 through 67. "Open" built-in stitches, like the three-step zigzag, blind hem, or most utility programs, are usually sewn at a stitch length longer than 1.5. Still others are the reverse-cycle stitches, which have a forward and reverse motion in addition to the zigzag action. Preselected stitch lengths and widths are programmed in the computer.

To practice the built-in stitches and make a record of them, first set up your machine as indicated at the beginning of the lesson.

Program: as selected
Stitch width: preprogrammed
Stitch length: preprogrammed
Pattern length: preprogrammed
Needle: #80/12
Needle stop: up
Presser foot: as indicated by visual readout key
Dual feed: as indicated by visual readout key
Feed dogs: up
Tension: *top*, as indicated by visual readout key; *bobbin*, normal
Fabric: medium-weight striped cotton
Thread: *top*, machine embroidery to contrast with fabric; *bobbin*, same, but different color
Accessories: fine point marker; tear-away or freezer paper

Stitch lines of the built-in stitches found on your machine; using striped fabric will help you keep them straight (Fig. 2.1). Start by using the settings suggested in

13

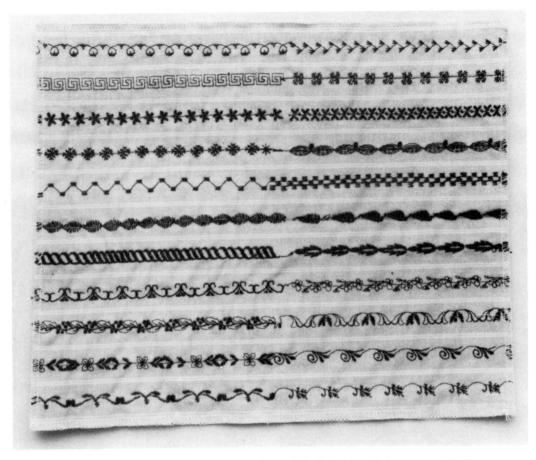

Fig. 2.1 Striped fabric is used to make a record of all the built-in stitches on my Pfaff Creative.

the manual. Vary the settings as you stitch, using the plus or minus keys, making the stitches wider and narrower, longer and shorter. If there is a setting you like better than the preprogrammed setting, mark it right on the fabric with a marker to show where it begins, and write down the preferred settings.

The machine is preprogrammed to give you the best length and width settings on all stitches, but you are perfectly free to override the computer if you like something else better.

Using different colors of thread on top and bobbin will help you adjust the machine to find the perfect stitch. Adjust tension by loosening the top tension slightly and leaving the bobbin tension normal. Again, your visual readout key tells you where to set the tension. The top thread should be pulled down and show underneath the fabric and should mound slightly on top when making satin stitches.

Start by stitching the zigzag, with the widest stitch width, stitch length as programmed. Adjust the length as you stitch

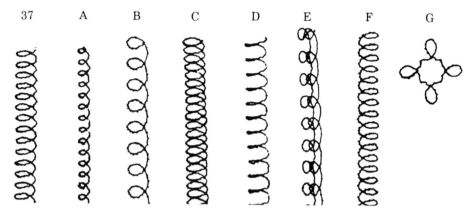

Fig. 2.2 Program 37 stitches can be changed with function keys. A. Narrowed with width key. B. Lengthened with length key. C. Closed with balance key (+7). D. Opened with balance key (−7). E. Stitched with double needle, elongated. F. Mirrored. G. Stitched in a square, pivoting clockwise, then counterclockwise.

until the satin stitch is perfect. This will be between 0.35 and 0.45, depending on the weight of the thread you are using. Write the setting on the sample.

When you finish your record of the built-in stitches, practice mirror images. This is as simple as pushing a button on your Pfaff.

There are a number of variables with mirror images. Are you feeding the fabric through exactly? Don't pull on one side when the other has been fed through free-

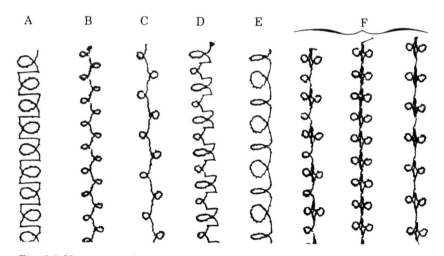

Fig. 2.3 Use memory keys to alter Program 37, creating other stitches. A. Alternately mirrored. B. Narrowed, then alternately mirrored. C. Narrowed, lengthened, alternately mirrored. D. Alternately widened and narrowed. E. Alternating short and long. F. Three versions using programmable straight stitches.

15

ly. Did you start the second row at exactly the right spot? Just one stitch off will make a difference. Do you have the same thickness of fabric under both sides of the design? If you're stitching on top of a seam allowance, the needle may go off the two layers.

Not only can you make a mirror image by pushing a button, but you can also have the machine stop after the last stitch of the program by pressing the tie-off key while you are sewing. Designs can be elongated, narrowed and balanced, as well as varied in other ways. See Figs. 2.2 and 2.3 for a sampling of the variations on a single program. Make a sample of each possibility and mark the settings.

As you sew line after line of practical and decorative stitches, imagine how they can be used. For example, the blind-hem stitch is used for blind hems and for the tricot scalloped hem. But it can also be an invisible way of stitching on a patch pocket or an appliqué, or the stitch to use when couching down heavy cords.

Lesson 2. Using free-machining: darning, whipping, feather stitching

In free machining, you — not the feed dogs — control the movement of the fabric, which in turn determines the length of the stitch. With fabric stretched tightly in a hoop, it is easy to move your work forward, backward, in circles, whatever way you wish.

I suggest working with a wooden hoop when first learning machine stitchery. Choose one that has a smooth finish, and slips easily under the darning foot. But whatever wooden hoop you use, be sure it is the screw type, as that will hold the fabric tightly. To be sure that it does, the inside ring of the wooden hoop should be smoothly wound with narrow twill tape. This keeps the fabric from slipping. Take a few hand stitches at the end of the tape to hold it firmly.

If your needle will not clear the hoop you've chosen, turn the hoop on its side and slip it under the darning foot or put the hoop together and carve out a small wedge to make it easier. Then wrap the inside part with tape.

Fabric is placed in the hoop upside-down from the way you would put it in a hoop for hand embroidery (Fig. 2.4). Pull the cloth as tightly as you can. Tighten the screw; pull again; tighten. Tap on the fabric. If it sounds like a drum, it is tight enough. You may or may not want to use a stabilizer under a hoop, depending upon the effect you want and the weight of the fabric.

You can stitch with a darning foot on or without a presser foot, removing the foot and shank (but keep your fingers a safe distance from the needle!).

It is possible to stitch freely without a hoop if you use your fingers to hold the fabric taut while stitching. If you don't use a hoop — or if you use a spring-type hoop — use the darning foot to prevent skipped stitches. It will hold the fabric down each time the machine makes a stitch so the threads interlock correctly underneath. Also, use a stabilizer under the fabric to keep the stitches from puckering.

Program: 10
Stitch width: 0.0 to 6.0
Stitch length: 0.2
Needle: #80/12
Needle stop: up
Presser foot: remove presser foot and shank; or use darning foot #6

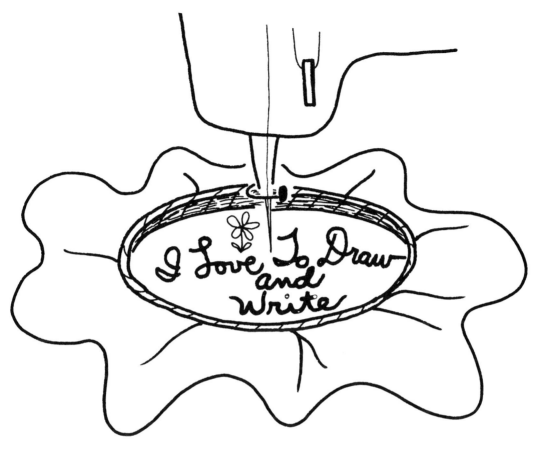

Fig. 2.4 Tighten fabric in a hoop. The fabric rests against the bed of the machine, with the material topside up for machine embroidery.

Dual feed: disengaged
Feed dogs: lowered
Tension: *top,* 3; *bobbin,* normal
Fabric: light colored, medium-weight poplin
    scrap for practice; 18″ × 18″ (45.7cm ×
    45.7cm) square for notebook
Thread: *top,* contrasting color; *bobbin,* con-
    trasting with fabric and needle thread
Accessories: wrapped wooden hoop, 7″
    (17.8cm); fine marker
Stabilizer: tear-away or freezer paper

The two samples in this lesson will give you practice in control and coordination.

One sample will be for practice; the other, for your notebook. Keep a record of the new-found stitches you create with your machine and your imagination.

Free machining—darning, whipping and feather stitching—takes practice, but it is worth every minute. It opens up a new world of stitchery to you.

First, you are going to learn to draw, write, and sketch with your machine. It's called the darning stitch.

Always begin by dipping the needle into the fabric and bringing the bobbin thread to the top. Lower the presser foot lifter

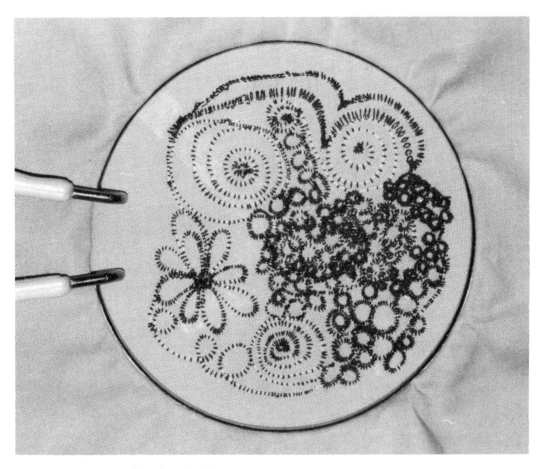

Fig. 2.5 Whipping and feather stitching.

halfway. There is a little notch that keeps it in place, and keeps the dual feed and bar mechanism out of the way while still engaging the tension. Hold both threads to the side while stitching in one place several stitches to anchor the thread. Clip off the ends. When you begin your stitchery, start slowly. Practice moving the hoop slowly, as well. You must coordinate the speed at which you move your hoop and your sewing speed. It is not necessary to stitch at top speed—moderate speed is fine. You'll soon learn how fast is right for you and for the particular stitching you are creating.

Move the hoop back and forth, then in circles—remember the old Palmer Method exercises for handwriting? Stitch faster; move your hoop faster. Then write your name, draw a picture of a tree, your dog, an old flame. It doesn't matter how well you draw; you are really practicing control.

Change to zigzag and try it all over again. Yes, it will take awhile to gain absolute control, but don't give up. Stitch tiny fill-in spirals, figure eights and jigsaw patterns.

Now stitch, hesitate, stitch. The bobbin color may come to the top. Good! That's

Fig. 2.6 Draw 36 squares on a piece of fabric, then fill them in with the new stitches and techniques you've learned and will learn. Be sure to record machine settings.

what we want. To make sure it does, tighten the top tension slowly. When you see the bobbin thread, note where the tension dial is set and write this on the sample. This type of stitchery is called whipping. If the hoop is moved slowly and the machine run very fast, a nubby, thickened line of bobbin thread will appear on the surface. It can be used in place of the darning stitch when embroidering—or used with it for variety. Whipping can be seen in the tiny circles of dark bobbin thread in Fig. 2.5.

With the top tension very tight and the bobbin tension loosened, stitch straight lines, circles and spirals. Move the hoop quickly. The top thread is visible as a straight line on top of the fabric. Covering it are looping, feathery bobbin stitches. This is an exaggeration of whipping, which is called feather stitching. This can be seen in the hoop in some of the small circles as I went from tight to tighter top tension, and in the larger, spiky spirals (Fig. 2.4) that occurred when I loosened the bobbin tension until there was no resistance on the thread. You may have to use a heavier, stronger thread in the needle if you tighten your top tension a lot.

Practice is the only way to learn control. When you feel you have accomplished co-ordination between moving the hoop and the speed of the machine, make the following record of what you've learned: On the 18" x 18" (45.7cm x 45.7cm) square of fabric, draw a grid of 3" (7.6cm) squares, six across, six down (Fig. 2.6). Then fill in your squares with examples of free machining—darning, whipping and feather stitching. Use both straight stitches and zigzag stitches in your squares. Try built-in stitches, too. You can stitch your own designs or use mine. But as you practice, write the machine settings on the fabric. Slip this into your notebook. Add new stitches as you discover them and refer to your notebook regularly for stitches you want to use on a project.

For variety, thread your needle with two colors, or try a double needle. But remember to press the twin needle button so your double needle will fall inside the hole of the plate when setting it on zigzag.

Project
Buttons and Pendants

The following one-of-a-kind project includes free-machining, stitching with the feed dogs up, and using some of the decorative stitches on the machine. They are an "anything goes" project, fun to do, and every one different. See color section for finished samples.

For the round button in Fig. 2.7, I used a No. 75 Maxant button form, which is about 2" (5.1cm) in diameter, while the rectangular and free-form designs in Figs. 2.8 and 2.9 are mounted on cardboard which has been padded with poylester fleece.

Program: 00, 10, 64, 82, 85 and various dec-
    orative programs
Stitch width: 0.0 to 6.0
Stitch length: As programmed
Pattern length: varies
Single pattern: varies
Needle: #90
Needle stop: up
Presser foot: fancy stitch foot #2, darning
    foot #6, or none
Dual feed: disengaged
Feed dogs: up or lowered

Fig. 2.7 Pattern for embroidered button (see color insert).

20

Fig. 2.8 Use whip stitches to make a pendant using this pattern (see color insert).

Fig. 2.9 Pattern for free form machine-embroidered pendant (see color insert).

Tension: *top,* varies — sometimes tightened; *bobbin:* varies

Fabric: tightly woven smooth linen or polyester

Thread: *top,* machine embroidery cotton or rayon; *bobbin,* same

Accessories: spring hoop; button form; cardboard; glue; fleece or padding; cord; beads (optional)

Stabilizer: tear-away

If you use the round design in Fig. 2.7 with the button form, you may use the pattern on the back of the card of buttons, or you may draw two circles with the same center point, the outer one being ½" (12.7mm) larger than the inner circle. The ¼" (6.4mm) area between the lines will not be embroidered. Use a piece of fabric large enough to go into a spring hoop, and place a piece of tear-away stabilizer underneath.

The round design is mostly whipping, starting with the little circles. I started in the center and gradually worked my way out until they were about ¼" (6.4mm)

wide, and without breaking the thread, moved to the next one and did the same thing.

The next step was to stitch the dark lines which divide the area into sections. Rather than make a perfectly straight line, I wiggled my way across the button. The same stitch was used throughout.

After putting in the dark lines, I filled the background in with wiggly lines, making sure that occasionally some of the fabric was still peeking through, as this was an especially nice piece of linen.

The rectangular pendant in Fig. 2.8 was made on a scrap of *peau de soie* left over from a dress. I loved the color and loved the dress, and could never bear to part with the leftover fabric.

I started by making two tapered satin stitch forms on either side of the pendant area, one elongated and tapered, and the other sort of curled around itself as it tapers. Then, with a lighter colored thread for contrast, I stitched a row using Program 64 just as it is in the machine. Be-

21

cause I wanted a raised and corded effect down the center, however, I again loosened bobbin tension sufficiently so that the bobbin thread pulled up and surrounded the needle thread. If you are using rayon thread, you may find it necessary to use a heavier thread in the needle, because the upper tension should be tightened somewhat. At first this caused the needle thread to break, but with heavier thread I was successful in getting the corded effect in the center to stand out.

The little diamonds were then outlined with satin stitch, freely stitched to surround the automatic design. Little blobs of thread the same color as the original satin stitch forms were added, and these were outlined with a dark whip stitch.

The entire embroidery was then outlined with gold-colored whip stitch. This was kept fine enough so it looks like a fine gold wire, something like cloisonné. Lots of fabric was left showing on this pendant, because I do love that particular shade of blue.

I discovered one trick when covering the cardboard backing for this pendant: I ran a line of straight stitching ¼″ (6.4mm) in from the edge of the fabric, almost right at the edge of the stitchery, and then pulled the bobbin threads tight so the fabric wrapped around the cardboard and stayed in place while everything was being glued. A piece of batting was glued on the cardboard first, then the stitchery was shaped around it. The gathering thread made it possible to ease the fabric at the corners. The edges of the fabric are then glued to the cardboard, and you do not have to try to hold them in sixteen different places at once, while worrying about glue spotting the stitchery and spoiling your work.

The backing piece is handled the same way, and then the two pieces are put together. A heavy cord is then whipped around the outside edge to conceal the place where the sections are joined.

The cord, in this case, was made on the sewing machine. Instructions for this are given in Chapter 10, Lesson 35. Three lengths of the cord were used for the "chain," and they are knotted every 2″ (5.1cm).

The freeform design in Fig. 2.9 used a single Program 82, with a pattern length of 30. A single Program 85, with a length of 8, was used at the opposite end, and whip stitching was freely stitched around it with the addition of some free satin stitches in a slightly darker shade. These areas were all outlined with whip stitching in gold. Some of the areas were then filled in with darker colors. A single gold bead was attached by machine.

The pendant was mounted on cardboard in the same way as the rectangular one, and then purchased rayon cord was whipped around the outside edge and used as a neckchain.

CHAPTER 3

Adding Texture to Your Fabric

- **Lesson 3. Building up sewing stitches**
- **Lesson 4. Applying thick threads from top and bobbin**
- **Lesson 5. Fringing yarn and fabric**
- **Lesson 6. Adding buttons, beads, shisha**
- **Lesson 7. Smocking and gathering**
- **Lesson 8. Pulling threads together**

Add to or create texture on fabrics by building up sewing stitches, using thick threads, attaching fringe or objects like buttons and beads, gathering fabric for smocking or for utilitarian purposes—to stitch elastic on sleeves or bodices, or to make ruffles for curtains.

You'll make samples for your notebook; stitch up a fabric greeting card; cable stitch a tote bag square; make fabric fringe for rugs and doll hair; and make a framed picture. Both projects and samples will suggest numerous other ways to use these stitches.

Lesson 3. Building up sewing stitches

One of the simplest ways to build up texture is to sew in one place many times. Sounds simple and it is. But you can do this in so many ways that even though it is simple, the results aren't. Texture can look studied and exact or free and wild.

I use the following techniques for landscapes, monograms, and flowers. Practice each one for your notebook, recording your machine settings and any notes on how you might use the stitches later.

Begin with my suggested settings, but change them if they are not to your liking.

Program: 10
Stitch width: 6.0
Stitch length: 0.0 to 0.5
Needle: #90/14
Needle stop: up

Presser foot: darning foot #6; fancy stitch foot #2
Dual feed: disengaged
Feed dogs: raised or lowered as required
Tension: *top*, −3+; *bobbin*, normal
Fabric: varied
Thread: *top*, varied—experiment with many types and colors; *bottom*, machine embroidery, pearl cotton, cordonnet
Accessories: 7″ (17.8cm) spring hoop
Stabilizer: tear-away or freezer paper

With the feed dogs up, and embroidery foot on, select program 10 at 6.0 width, then press the tie-off/buttonhole key. Sew a block of 6 or 8 satin stitches. Anchor them by pressing the tie-off/buttonhole key while the machine is running. Move the hoop and do another block of satin

Fig. 3.1 Use satin stitches for flower centers or fill-in background stitches.

Fig. 3.2 Blobs and loops.

Fig. 3.3 Straight-stitching around blobs.

stitches. Keep them quite close together, but all at different angles (Fig. 3.1). Use these to fill in areas in designs (see Fig. 3.29).

For the next sample, lower the feed dogs and use darning foot #6. Use the same wide zigzag, press the tie-off key, but sew in one place to build up 10 or 12 stitches. Move to another spot close to the first blob of stitches and stitch again. If you wish to achieve the effect in Fig. 3.2, pull the threads into loops as you move from place to place and don't cut them off. You can make flower centers this way. Or finish by clipping between the satin stitches and then, using a different color on top, outlining with straight stitches (Fig. 3.3). Using variegated thread is especially effective.

In the next experiment, with feed dogs up, place the fancy stitch foot #2 on, and set your machine on the widest satin stitch, 6.0. Press the tie-off key and sew a block of satin stitches at the left of the practice fabric. Pull the fabric down about three inches and over to the right slightly. Stitch another block of satin stitches. Pull up and over a bit to the right to stitch another block of satin stitches. Pull down and over for the third block. Continue across the fabric. Change threads and come back with another color. Cross the threads from the first pass as you do (Fig. 3.4). This is a good filler for garden pictures—the stitches become hedges of flowers—or use layers of these to crown trees (Fig. 3.5).

Speaking of flowers, try the ones in Fig.

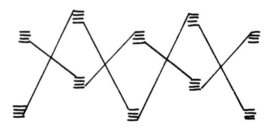

Fig. 3.4 Crossed threads and satin stitches.

Fig. 3.5 This tree was stitched on cotton net. The trunk is encroaching zigzags, the crown of the tree is satin stitches and crossed threads.

Fig. 3.6 Zigzag star flowers.

press tie-off key to anchor the thread and make a satin stitch blob perpendicular to the edge of the circle. Pull the thread across to the other side of the circle and make another blob. Press tie-off key with machine running to anchor thread. Cut off the thread. Go to another place on, just within, or just without the circle and stitch another blob. Pull the thread over to the

3.6, with feed dogs lowered, using the same machine settings, except that you engage the needle down button. Press the tie-off key. Stitch one blob of about 10 or 12 satin stitches in one place and, ending on the left side, the needle still in the fabric, turn the hoop. Do another blob and end on the left side. Turn the hoop and do another and another. Lay in about five or six of these to create a satin-stitch flower. The satin stitches will all have that common center — at needle left.

Make the next satin stitch flower (Fig. 3.7) by first tracing around a drinking glass with a water-erasable marker. With feed dogs lowered, needle stop up, again

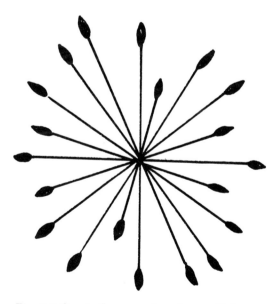

Fig. 3.7 Create flowers using zigzag stitches and crossed threads.

other side, make another satin stitch blob, anchor it, and cut off the thread. Begin again and continue until you have made a flower head.

Now you'll practice filling in shapes, another way to bring texture to your base fabric. Zigzagging is probably the most widely used method to fill in designs. You can use any stitch width, but the wider the setting, the looser the look. I feel I have more control if I use a 2.0 width — or better yet, I sew with straight stitches to fill in backgrounds. It is more like drawing with a pencil.

The drawback to straight-stitch filling is that the stitches are very tight to the fabric. Sometimes I want a lighter, loopier look, so I may start with zigzagging to fill in a design and then draw on top of that with straight stitches to emphasize a color, to outline, or to add shading to my embroidery. So I've included three ways to add texture to fabric by filling in designs with zigzag stitches.

Method A

In this method you will follow the contour of your design with zigzag stitches, changing a flat circle into a ball shape.

Program: 10
Stitch width: 6.0
Stitch length: 0
Needle stop: up
Needle: #90/14
Feed dogs: lowered
Presser foot: darning foot #6 or use a wooden hoop with no foot
Tension: *top,* slightly loosened; *bobbin,* normal
Fabric suggestion: medium-weight cotton
Thread: sewing thread for practice
Accessories: large hoop at least 7" (17.8cm); water-erasable marker

Using the marker, draw several circles on the fabric in the hoop (I drew around the base of a large spool of thread). Place stabilizer under the hoop. Zigzag the first

circle into a ball shape by stitching in curved lines. To make it easier, first draw stitching guidelines inside the circle (Fig. 3.8, method A, *left*).

Start at the top of the circle, stitching and moving your hoop sideways and back while following the curves you've drawn (Fig. 3.8, method A, *right*). Move from top

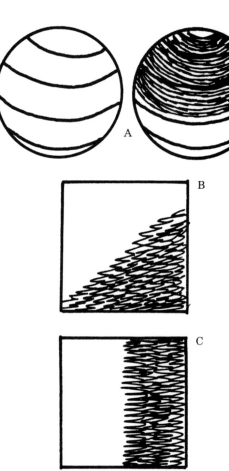

Fig. 3.8 Filling in designs with zigzag stitches. A. Draw guidelines in the circles, then move sideways and back, following the guidelines.
B. Stair-step method. C. Encroaching zigzag.

to bottom, creating the ball shape as you stitch. Don't build up stitches too fast in one place. Move the hoop evenly, slowly, and practice coordination.

Try other stitch widths on the other circles you've drawn. Put the samples in your notebook.

Method B

This has been described as the stair-step method. Designs can be filled in by zigzag stitching from lower-left corner to upper-right corner and back again (Fig. 3.8, method B). To practice this, set up your machine as you did in method A. Draw several 1½″ (3.8cm) squares on your fabric. Although you will start with the widest stitch, experiment with other widths as you did before. Each line of zigzags blends into the one before it. Add your experiments to your notebook.

Method C

Encroaching zigzag is another way to fill in a design (Fig. 3.8, method C). Set up your machine as follows:

Program: 10
Stitch width: 6.0
Stitch length: 0
Needle: #90/14
Feed dogs: lowered
Presser foot: darning foot #6 or no foot
Tension: *top*, slightly loosened; *bobbin*, normal
Fabric: medium-weight cotton
Thread: sewing thread for practice
Accessories: 7″ (17.8cm) hoop, tear-away stabilizer, water-erasable marker

This time, draw only one 2″ (5.1cm) square on the fabric in the hoop, and place stabilizer under it. Keep the hoop in the same position in front of you; don't rotate it. Instead, move it backward and forward as you stitch. Start at the top of the right side of the square you've drawn and stitch down to the bottom, moving the hoop slowly to keep the stitches close together. Move the hoop to the left a bit and stitch back up to the top, overlapping the first stitching slightly. Continue until you have covered the square. Go back and stitch on top of stitches for more texture. Do a sample for your notebook.

Lesson 4. Applying thick threads from the top and bobbin

We created texture with regular sewing threads in Lesson 3, but in this lesson we'll change sewing and machine-embroidery threads for thicker threads, such as pearl cotton, cordonnet, and crochet cotton. We'll explore four different ways to create texture by attaching these thick threads to fabric, including using them on the top spool, couched down on top of fabric, threaded up through the hole in the throat plate of the machine, and wound on the bobbin.

Adding texture adds interest to sewing and embroidery. Perhaps it's not essential—a dress is still a dress without textured decoration—but it is a long-cut, that something extra that takes your dress from ordinary to special. Adding cords, fringe, objects, and gathers to the background fabric are all easy techniques once you know your machine.

Applying thick thread through the needle

Thread as large as cordonnet can be sewn with a #110 needle. Topstitching needles also have eyes to accommodate double threads or thick threads like buttonhole twist, and are available in #80–#110 needles.

Whatever you use, the thread must slip through the needle easily and the needle must make a hole in the fabric large enough to keep the thread from fraying.

Couching thread down on top of fabric

If thread is too thick for the needle, try couching it down on top of the fabric using the single cording foot. Place the cord under the center slot on the bottom, front to back. If you use the single cording foot, as soon as you start stitching the thread will be fed through this slot with no help needed. It will stay exactly in place as you satin stitch over it with a zigzag or other decorative stitch. Cover the cord as closely or sparsely as you wish, using different stitch lengths.

You can substitute other feet—fancy stitch foot #2, 5-groove and 7-groove cording feet, appliqué foot, or for very thick cords, the knit edge sewing foot. Unlike the cording foot which feeds the thread automatically, you may have to guide the cord if you use one of the other feet mentioned.

Try multiple cords as well. There are slots on the right and left sides on the top of the single cording foot in which you can lay the cords, or use foot #1, which has parallel grooves underneath. Foot #1 can be used with or without the dual feed.

The next project will give you practice applying thick threads. You will also practice making circles with the tack-and-tape method. But how do you stitch perfect circles without tack and tape? The following directions will show you how. As with all sewing, precision is most important.

Stitching perfect circles

The perfect circle is made with the tape-and-tack method described in Chapter 1 (see Fig. 1.2). Without this help, it takes practice and confidence to satin stitch a perfect circle. It's not necessary to practice stitching one hundred circles: rather, you gain confidence by using your machine often and by teaching yourself to precision stitch, even if it is only a simple dress seam.

Stabilize your appliqué fabric before drawing the circle and cutting it out. I usually use a fusible, so there will be no creeping or pleating when the circle is stitched down to the background fabric.

Be sure you start by drawing a perfect circle. I've used templates such as spools, cups and plates. If you plan to stitch a lot of circles, buy a plastic template at an art or office supply store (you'll need a fine-line marker or sharp pencil, too). The template is thick, but transparent, with cutout circles that range from too-tiny-to-be-of-any-use to 3″ (7.6cm) in diameter. Use the cups and plates for larger circles.

You'll find that large circles are easier to stitch than small ones, and it's easier to maneuver narrow satin stitches than it is wide ones. Use the fancy stitch foot or appliqué foot. I usually prefer a satin stitch no wider than 3mm for an appliqué, but the fancy stitch foot for your machine will accommodate the width of your machine's satin stitch. The appliqué foot is used when stitching a satin stitch no wider than 2mm.

It's important to have a reference point on the foot you use. The fancy stitch foot has a line in the center. To cover the fabric edges of a circle using this foot, use Program 11 with needle position to far left, stitch width 3.0, stitch length 0.35, and I place the center line on the edge I want to cover. Then I watch the mark and fabric edge closely as I guide my fabric clockwise around the circle. When stitching counterclockwise, I line up the foot and fabric edge the same way, but stitch with needle far right.

The transparent appliqué foot is a short-toed foot, which keeps the fabric ahead readily visible. The center groove, which is visible from the top of the foot, is flared on both sides at the back, behind the needle, to allow you to stitch around curves more easily. The groove in front of the needle is straight. I place the edge of the center groove directly over the edge of the fabric I will be satin stitching—that may be to the left or right side of the groove—depending upon whether I am stitching clockwise or counterclockwise. This foot should be used with Program 10, needle position in the center and engage the needle down key.

To get a more perfect edge when you stitch wovens, use a sharp (sometimes called a jeans needle); to produce a more beautiful satin stitch, always use machine embroidery thread and back your work with freezer paper or tear-away stabilizer.

Before I begin stitching my circle, I hand-walk the machine to be sure the needle swing has been set up correctly. I want the needle to go into the background fabric exactly at edge of the appliqué. The satin stitches are on the appliqué fabric. Never satin stitch out beyond the appliqué, attaching the circle with stitches that barely catch the edge.

Pivot as you stitch around the circle. The smaller the circle, the more pivoting and the harder it is to stitch a perfect circle. Keep this in mind: If the curve is an outside (convex) one, your pivot points will be on the outside of the circle. If your curve is inside (concave), then the pivot points will be on the inside edge. Always pivot whenever you see the satin stitches slanting instead of radiating (imagine your circle has lines radiating from the center and you are stitching only the edges of those lines). You may have to go back to the same pivot point several times as you complete the continuous curve. Do this with needle down in the pivot point, turn the fabric slightly, stitch, needle down in the same pivot point, move the fabric again, and so on until the curve is smooth and

covered evenly with satin stitches. Yes, it is slow going, but never stitch a circle if you are in a hurry—it won't work. Circles are a slow, stitch-by-stitch process if you want perfection.

Practice on several circles, playing with stitch width and the needle position to find what works best for you and your machine. Experiment with presser feet as well. Place your samples in your notebook.

Project
Greeting Card

Practice applying thick threads and making perfect circles on the greeting card shown in Fig. 3.9.

Program: M (Memory); Enter: [Program 10, mirrored width 1.5, length 1.0] 1 time; [Program 01, needle position 1϶ length 1.5] 3 times
Needle: #90/14
Feed dogs: up
Presser foot: blindstitch foot #3
Dual feed: engaged
Tension: *top,* loosened; *bobbin,* normal
Fabric suggestions: 12″ (30.5cm) square of white polished cotton, 6″ (15.2cm) square of green polished cotton, 12″ (30.5cm) square of yellow organdy
Thread: rayon in rainbow colors—yellow, red, green, purple, blue; #3 pearl cotton in the same colors; monofilament
Accessories: thumb tack, transparent tape, cork or eraser; water-erasable pen; greeting card folder (available at craft, art, and needlework shops) or picture frame; dressmaker's carbon; empty ball-point pen
Stabilizer: tear-away

Use the pattern in Fig. 3.10 as a guide, changing measurements to fit the card folder or frame. Trace the pattern from the book, then place the drawing on top of the

Fig. 3.9 "Even the Rainbow is Upset" greeting card.

edge of the green about ½" (12.7mm) and press it. Hold it in place with pins and apply it using the blindstitch foot #3, with monofilament thread on the top and bobbin, and the machine set on the memory program shown in the settings list.

Next, place three layers of yellow organdy over the white and green fabric. Back this with tear-away. Place the thumb tack, point side up, on the arm of the machine, so that when you bring it up through the 3 layers of organdy it will be in the center. This will be about 1" (2.5cm) from the needle. Place the ordinary presser foot #0 on the line of the inner circle. Stitch on that line around the circle with a straight stitch, allowing the machine to feed the fabrics in a perfect circle. Cut back only the top layer of organdy to the stitching.

Place the greeting card back under the presser foot with the tack back in its original hole. Satin stitch with the machine set on a width of 2.0, length 0.4.

Then move the tack so the line of the next circle will be centered under your presser foot. Straight stitch around the circle, cut back and satin stitch again as you did with the first. Do the same for the last layer of organdy.

Place tear-away stabilizer underneath while you stitch over the cord. Each cord is a different color; use the single cording foot to guide the pearl cotton. If you don't have a single cording foot, then use the fancy stitch foot #2 or appliqué foot. Fitting the pearl cotton into the slot, and guide it as you stitch. Stitch over the cords, using close satin stitches. I prefer to stitch in two passes, attaching the cord first at a width of 1.5, then stitching in close satin stitches to cover it evenly and smoothly on the second pass with a width of 2.0.

When the last cord has been covered, change to the darning foot #6, feed dogs lowered, straight stitch. Use the color you have on your machine—unless it's yellow—to write a message along the top of one of the cords. I wrote "get well," and on

white background fabric, with dressmaker's carbon between. Transfer it, using the empty ballpoint pen.

Cut a piece from the green fabric large enough for the area at the bottom of the design, plus 1" (2.5cm). Fold under the top

30

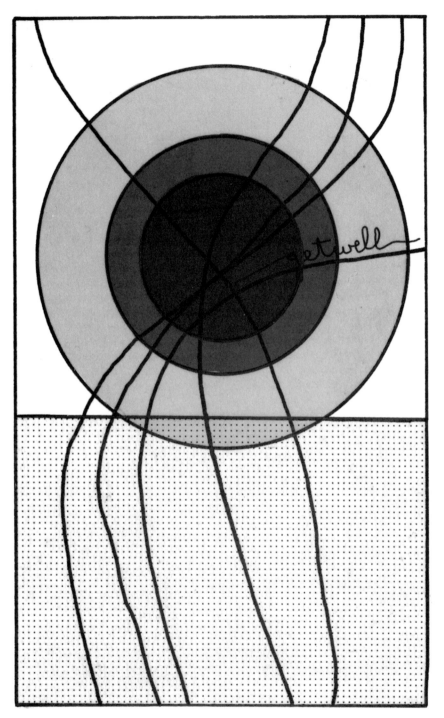

Fig. 3.10 Greeting card pattern. Enlarge or reduce to fit your card folder.

31

the inside I'll write the message: "Even the rainbow is upset."

Finish the edge with a straight stitch. Trim close to stitches and slip into the card folder or finish it for a framed picture.

Also try the knit edge foot for sewing down bulky yarn or cords invisibly. Use the blind hemming stitch, Program 17 (Fig. 3.11). Set up your machine as follows:

Program: 17
Stitch width: 2.0
Stitch length: 2.5
Needle: varies
Feed dogs: up
Presser foot: knit edge, fancy stitch foot #1, or #2
Tension: *top*, normal; *bobbin*, normal
Thread: monofilament on top, polyester on bobbin
Stabilizer: tear-away

Stitch alongside the cord. At the wide bite of the needle, the cord is sewn down with a narrow, almost unnoticeable stitch. When the line of stitching is completed, go back and gently nudge the cord over toward the stitching line. Now your monofilament will be completely hidden.

Or, using the 7-groove cording foot, line up several threads of pearl cotton next to each other. Use a zigzag or Program 13, width 4.0, to attach them with monofilament or with a colored thread. Make colorful shoelaces this way.

Soutache is like a thick cord, and can be attached perfectly using the single cording foot. It is not easily done without this special foot, as there is no way to hold the braid in place so the needle will enter exactly in the center each time. It's sometimes possible to feed other cords, narrow braids or rickrack through the slot in this foot. To attach soutache, trace the design on the topside of your fabric, using a water-erasable pen. Place stabilizer under the fabric.

Corners are not impossible if you walk the machine around them. Stop at the cor-

ner, needle down, presser foot raised. Turn the fabric 45 degrees, lower the foot, take one stitch; then, needle down again, raise the presser foot, turn the fabric to complete the corner. You'll get a good angle. If you can, though, choose a design with undulating curves, which are easier to accomplish. Look at the appliqué foot, also. You'll see this is very short, which helps turn corners. The groove on the bottom of the foot is flared in back, making it easy to turn in either direction.

Use soutache and other braids down jacket and vest fronts, around sleeves, to decorate belts and handbags.

If the braid crosses and recrosses itself, threading in and out like a Celtic interlacing cord, it is easy to use the appliqué foot. The braid should be hand basted in place on the fabric, then fit within the groove as you carefully ride over it and stitch it down.

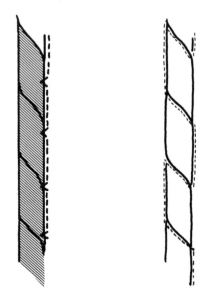

Fig. 3.11 Use the blind-hem stitch to attach cord invisibly.

Fig. 3.12 Stitch alongside, then across the twist, to attach cord.

For your next sample, use the darning foot #6 when freely couching down yarn. This darning foot has a guide in the front to hold the yarn as you freely attach it. To get the feel of the foot, use straight lines or gentle curves on your first samples. Try a smooth, sport-weight yarn for your first experiment. Add the result to your growing notebook.

Here's another invisible way to attach thick, twisted cord or yarn to fabric (Fig. 3.12). Leave the machine set up for free machining, but remove the presser foot or use a darning foot. Use monofilament thread on top. Iron a piece of freezer paper onto the back of the fabric. Begin by drawing the bobbin thread to the top and anchoring the threads. Stitch the end of the cord down. Then move along one side of the cord with a straight stitch. When you reach a twist in the cord, follow it to the other side by stitching in the twist. Once on the other side, follow along that side for a few stitches until you reach the top of the next twist. Cross over again, following the twist. Continue in this manner until the cord is attached.

Attaching cord pulled through the needleplate

You can also attach thick cords to the surface of fabric by threading them through the hole in the needleplate. Of course, this method attaches the cord underneath the fabric, so you must stitch with the top-side of the fabric against the needleplate.

Your Pfaff needleplate snaps off easily and I recommend also removing the bobbin case, so the thread does not get caught between the bed of the machine and the plate when it is snapped back into place.

Thread the cord through the hole in the plate. Once you have it threaded through, tie a knot at the end so it does not slip out again. Snap the plate back on the machine. I've used this method of attaching cords

through the needleplate for collages, when I want to add long lines of cords easily and fast. I draw on the stabilizer, which is on top of the wrong side of the fabric, to indicate where I should stitch. The cord is fed evenly through the plate and attached to the fabric with straight or zigzag stitches.

Stitch a record of your experiments with straight stitch and zigzag. Also try cord through the needleplate with some of the built-in stitches intended for decorative edgings, like the scallop stitch, Program 38.

You can also apply round elastic or flat ⅛″ (3.2mm) elastic with this method.

Use pearl cotton through the needleplate for pintucking with double needles (see Chapter 5). Make samples using each cording foot you own. Stitch many rows, spacing them according to the spacing on the cording feet. Mark them for your notebook.

Using thick thread from the bobbin

Cable stitching is an embroidery technique using thick thread on the bobbin. The topside of the fabric will be against the bed of the machine. It can be done with feed dogs up, using an embroidery foot for straight or built-in stitches, or it can be done freely with feed dogs down, using a darning foot or using no presser foot at all.

Cabling can look like a tightly couched thread or like fluffy fur, depending on the thread you choose. A hard twist thread like crochet cotton will lay flatter, with less beading or looping than a soft, loosely twisted yarn like mohair. The effects you get will depend not only on top and bobbin tension, but on stitch width, stitch length, color and size of cord, color of top thread, feed dogs up or down, color, weight, and type of fabric, how fast you stitch and how fast you move the hoop.

When I say you can use thick threads, I'm not kidding. Did you know that you can use up to a four-ply yarn in the bobbin? Of course, the thicker the yarn, the less you can wind on the bobbin. Usually the bobbin can be put on the machine and wound slowly while you hold the yarn or cord to control it. If you are more comfortable winding it by hand, do so evenly without stretching it.

To use the thicker threads this embroidery requires, you must override that panicky feeling that accompanies loosening and tightening the tension on the bobbin. Perhaps you've already discovered, as you've changed bobbins, that you can recognize the feel of normal tension. If not, put a bobbin full of sewing thread into the bobbin case and click the thread into the spring. Hold on to the end of the thread and let the bobbin case hang from it like a yoyo. It should not slide down by its own weight but drop slowly when jerked. Memorize how this feels with normal tension before you begin to loosen the bobbin spring for cabling. Loosen the spring over an empty box, as the screw has a tendency to pop out and disappear forever. I've purchased several extra screws just in case.

Do not use a screwdriver, but use the ball of your thumb or the tip of your finger. This way the screw is less likely to take off for parts unknown.

Always turn the screw just a hair's breadth at a time. Just a fraction will tighten or loosen the tension considerably.

When adjusting tension for heavy threads, remember that the cord must feed through the bobbin case smoothly. Loosen the bobbin tension by turning the screw counterclockwise until the tension feels normal to you.

You may have to bypass the tension spring altogether if the cord or yarn is too thick. This is easy to do. Simply poke the end of the cord or yarn through the little opening where the end of the tension spring fits into the bobbin case. Pull it through and place the bobbin case in the machine in the usual way.

Practice cabling on a piece of scrap fabric. Set up your machine with feed dogs up, using an embroidery thread on top or regular sewing thread. Place your fabric in a hoop and use the darning foot #6. Stitch and then look under the fabric to be sure the tension is set correctly—do you want tight, stiff stitches or loosely looping ones? Manipulate the bobbin tension for different effects.

Don't forget the top tension. It must be loose enough so the bobbin thread stays underneath the fabric; but if it is too loose, it may keep the stitches from staying neatly in place.

Write on your sample fabric which is the topside, which is the back. Also record bobbin and top spool tensions by using + and − signs, and the numbers from your calibrated tension dial.

Most embroiderers I know, if they own machines with removable bobbin cases, buy extra bobbin cases to use for embroidery only. Buying an extra case is a good idea. It's possible to tighten and loosen the spring screw—or even remove the spring altogether—without the time-consuming adjustments needed to return to normal sewing tension.

Whatever you choose to do, don't be afraid of your sewing machine. Change tensions, lengths, speeds, and use it to its full potential. Get to know your machine.

Now prepare a cabling sample for your notebook. Choose a medium-weight cotton or blend. Use some of the built-in stitches with #3, #5, and then #8 pearl cotton. Try ribbon and yarn as well, overriding the computer settings if necessary. Keep the stitches long enough to prevent the cord from bunching up under the fabric. Open built-in stitches work best and simple zigzag is very effective. Program 10 is a good starting point and you can easily change both length and width to 6.0 for a rickrack effect. Some programs, such as 52 and 95, are designed for very fine thread and would not be suitable for cabling, but ex-

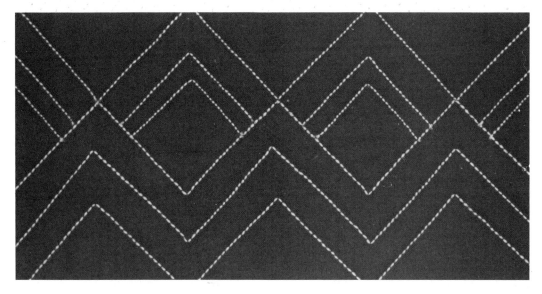

Fig. 3.13 Stitching in the style of Japanese Sashiko.

perimentation will show what you can and cannot do.

Don't use a stabilizer underneath. Instead, use a stabilizer on top to keep your stitches from pulling. Draw lines or designs on the stabilizer. This is actually the back of your work.

Dip the needle into the fabric, drawing the bobbin thread or cord to the top. Hold the threads to the side as you begin. If you can't bring the cord up through the fabric, then pierce the cloth with an awl or large needle and bring it up. Don't anchor the threads with a lockstitch at the end. The machine will automatically take a stitch to secure the threads at the beginning of a program. Instead, pull the threads to the back each time you start; when you stop, leave a long enough tail to be able to thread it up in a hand-sewing needle and poke it through to the back. Later you can work these threads into the stitching by hand.

It is also possible to quilt with this technique. Using a white pearl cotton in the bobbin and a top thread to match the fab-

ric, you can get an effect which looks much like Japanese Sashiko (Fig. 3.13).

Apply ⅛″ (3.2mm) double-faced satin ribbon as shown in Fig. 3.14. Wind the ribbon onto the bobbin. The end of the ribbon

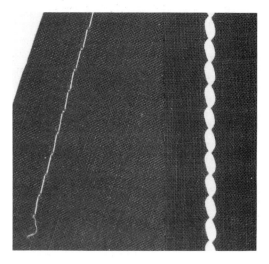

Fig. 3.14 The top and underneath of a ribbon attached by machine stitching.

will bypass the tension spring. Then place the bobbin in the case. Use the regular presser foot, needle right, stitch length at 6.0.

When you start and stop in this type of couching, the ribbon is brought to the underside and finished off by hand. This technique is used on the infant's bonnet in Chapter 5.

Next try cabling with free embroidery. Place a medium-weight fabric in a hoop with a stabilizer on top. Lower the feed dogs and, using the darning foot #6 or bare needle, freely straight stitch, then zigzag.

Plan the lines of stitching before you begin. As you work, sew and peek under your hoop so you can regulate the bobbin and top tensions to your liking. Practice turning, pushing and pulling the hoop, sewing circles and straight lines. When your stitching changes direction, the tension is also changed, so practice how fast you should move your hoop for the effects you want. Often a design can be seen from the back of printed fabric. Take advantage of that to stitch a sample piece for your notebook. Stretch the fabric in a hoop. Water-soluble stabilizer can be used underneath if the fabric is washable. Otherwise, don't use a stabilizer. Instead, be sure your fabric is very taut, and use the darning foot. Embellish these prints by outlining the designs with pearl cotton or thick rayon thread on the bobbin.

Use bridal veiling as your fabric and create original lace. Or, decorate velveteen using velour yarn on the bobbin and monofilament thread on the top.

Project
Tote Bag
Square (Cabling)

Think "spring" with a tote bag square; the pattern is provided in Fig. 3.15. Re-member that directions for making the tote and finishing the squares are in Chapter 12.

Program: 00
Stitch width: 0
Stitch length: 0
Needle: #80/12
Feed dogs: lowered
Presser foot: darning #6
Tension: *top*, normal; *bobbin*, normal, then loosened for #5 pearl cotton
Fabric suggestions: 9″ (22.9cm) square medium-weight white fabric
Thread: green, red and yellow machine embroidery thread; three bobbins wound with #5 pearl cotton (red, yellow, green)
Accessories: tracing paper, dressmaker's carbon, empty ballpoint pen, water-erasable pen
Stabilizer: freezer paper

Transfer the design in Fig. 3.15 to tracing paper and then, using dressmaker's carbon and the ballpoint pen, transfer the design to freezer paper. Color in or mark each flower to indicate color. Press this to the underside of your fabric. Always do a sample first, using the same fabric, stabilizer and threads as you will be using on your finished copy. Peek under the sample and adjust the tensions as needed. When cabling, you always work with underside up.

Use yellow machine embroidery thread on the spool and pearl cotton on the bobbin. With feed dogs lowered, darning foot on, pull the thick pearl to the top but do not anchor it.

Manually move the hoops in tight spirals, laying in lines of cabling to make the flower centers. Pull all ends through to the back as you finish the centers.

Change to red thread and pearl and freely stitch the petal lines. Don't worry if your lines are not exactly the same as mine. Finish off the ends as before.

Change to green thread and pearl cotton and do the inner accenting lines, ending as

Fig. 3.15 Pattern for tote bag square.

before and leaving threads long enough to poke to the back and work into the stitches there later.

When you've finished, pull off the freezer paper and work in the pearl cotton beginnings and ends by hiding them in the stitches on the underside. Finish as explained in Chapter 12.

Lesson 5. Fringing yarn and fabric

In this lesson you will learn to make fringe with a fringing fork, as well as with strips of fabric sewn together and clipped into fringe. Start by using a fringing fork to make yarn fringe. It can be used for wigs, costumes, rugs, and decorating edges of garments. Fringing forks are available in many different sizes. Or, you can make your own using wire, ranging from the thickness of a coat hanger to fine as a hairpin.

Wrap the fork as shown in Fig. 3.16, sew down the center, pull the loops toward you, and wrap some more. If making yards and yards of fringe, use Robbie Fanning's method of measuring. Robbie measures the length she wants from a roll of adding-machine tape and stitches her fringe right to the tape. This also keeps the fringe from twisting. When you're finished, tear off the paper and apply the fringe.

Sometimes you may not want the fringe sewn in the middle (Fig. 3.16A). Stitch it at the edge of the fork to make fringe twice as wide as that made by sewing down the center (Fig. 3.16B). As you work with the fork, you will understand when to use each method. And don't limit yourself to yarn or string alone. Try fabric. I used it for doll hair for my denim doll.

Program: 10
Stitch width: 4.0
Stitch length: 2.0
Feed dogs: up
Presser foot: fancy stitch foot #2

Tension: *top*, normal; *bobbin*, normal
Fabric suggestion: 1"-wide (2.5cm-wide) bias strips, several yards
Thread: polyester to match bias
Accessories: large fringe fork
Stabilizer: adding machine tape

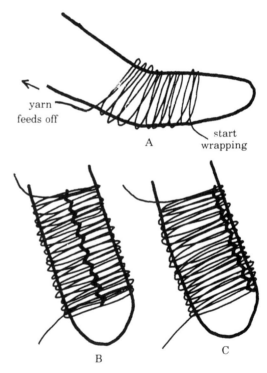

yarn feeds off

A

start wrapping

B   C

Fig. 3.16 The fringe fork. A. Wrap with yarn or fabric strips. B. Sew down in the middle. C. Or sew at the side of the fork for wider fringe.

Fig. 3.17 The doll's hair is fabric fringe, her eyelashes are thread fringe done with the tailor-tacking foot.

I wrapped the fork with red denim and sewed down the center over adding-machine tape. When I had enough for hair, I tore the paper off the fringe and pinned the hair to her head in various ways to decide what hairdo I liked best. I sewed it on by hand; I could have left it as it was, but I decided to clip the loops (Fig. 3.17).

But you can achieve almost the same effect with fabric without using the fringing fork. Work with strips of fabrics, but don't clip them into fringe until after they are sewn to the item you are making.

Project Fringed Denim Rug

This fabric-fringe project, a little rug, ate up yards of old jeans and denim remnants I picked up at sales; I kept cutting 2½" (6.4cm) strips on the bias until I had finished the rug.

Program: 01
Stitch length: 2.5
Needle position: 6 to left

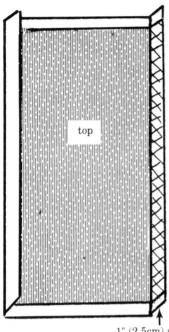

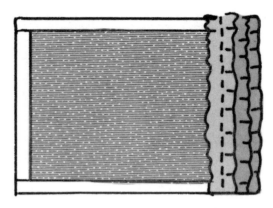

Fig. 3.18 Place a 1" (2.5cm) strip of fusible webbing along each edge. Fold toward the topside of the fabric and press in place.

1" (2.5cm) strip
fusible webbing

Fig. 3.19 Stitching bias strips onto the rug.

Needle: jeans needle #110/18
Presser foot: zipper foot #4, placed in right
    position
Dual feed: engaged
Tension: *top,* normal; *bobbin,* normal
Fabric suggestion: denim, cut into 2½"
    (6.4cm) bias strips of blues and red; use
    remnants and old jeans to cut quantity
    needed for rug size you want; heavy up-
    holstery fabric for rug backing
Thread: matching polyester thread
Stabilizer: 1"-wide (2.5cm-wide) fusible web-
    bing (measure circumference of rug)

You'll need a piece of heavy fabric the size of the finished rug, plus an inch all around. Measure the perimeter and cut a piece of 1"-wide (2.5cm-wide) fusible webbing. Using a Teflon pressing sheet, press the fusible webbing to the topside of all the edges and fold them back on the topside of the fabric, pressing again (Fig. 3.18). This is the top of the rug, so the edges will be finished when the last strip is stitched down.

Fold the first bias strip lengthwise to find the center, but open it again and place it ⅛" (3.2mm) from the edge of the upholstery fabric. Stitch down the center crease of each strip from top to bottom (Fig. 3.19). Fold the left side of the strip to the right. Push the next strip as close as you can get it to the first. Sew down the center again; Fig. 3.19 shows the first three fabric strips stitched down. If you run out of fabric for a strip, add another by overlapping the last strip at least 1" (2.5cm).

When you're all done stitching, clip each strip every ½" (12.7mm), staggering the clips for each row. My rug (Fig. 3.20) went into the washer and dryer to soften.

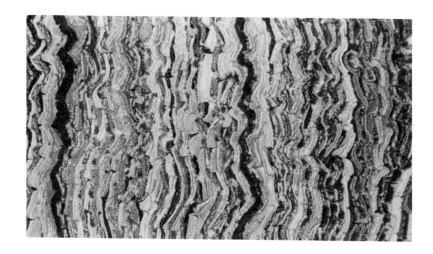

Fig. 3.20 The bias strips are clipped into fringe.

Lesson 6. Adding buttons, beads, shisha

Attaching buttons

Once you've attached a button by machine, you won't want to do it any other way, it is so speedy. If you are applying buttons to a garment you've made, be sure the button area is interfaced. Dab glue stick on the underside of the button and position it.

Program: 89
Stitch width: space between holes in the button, usually 4.0
Stitch length: 0
Needle: #80
Feed dogs: lowered (automatic)
Presser foot: tailor tack, fancy stitch #2, or bare shank
Dual feed: disengaged
Tension: *top,* normal; *bobbin,* normal
Thread: polyester
Accessories: button elevator, or toothpick are optional, transparent tape, glue stick, scrap fabrics, buttons, beads and shisha mirrors (see Sources of Supply)

Place the foot or shank on top of the button and lower the needle in the hole to the left. The machine will anchor the threads, then swing the needle to the right needle position. Pause here to be sure the needle clears the button and falls into the hole at the right. Stitch back and forth several times, until the machine stops by itself. The needle will again be in the left position, ready for the next button. That's all there is to it.

If the garment fabric is thick, such as coating, you will need to make a button shank; otherwise, the buttonhole will pucker whenever the coat is buttoned. Raise the stitches to create a shank by taping a darning needle or round toothpick between the holes on top of the button before you stitch (Fig. 3.21A). When finished, pull off the tape and remove the darning needle. Leave a long thread to wrap around the shank and anchor with a hand needle, strengthening the shank.

A button elevator, which is a small gadget made to slip under the button and raise it, is available at notion counters. The fringing foot can also be used, to make a thread shank.

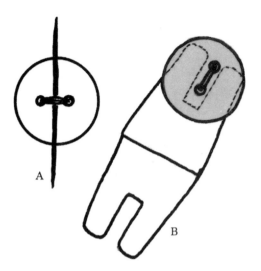

Fig. 3.22 If beads
are stitched down
on only one side,
they can be nudged
to stand up.

Fig. 3.23 Stitching
down both sides to
make beads lie flat.

Fig. 3.21 Sew on a button with a shank.
A. Use a toothpick on top of the button.
B. Use a button reed.

Attaching beads and baubles

Beads can be attached by machine if the hole in the bead is large enough and your needle fine enough. The thickness of the bead also matters if you zigzag it in place. Lower the feed dogs, remove the presser foot, adjust the stitch width as directed. Hand-walk the machine first to see if the needle will clear the bead, and if the sizes of the bead and needle are compatible. If attaching the bead by hand-walking only, attach the rim of the bead to the fabric by first holding it in place with a dot of glue from a glue stick. Anchor the thread in the center of the bead by stitching in place three or four times. Raise the needle. Move the fabric over to anchor the thread on the side of the bead. Go back to the center and anchor again. Repeat until the bead is securely sewn in place and will stand up (Fig. 3.22). Nudge the bead to stand on its outside rim when you finish stitching. Wipe off the glue.

If you go back and stitch down the other side as well, your bead will lay flat, hole up (Fig. 3.23).

Attaching seed beads, or other fine or oddly shaped beads can be done in the following way. First string the beads onto a thread. Using monofilament, stitch one end of the beaded thread down on the fabric. Stitch along the thread the width of one bead. Push the first bead near that end and then stitch over the thread to keep the bead in place. Stitch again the distance of the next bead. Push the bead up to the first, stitch over the thread and repeat, as shown in Fig. 3.24.

Or sew beads down by stringing them singly on thick threads and stitching both ends of the threads down (Fig. 3.25).

You can attach beads invisibly, using monofilament thread to couch them down or to string the beads on. Or choose your thread wisely and use the stitching as a part of the decoration.

Another way to hold down beads is to first stitch strips of needlelace on water-soluble stabilizer. You might try mending Program 09 to make strips of needlelace 2″ to 3″ (5.1 to 7.6cm) long. Allow the machine to stitch forward for the desired length over a double thickness of water soluble stabilizer. Touch the reverse button and the machine will weave forward and back, then stop. When the lace has been stitched, merely pull off the excess stabilizer and hold your work under a faucet to wash out most of what remains, but leave

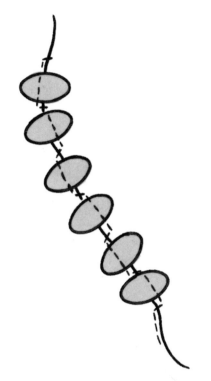

Fig. 3.24 *A string of seed beads, attached by machine along dotted line (solid line is thread).*

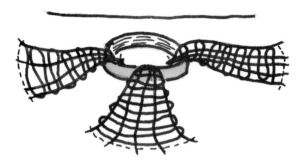

Fig. 3.26 *Using needlelace to attach beads.*

a bit of the sticky residue. When it is almost dry, shape the needlelace strips and they will dry in that shape. Use two or three of these strips to hold down beads or washers (Fig. 3.26). Thread a strip through the object and stitch down one

end. Move the bauble down over your stitching. Arrange the strip, twisting it if you wish. Then stitch down the other end freely and invisibly. Use this method, as I have, on decorative box tops and collages (Fig. 3.27).

Another method of using stones and jewels for wall hangings or pictures is to cover them with net or transparent fabrics, and then stitch down the fabric. Then cut holes in the fabric large enough to let the objects show through and small enough so they don't fall out.

Or make needlelace in the center of wire bent into a circle, rectangle, or other shape. Stretch the lace over an object placed on a background fabric. Attach the lace to the fabric by stitching freely, close to the wire, around the inside of this frame, and cutting off the wire. Embroider the edges if you wish.

Attaching shisha mirrors

Shishas are small pieces of mirrored glass. They are about 1″ (2.5cm) in diameter, but are never exactly circular. It is possible to attach them to fabric if you follow the methods Caryl Rae Hancock of Indianapolis, and Gail Kibiger of Warsaw, Indiana, invented.

This is Caryl Rae Hancock's method, illustrated in Fig. 3.28. First, stretch organdy in a hoop. The shisha is placed on top of the organdy and its outline traced. The

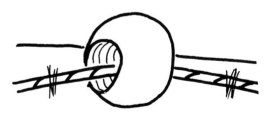

Fig. 3.25 *Attach a large bead by threading a cord through it and stitching on either side of the cord.*

Fig. 3.27 "The Flop Box," made by Pat Pasquini, has a machine-embellished top by the author. It includes beads held down with needlelace, other beads strung with cord and porcupine quills and couched in place, textures created by stitching cords down, using a double needle to pintuck suede, and stitching blobs and satin stitches in the background. Photo by Robbie Fanning.

back of the shisha is dabbed with glue stick and placed on a background fabric, not the organdy.

Sew around—and about ⅛" (3.2mm) inside—the drawn circle. Stitch around two more times. Without taking the fabric out of the hoop, cut out the circle of fabric within the stitching. After anchoring threads, the machine should be set on Program 10 without changes, and the circle

stitched freely around the cut edge. Turn the hoop as you sew around it, letting the stitches radiate from the edge of the hole to about ½" (12.7mm) beyond. The organdy must be covered with stitches at this time. Anchor threads and take the organdy out of the hoop. Cut very closely around the outside stitching.

With the machine changed back to straight stitch, place the piece of embroi-

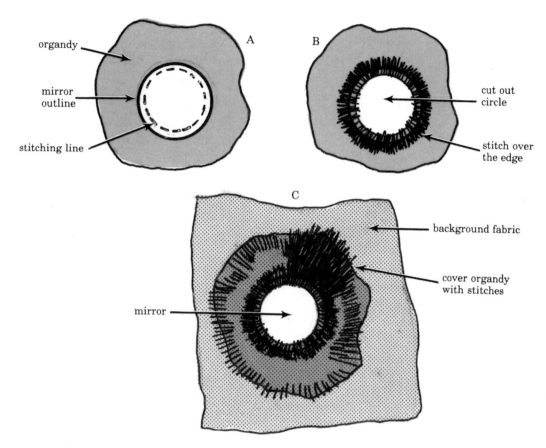

organdy

mirror
outline

stitching line

A

B

cut out
circle

stitch over
the edge

C

background fabric

cover organdy
with stitches

mirror

Fig. 3.28 Glue the shisha to the background fabric. A. On organdy, stitch around a circle slightly smaller than the shisha. B. Cut out the center and embroider over the edge. C. Place the organdy over the shisha and stitch it in place on background fabric by straight stitching. Embroider the background to conceal the edge.

dery over the shisha and background fabric and pin organdy in place. Stitch around outside edge of the shisha. Be careful: if you stitch into the glass, the needle and probably the shisha will break.

Leave the machine as set or change to zigzag again and stitch over those straight stitches, following the radiating direction of the original zigzagging. Blend the outside edge of the organdy with the background fabric by radiating stitches onto the background fabric.

Gail Kibiger has a slightly different method. She applies shisha by first placing the mirror on the background fabric, not on organdy, and tracing around it. Removing the shisha, she stitches ⅛" (3.2mm) within this circle three times and cuts out the circle. Gail embroiders on the background fabric as Caryl Rae did the organdy.

The shisha is then glued to a piece of organdy and placed under the finished hole. After pinning it in place, she straight stitches around the mirror to hold it in place.

One of Gail's variations is to work a spiderweb across the hole before the edges are zigzagged.

Silver bangles, the large sequins found in craft and knitting shops, are an excellent substitute for shisha. Not only are they exactly round, unlike the uneven shape of shishas, but they are durable. If you sew into them, your needle doesn't break. Make a record for your notebook of how you have applied buttons, beads and shishas.

Project
Bird Collage

I work with transparent fabrics almost exclusively, so I collect them. Besides fabric stores, garage sales and thrift shops are wonderful sources. I check out the chiffon scarves, colored nylons, lingerie, curtains, as well as glitzy dresses—though it takes courage to buy some of these because of the double-takes at the checkout counter.

This is a beadwork project, which includes appliqué as well. Bird shapes are my

Fig. 3.29 Bird collage.

favorites. I like them plump like baby chicks, sleek like soaring eagles, even whimsical like African Dahomey appliqués. I've used them on quilts, wall hangings, and in fabric collages.

In this small picture, shown in Fig. 3.29, I added small clay beads by machine to the appliquéd picture.

Program: 00
Stitch length: 0
Needle: #90/14
Feed dogs: lowered
Presser foot: darning foot #6
Tension: *top,* slightly loosened; *bobbin,* normal
Fabric suggestions: green and gold suede or felt for bird's body and wings; transparent fabrics, such as organdy, chiffon, yellow mesh grapefruit bag, for the wings; moss green bridal veiling to cover the picture; 12" (30.5cm) square of coarse beige upholstery linen for background; loosely woven taupe-colored fabric for the nest; gold lamé for the eggs; nude-colored nylon stocking; also needed are small clay beads
Thread: several strands of brown and beige coarse thread or string, cut into 1" (2.5cm) pieces; brown, green and beige shiny rayon; monofilament
Stabilizer: freezer paper

If this sounds overwhelming, you can substitute any colors you wish, and use only one, instead of a variety, of transparent fabrics. Although I used transparent thread for most of this collage, I added browns, greens and beiges in rayon stitches when my piece was almost complete.

Begin by pulling off a half-dozen threads from the square of background fabric. Cut these threads into small lengths of 1" and 2" (2.5–5.1cm) and add them to the other threads you've cut—you will need several dozen. Put them aside.

Iron freezer paper to the back of the linen fabric for stability, as you will not use a hoop for this project. Although not necessary, I always cut the background fabric at least 6"–8" (15.2–20.3cm) bigger than the finished size so I can practice stitching or layering on the edges. Also, I plan my pieces so they look as if they go on beyond the frame. I don't want them to look as if they end inside it.

Fig. 3.30 shows the arrangement, and Fig. 3.31 is the pattern; cut out the fabric pieces as follows: Cut out the oval nest from the taupe fabric and place that slightly below the center on the background. When I cut fabric for collages, I use a cut/tear method. By pulling slightly on the fabric as I cut, I fray the material a bit to keep the edges soft. The bird should be cut from green suede or felt so it will not roll when you cut it out. Be sure to use fabric that has some body, so it will be easy to control. Place the bird on the nest (Fig. 3.30). Cut a gold wing from suede and position that on the bird. Cut out the transparent wings. Place one on top of the gold wing, but shift it a bit so it is not exactly in the same place as the first. Do the same with the other sheers. Your wings will cross, meet, blend, as if in a watercolor. Over the last wing you will use one cut from a yellow mesh grapefruit bag or a coarse yellow net. Rearrange until the wings look pleasing to you.

Cut the foot and top off a nude-colored nylon stocking and slit the stocking from top to bottom. Stretch it over the picture and pin it down just beyond the image area. As you stretch the stocking, it will lighten in color. It should be almost invisible, but not stretched so tightly it buckles the picture. This holds all the pieces in place, and softens, but does not change, the colors of your picture.

Lower the feed dogs on your machine. Use a darning foot, as you will have many layers to stitch together. Begin by freely sewing around the bird with transparent thread. Stitch just off the edge of the body and wing pieces. It is not important to be

Fig. 3.30 Follow this design for assembling the bird picture.

completely accurate; it's fine if you stitch into the body or wings. You might want to stitch in a few feathers on the gold wing as well, giving the bird an attractive, padded look. Stitch to the outside of the nest and sew that down freely. Then sew all around the outside edge of your picture. Cut off the stocking from the outside edges.

Add three gold lamé eggs under the bird. Over the edge of the nest, scatter half the thread pieces you've cut. Hold all this down by laying a piece of moss green bridal veiling over the picture and pinning it in place.

Again, with transparent thread and a free machine, sew around the eggs, around the outside of the bird and around the nest, managing to catch threads to anchor them. Yes, you will be sewing in a haphazard manner around the nest — and you do not have to sew every thread in place. With a very fine embroidery scissors, cut out the veiling from in front of the bird and the eggs.

String the small clay beads onto some of the remaining "nest" threads. Arrange the threads around the nest on top of those you have already sewn in place. Be very careful as you sew these threads in place; you don't want to hit beads with the darning foot. With transparent thread, sew above and below the beads to hold them in place (see Fig. 3.25).

An alternative method is to remove the darning foot. Press the fabric firmly against the needle plate as you sew down the threads. Be careful of your fingers. Thread up with a shiny brown rayon thread. With your machine set up for zig-zag stitching, add texture and color to the nest by stitching a blob, lifting the presser foot lever and pulling the picture to stitch again in another spot. Cross and recross threads. I change colors several times (browns, beiges and greens). This also helps anchor the coarse threads.

The bird's eye can be added by sewing on a gold bead by hand, or with your machine,

48

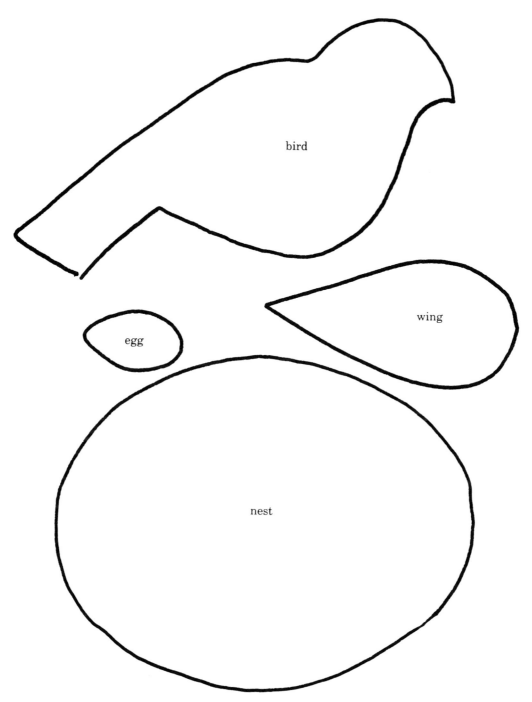

bird

wing

egg

nest

Fig. 3.31 Patterns for the Bird Collage.

by building up a blob of thread. Your picture is complete. Pull off the freezer paper, or leave it in place. Cut off that extra margin from around your piece. Stretch the picture over a piece of batting and plywood and frame it. These pictures are so much fun to put together, and no two are alike.

Lesson 7. Smocking and gathering

Smocking

In hand smocking, fabric is gathered tightly into channels and embroidery is worked on top of the channels. Stitches chosen are open and stretchy.

Smocking by machine, on the other hand, will not be stretchy like hand smocking. After gathering with thread or cord, machine embroidery stitches usually hold the gathers in place. But if you use elastic, the gathering will stretch—but then, of course, you won't embroider over it.

There are at least a dozen ways to smock on your sewing machine, varying the method of gathering or embroidering, or varying the threads used. Here are several methods you can try. In each one, start with at least 2½ times the width needed for the finished pattern. For any garment, do the smocking first and then cut out the pattern.

Program: 00; others as desired
Stitch length: 4.0–6.0
Needle: #90/14
Feed dogs: up
Dual feed: engaged
Presser foot: ordinary sewing foot #0
Tension: *top*, −3+; *bottom*, normal
Fabric: 2 or more 18″ × 45″ (45.7 × 114.3cm) pieces of medium-weight cotton; 1 yard (.9m) strip for gathering ruffles; several 12″ (30.5cm) or larger pieces of scrap fabrics
Threads: regular sewing thread; machine embroidery; monofilament
Accessories: water-erasable marker

Simple gathered smocking

First draw at least four lines across the 45″-wide (114.3cm-wide) fabric with a water-erasable marker. The lines should be about ½″ (12.7mm) apart. Leave the seam allowances free of stitching. Anchor the threads, and then straight stitch along your drawn lines, leaving long ends of thread at the ends of the rows (Fig. 3.32A). Pull on the bobbin threads to gather the fabric to 18″ (45.7cm) and knot every two threads together.

Choose a decorative stitch, change to fancy stitch foot #2, and embroider across the fabric between the gathering lines of stitching (Fig. 3.32A). Then take out the gathering stitches.

Smocking with cordonnet

Use another piece of 18″ × 45″ (45.7 × 114.3cm) fabric. Thread the cordonnet through the throatplate of the machine. To gather, sew across the fabric, using a double needle (1.6mm) and the 7-groove cording foot (Fig. 3.32B). Again, leave the seam allowances free of stitching. Use the presser foot as a width guide to sew at least three more rows. Stitch an even number of rows, at least four. Leave tails of cord at the beginning and end of each line.

Tie off pairs of the cords at the start. Pull the cords to gather the material to 18″ (45.7cm). Then tie a knot at the end of each. Remove the cordonnet from the machine.

Place a stabilizer under your work. Em-

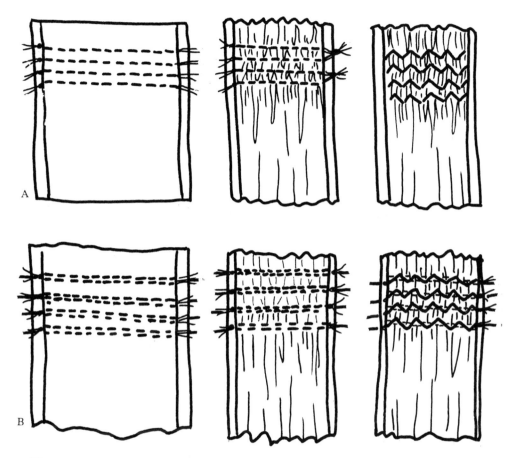

Fig. 3.32 Two ways to machine smock. A. Gather up rows of stitching and embroider between them. B. Gather the fabric, then using a cord and double needle, embroider over the gathers.

broider over the cords and then remove the stabilizer.

Embroidering with thick thread in the bobbin

This may be used with either of the preceding methods for gathering. First complete the gathering. Turn the fabric over, topside down on the bed of the machine. Place water-soluble stabilizer under the gathers.

Program: 10, 27, or 29
Stitch width: 6.0
Stitch length: 6.0 on Program 10; as set by computer on 27 or 29
Needle: #90/14
Feed dogs: up
Presser foot: fancy foot #2
Tension: *top*, normal; *bobbin*, varies with cord
Fabric: medium-weight cotton
Thread: sewing thread for top; #5 or #8 pearl cotton for bobbin
Stabilizer: water-soluble

When you stitch up the samples, sew, look underneath to see if the pearl cotton is attached evenly and smoothly. Adjust tensions and stitch width as necessary.

Open built-in stitches look best — the simple zigzag is effective. Remove the stabilizer when your stitching is completed.

Smocking with elastic

Wind the bobbin with fine, round elastic. Do this by hand so it doesn't stretch. Again, stitch down rows ½" (12.7mm) apart, gathering as you sew. The thread on top will show, so choose the color carefully. You can use this for bodices of sun dresses, nightgowns or swimsuits. This works best on delicate to lightweight fabrics.

Another way to make fabric stretch, giving a shirred effect, is to use a round elastic through the hole of the throat plate. Use regular thread on top and bobbin, and a zigzag setting that clears the elastic.

Alternately, stitch with a double needle and a straight stitch. Stitch several rows across the fabric using the presser foot as a guide, or draw the rows on the fabric with a water-erasable marker before stitching. Don't pull the elastic for gathering until all the stitching is completed. I use this method at the top of children's knit skirts, as well as on waistlines of T-shirt dresses.

With ⅛" (3.2mm) flat elastic, use either Program 12 or 13 (Fig. 3.33A and B); use width 4.0, length 2, or as set in the computer. Thread the elastic through the hole in the throat plate and follow the stitching line.

With these programs, the gathers can't be changed after they are sewn in, because the needle stitches into the elastic. Stretch the elastic while sewing. The more you stretch it, the more gathers it will create.

The zigzag stitch, Program 10, will sew on either side of the flat elastic and will not pierce it as will Programs 12 or 13. After stitching, adjust the gathers.

Gathering

Using cord

To gather light- to heavy-weight materials, use this, my all-time favorite method.

Program: 10
Stitch width: 2.0
Stitch length: 2.0
Feed dogs: up

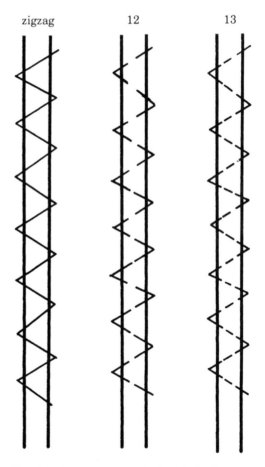

zigzag   12   13

Fig. 3.33 Two ways to attach flat elastic. Zigzag stitch does not penetrate elastic. Programs 12 and 13 stitch into elastic.

Zigzag over a cord, such as gimp or cordonnet. To keep the cord in position while stitching over it, use the single cording foot. Place the cord in the groove and it will be fed through and covered perfectly (Fig. 3.34). Pull up the cord to gather the fabric. Leave the cord in the fabric.

I use this for everything from skirts to dust ruffles to slipcovers. You won't break the gathering stitch as you often do when pulling on a basting thread. It saves hours.

Using elastic

Using the same settings as you did for cord, thread the elastic through the slot under the cording foot. Hold the elastic

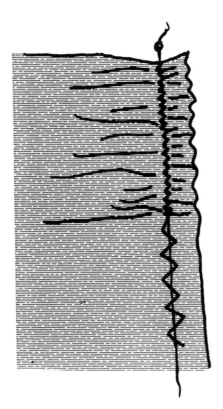

Fig. 3.34 Use an embroidery foot when zigzagging over cord to gather fabric.

gently in back. Pull on it from the front while sewing a zigzag over it. I use this for quick sleeve finishes for little girls' dresses. If sewn about 1″ (2.5cm) from the finished edge, it creates a ruffle.

Using a gathering foot

Gathering yards of ruffles is easy with a shirring foot. It simultaneously gathers and applies the gathered fabric to another flat piece of fabric. The only drawback is that without seeing your fabric, I can't give you an iron-clad formula for how much fabric is needed to gather into, say, a 15″ (38.1cm) ruffle.

The key to your estimates is to stitch a sample. Work with the same material you're going to use for the ruffle. Finer materials need to be gathered more fully than heavy fabrics do. Gathering depends upon fabric weight, tension and stitch length. The tighter the tension, the more gathering. The longer the stitch, the more fullness that can be locked into each stitch and the tighter the gathers—and the more fabric you'll need. I admit I'm a coward and always add inches to be sure.

Even though this foot will gather a ruffle and apply it to fabric at the same time, I prefer gathering and attaching the gathers in two steps because of the difficulty in estimating the yardage I'll need for the ruffles. But, to do both steps at once, place the fabric to be attached to the ruffle in the slot of the gathering foot and the ruffle fabric under the foot. Keep the edges of both pieces of fabric even.

If you do not intend to attach your ruffle to the fabric all in one step, you may want to take advantage of a favorite trick. This is an oldie but goodie, in that you can do this on any model Pfaff that has the dual-feed feature. The machine will shirr and gather by simply disengaging the dual feed, increasing your stitch length and tightening the upper tension. For light-weight fabrics, I generally set the tension between 5 and 6, or approximately where the color separation line is on the tension dial. Then the amount of fullness on that particular type of fabric can be regulated by simply changing the stitch length.

Program: 00
Stitch length: 3.5 to 6.0
Needle: #80/12
Presser foot: ordinary foot #0
Dual feed: disengaged
Feed dogs: raised
Tension: *top*, 5 to 9; *bobbin*, normal
Fabrics: light, medium, and heavy weight
Thread: regular sewing thread
Accessories: rotary cutter and mat; ruler; vanishing marker

To make the samples for your notebook, cut several strips of fabric 1" (2.5cm) wide by 12" (30.5cm) long. Mark them by drawing a line across each end 1" (2.5cm) from the end of the strip. This will leave an area in the middle 10" (25.4cm) long. Stitch down the center of each of these strips from one end to the other, with the machine set up for shirring.

You might start one set of strips with the tension set between 5 and 6, and another set with higher tensions, and change the stitch length for each one of the strips in the set. Mark them so you will know exactly how much your machine will shirr at any given setting on that particular fabric. You will measure the marked 10" (25.4cm) area between the two lines. If, for example, you have shirred the length down to 8" (20.3cm), you will be able to estimate the amount of fabric needed.

You can use this shirring in many ways, all of them decorative. Most of these I learned years ago, when I first started selling sewing machines. At that time, the company I worked for did not have a zigzag machine, but we made use of the attachments, and the special shirring foot was one of them.

I do like to make pretty blouses, and

shirring on the yokes, or even the cuffs, can be a long-cut that will garner lots of compliments.

One way of shirring is to stitch many rows about ⅝" (15.9mm) apart. When you have covered the entire piece of fabric, shirr again at right angles. This makes a puffy, textured effect called waffle shirring (Fig. 3.35).

Rows of shirring can be grouped and spaced in various ways and ribbon or lace sewn between alternate rows. Try this on the bodice of little girls' dresses. The effect is almost like French handsewing, but it is considerably more durable.

Project:
Closet Sachet

Sachets are quick to make, and you can often use scraps of shirred fabric from other projects. Remember to always do the shirring *before* cutting out garment sec-

Fig. 3.35 Waffle shirring gives a puffy, highly textured effect.

tions, and you're sure to have lots of shirred fabric on hand. Nevertheless, I will give instructions and measurements for making the sachet in Fig. 3.36 from scratch.

Program: 00; 97 or other decorative stitch
Stitch length: 3.5
Dual feed: disengaged, engaged
Tension: *top,* 5 to 6; *bobbin,* normal
Fabric: lightweight lawn, batiste or broadcloth; nylon net; fleece (optional)
Thread: regular sewing thread; variegated machine embroidery thread (optional)
Accessories: glue stick; ribbon; potpourri

Cut a piece of fabric 6½″ (16.5cm) wide and 10″ (25.4cm) long. With the vanishing marker, draw a line ¾″ (19.0mm) in from the long edge on one side. Draw a second line parallel to the first, spaced the width

Fig. 3.36 Shirred and ruffled closet sachet.

of your ribbon. Draw third line ¾″ (19.0mm) away from, and parallel to, the second line. Continue across the width of the fabric, alternating the ribbon width and ¾″ (19.0mm) measurements.

Set up the machine for shirring and stitch each of these parallel lines. Be sure to let the fabric feed easily so that the machine will shirr the same amount on each stitching line.

Reengage the dual feed, change the stitch length to 2.0, set the tension between 4 and 5 (normal setting) and staystitch the end rows to secure the shirring.

Place the ribbon over the double rows of stitching and, using thread to match the color of the ribbon, stitch in place along the edge of the ribbon. It is easier to use the ordinary presser foot #0 for this, as the center of this foot is an excellent guide.

Cut a paper square 4½″ × 4½″ (11.4cm × 11.4cm) and center this over the shirring. (If you wish, you can position your rows of shirring on the diagonal.) Mark around this square with the vanishing marker, then staystitch these lines. Trim away the surplus shirring to within ¼″ (6.4mm) of the stitching.

You can use the extra pieces to experiment with some of the decorative programs on the strips of ribbon. I used variegated rayon thread and Program 97. When you find one that you like, do the decorative stitching or, if you prefer, leave the ribbon plain.

Cut a strip of fabric 2″ (5.1cm) wide for the ruffle. You can decide how full you want to have this, and by consulting your samples in the notebook, set your machine accordingly. I kept the settings that I used on the main section of the sachet, and 16″ (40.6cm) should be more than adequate. First, attach the ribbon to the right side of one of the long edges of this strip using glue stick; then stitch down the edge of the ribbon. Fold the ribbon back, concealing the raw edge, and stitch down the opposite side of the ribbon. This ribbon may be decorated with the same fancy stitch used on the sachet or left plain.

Now set the machine for shirring, and shirr the opposite side of the ruffle. Leave about 6"–8" (15.2–20.3cm) thread at the beginning and end of your shirring, as you will want to adjust the ruffle when attaching it to the sachet.

Pin the ruffle to the square, right sides together matching the edges; join the ends of the ruffle where they meet. Stitch around.

Cut a second square of plain unshirred fabric. If you think you want extra body, cut a square of fleece the same size. Place these on top of the ruffle and square, then stitch, leaving an opening on one side for turning. Trim the corners and edges, then turn right-side-out.

To hold the potpourri, I cut a strip of nylon net about 8" × 4" (20.3cm × 10.2cm), and folded it in half the long way, then shook the potpourri mixture between the two layers as I stitched. The reason I made it long and skinny is that it was much easier to put through the hole I left for turning, and the "snake" could be coiled around, or simply allowed to fold up inside the sachet.

After whipping the opening shut, I attached the ribbon for hanging. Cut this approximately 20" (50.8cm) long, fold it in half and measure 4" (10.2cm) down from the fold. Attach the ends of the ribbon to the sachet at this point, using Program 89 (button sewing program), then tie a bow. Any surplus ribbon or uneven ends can be clipped off.

You can use circular shapes or ovals, too. Sachets are fun to make and are a nice gift when you want to make something, but do not want to spend a week doing it.

The shirring feature can also be used on heavy fabrics. While they will not shirr, it is possible to ease them by disengaging the dual feed and increasing the tension and stitch length drastically. I often do this when I have to set a sleeve into a tailored jacket. Stitching around the cap of the sleeve makes tailoring a snap, because it will ease in perfectly every time, with no unwanted pleats or puckers.

Lesson 8. Pulling threads together

Satin stitching on top of loosely woven fabric builds up texture quickly by drawing the threads of the fabric together into ridges. Then you can connect the ridges for even more texture. As you can see in the sample (Fig. 3.37), this technique looks like lace.

If you're hesitant about stitching in open areas, place water-soluble stabilizer behind the fabric before stitching.

Program: 10
Stitch width: 4.0
Stitch length: 0.0
Needle: #90/14

Feed dogs: lowered
Presser foot: darning foot #6
Dual feed: disengaged
Tension: *top*, slightly loosened; *bobbin*, normal
Fabric: loosely woven cheesecloth type
Thread: machine embroidery, desired color top and bobbin
Accessories: spring hoop, water-soluble stabilizer (optional)

To learn this technique, stitch an imaginary tree of satin stitches and lacy straight stitches. It's not necessary to trace my design, as this is done freely.

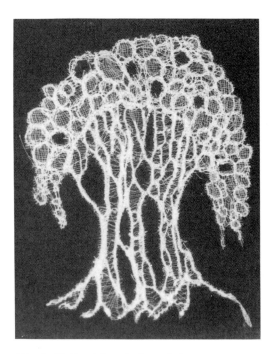

Fig. 3.37 Straight stitch and zigzag over loosely woven fabric produced both lacy and textured embroidery.

Put the fabric in a hoop. It must be stretched tightly. Bring the bobbin thread to the top and anchor the threads. Using the widest stitch setting, sew up and down in straight lines. At the down points, move the fabric over a bit and go up and down again. Continue until you have three or four rows of satin stitches. Then go back over them, zigzagging in between. This draws the previous lines together. Cut fabric threads if there is too much pulling and puckering.

Create branches on top and, when you come down to the bottom again, flare the line of stitching to resemble roots. Use the widest zigzags to stitch up and down again. Go back and zigzag over the whole tree again and again until the stitches are built up to your liking.

Change to a straight stitch and begin to stitch small circles at the top to crown the branches. Go from one to another. Cut or poke out the centers of some or all of the circles in the tree top, thus creating a lacy effect.

If you've used water-soluble stabilizer, then wash it out on completion of your work.

In the sample, I trimmed the tree from the background to show you the type of appliqué I add to my collages. It has a lacy look you can see through, which adds depth to the embroidery it's placed over. But sometimes I place the untrimmed appliqué over a background fabric and stitch it in place. After trimming it back to the stitches, I freely embroider over it with more satin stitches, with more ridges, building up more and more texture.

If you do a large enough square of threads pulled together with satin stitches, it can be used as a design for your tote bag. Or leave it untrimmed and still in the hoop for a window hanging.

CHAPTER 4

Adding Fabric to Fabric: Appliqué

- Lesson 9. Methods of applying appliqués
- Lesson 10. Appliquéing with feed dogs up
- Lesson 11. Appliquéing with feed dogs lowered

Once you know your machine as I know mine, you won't be satisfied stitching down all your appliqués with satin stitches. This chapter will show you several ways to place an appliqué onto a background successfully and teach a variety of methods for stitching it in place, including satin stitch, straight stitch, blind hem, and three-dimensional applications.

You'll make tote bag squares, Carrickmacross lace, and shadow work in these lessons. You will also work samples for your notebook to practice other appliqué methods.

Lesson 9. Methods of applying appliqués

Applying fabric to fabric takes two steps. Both are equally important. The first is to place the appliqué on the background in a way that keeps it in place, without puckering the fabric and with edges held down firmly, to enable you to do a perfect final stitching. The second step is the stitching. In Lessons 10 and 11, we'll try blind hems, edge stitching, straight stitching, blurring, scribbling and corded edges.

In appliqué, the best results are achieved when the applied and background fabrics have similar properties. For example, if using a cotton background fabric, it is best to use a similar weight appliqué fabric, and one that can be washed like the cotton. If washable, prepare the fabrics by washing and ironing them. They may be easier to work with if they are starched.

Match the grain lines of the appliqué to those of the background fabric. It's usually necessary to use a stabilizer under the fabric to prevent puckers when stitching. There are several methods for the first step. The first one wastes fabric, but the results are worth it.

Method A

Place the fabric for the appliqué on the bed of the machine and the base fabric on top, with the topsides of both fabrics down. Draw the design on the wrong side of the base fabric with a water erasable or vanishing marker, or place a paper pattern over it, pinning it carefully in position.

Program: 00
Stitch length: 1.5
Needle: #80/12
Presser foot: ordinary #0
Dual feed: engaged
Feed dogs: up

58

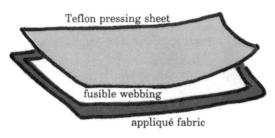

Teflon pressing sheet

fusible webbing

appliqué fabric

Fig. 4.1 To prepare an appliqué with fusible webbing, first place a piece of the fusible on the back of the appliqué fabric, cover it with the special Teflon sheet, and press in place.

Tension: *top,* normal; *bobbin,* normal
Fabric: varied
Thread: regular sewing thread on top and
    bobbin

With the machine set on straight stitch, single stitch around the design. Take the fabric from under the presser foot, turn it over, and cut the applied fabric back to the stitching line as closely as possible. Place the fabric under the presser foot with the appliqué on top this time. Use one of the methods for final stitching discussed in Lessons 10 and 11.

Method B

For the next method, fusible webbing and a Teflon pressing sheet are needed. This will produce a slightly stiffer appliqué than the first method, but if done correctly, it will never produce a pucker.

Cut a piece of fabric and a piece of fusible webbing slightly larger than the appliqué (Fig. 4.1). With the fusible webbing on top of the appliqué fabric, place the Teflon sheet over it and iron until the fusible webbing melts (Fig. 4.2). When it cools, the Teflon can be peeled away. Cut out the appliqué from this piece of fabric and then iron it to the background fabric, using a Teflon sheet on top to protect your iron.

Or use Wonder-Under, a fusible webbing that resembles appliqué paper (see Chapter 1).

Method C

An alternative to fusible webbing is the appliqué paper backed with "glue." To use this paper, cut a piece of it and fabric approximately the size of the appliqué. Draw the design on the non-adhesive side of the paper, then iron the paper to the back of

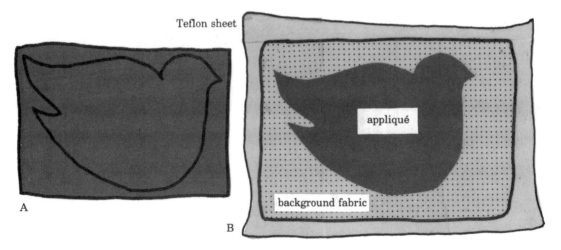

Teflon sheet

appliqué

background fabric

A

B

Fig. 4.2 A. Cut out the design from the appliqué fabric. B. Cover the design with the Teflon sheet again to press in place on the background fabric.

the fabric. After it adheres and cools, cut around the design and fabric, then peel the paper off the appliqué. The glue will have been transferred from the paper to the fabric. Iron the appliqué to the background.

If doing lettering or an appliqué where direction is important, then remember that this method gives you a flipped or mirror image of the original.

Method D

Plastic sandwich bags can also be used as a fusible—or try cleaners' garment bags. Cut out a piece of plastic the size of the appliqué and place it between the backing fabric and appliqué.

Put brown wrapping paper over and under this "sandwich" so any plastic that is peeking out will be ironed onto the brown paper and not your iron or ironing board. Press it with an iron hot enough to melt the plastic and fuse the fabrics together.

Method E

If you wish to blind hem around the edge of an appliqué for step two, the appliqué must be prepared in another way (Fig. 4.3).

First, straight stitch around the appliqué on what will be the fold line. Cut the appliqué from the fabric, leaving a ¼" (6.4mm) seam allowance. Clip the edges and turn under on the stitched line. Trim off more seam allowance wherever fabric overlaps or creates bulk and, if necessary, use Fray Check on any points to eliminate little "eyelashes" or fraying. Baste with stitches or a glue-stick. Press the edges flat. Baste in place on the background fabric—I find it more accurate when done by hand. There is a wash-away basting thread on the market. If you use this it eliminates the need to pull out the basting later, and if it gets caught in your final stitching, there's no problem because it simply washes away. Now you can blind-hem the appliqué to the foundation, using the specially written memory program given in the greeting card project.

If the appliqué is to be embroidered, it is sometimes best to do it first to prevent puckers in the background fabric. Embroidered patches can be appliquéd in many ways, the most common being satin stitching around the edge. But another way is to leave the edge almost devoid of stitching, cut out the appliqué and apply it with the

Fig. 4.3 To prepare and apply an appliqué for blind hemming, stitch all around it ¼" (6.3mm) from the edge (left). Fold under on the stitching, apply to the background and blind-hem-stitch in place (right).

same free stitches as the embroidery, to blend it into the background.

Even if fabric is to be heavily embroidered, embroider first on another piece of fabric, cut it out, and make it an appliqué. Use a glue stick or pin it in place. These appliqués are usually too thick to attach with fusible webbing.

Lesson 10. Appliquéing with feed dogs up

Satin stitches three ways

In addition to keeping your machine in excellent condition, the perfect satin stitch is achieved by matching of fabric, needle, and thread. Always sew a sample, using the same fabric, needle and thread that will be used on the finished piece. Don't watch the needle, but keep your eyes on the line you'll be stitching. Check to see if the fabric is being fed through evenly, but still covering the edges of the appliqué smoothly. As a general rule, the 0.35 stitch length setting on either Program 10 or 16 will give you a perfect satin stitch. Finer thread, however, may necessitate shortening the stitch length to 0.3. If you use heavier thread, a stitch length of 0.4 would be indicated.

Standard method

Keep a few things in mind when attaching an appliqué with satin stitches: First, the stitch width should not overpower the appliqué. I almost always use a setting no wider than 2, along with an appliqué foot, because the satin stitches fit perfectly inside the groove on the underside of the foot. The groove guides my stitching so that satin stitches are perfect. If I use a wider stitch setting, then I use a foot with a wider groove—such as the fancy stitch foot #2 or the knit edge foot.

Program: 10 or 16
Stitch width: 2.0 to 4.0
Stitch length: 0.35 or adjust for thread being used

Presser foot: appliqué foot, fancy stitch foot #2
Feed dogs: up
Tension: *top,* slightly loosened; *bobbin,* normal

While you may need to cover the edge of your appliqué in only one pass, if the fabric tends to fray you may find it more satisfactory with two passes, the second slightly wider.

Use a needle appropriate for the thread. The needle must be large enough to let the thread pass through freely and it must punch a large enough hole in the fabric to prevent the thread from fraying. For example, with rayon embroidery thread I use a #90/14 needle; on cotton embroidery thread, I use a #80 needle. On woven materials, I use a jeans needle instead of a universal point because I feel it gives me a more perfect edge. (The universal point is slightly rounded, so it deflects off the fibers and slips between them. When satin stitching on closely woven materials, this needle may create an uneven edge.)

Stained-glass method

Stained-glass is a type of satin-stitch appliqué in which your satin stitches are gray to black and extend out from the appliqué to the borders of the design. It is important to remember this, since not every design is appropriate for stained-glass.

Reverse appliqué

Reverse appliqué is the technique of layering from one to many fabrics on top of a background material. A design is straight-stitched through the layers, then the fabric is cut away from portions of the design to reveal the fabric beneath. It is finished by satin stitching over the straight stitches. Reverse appliqué can be combined with appliqué from the top as well. To do a perfect reverse appliqué, put both fabrics topsides up with your appliqué fabric underneath and use the ordinary presser foot #0 and dual feed. Draw the design on the top fabric or place the pattern on top of the fabrics and straight stitch around the design. Remove the paper.

Cut out the top fabric inside the design area. Slip stabilizer under your work, and then satin stitch the edges. When finished, you may want to cut away the extra appliqué fabric on the back to eliminate bulk.

This method often affords better control of the appliqué when applying small pieces to a design.

Project Tote Bag Square (Reverse Appliqué)

Here's a tote square to perfect your reverse appliqué technique. The pattern is provided in Fig. 4.4.

Programs: 00; then 10
Stitch length: 1.5 to 2.0 on Program 00; 0.35 on Program 10
Stitch width: 2.0 and 4.0 on Program 10
Needle: #90/14 jeans needle
Feed dogs: up
Presser foot: ordinary #0 on Program 00; appliqué or fancy stitch foot #2 on Program 10
Dual feed: engaged on Program 0; disengaged on Program 10
Tension: *top*, slightly loosened; *bobbin*, normal

Fabric suggestions: lightweight cotton, 9″ (22.9cm) squares of orange, yellow, and green
Thread: orange, yellow, and green machine embroidery cotton to match
Accessories: dressmaker's carbon; empty ballpoint pen
Stabilizer: freezer paper

Transfer the design in Fig. 4.4 onto tracing paper. Use the dressmaker's carbon to then transfer the design to the orange fabric.

Layer the three pieces of fabric with the marked orange on top, then the green and then the yellow. Pin together, then place all three layers under the presser foot with dual feed, and stitch around the outer framing line. The stitch length should be 1.5 to 2.0.

Remove the work from the machine and carefully cut out the orange layer from the center, leaving the green layer intact.

Take your traced pattern and place it over the square, making sure all the lines match. Pin the corners, then slip the dressmaker's carbon under the tracing, and trace the inner line of the frame, as well as the flower circles. Remove paper and stitch lines with a short straight stitch, making sure, when you stitch the frame, that the ends of the frame overlap the stitching on the outer frame. Clip the green fabric from the center, but don't clip it from the flowers. Leave the green flowers surrounded by yellow. Again placing your pattern on the fabric, trace the stem lines of the flowers.

Iron on a piece of freezer paper to the back of your work as a stabilizer.

Thread the machine with green thread and stitch the stems on the yellow background, as well as the line between the yellow and green area. With orange thread, stitch the outer line of the design (stitch width 2), then stitch the circles. Use a 4.0 satin stitch for the flowers, stitching around them at least twice. I chose to

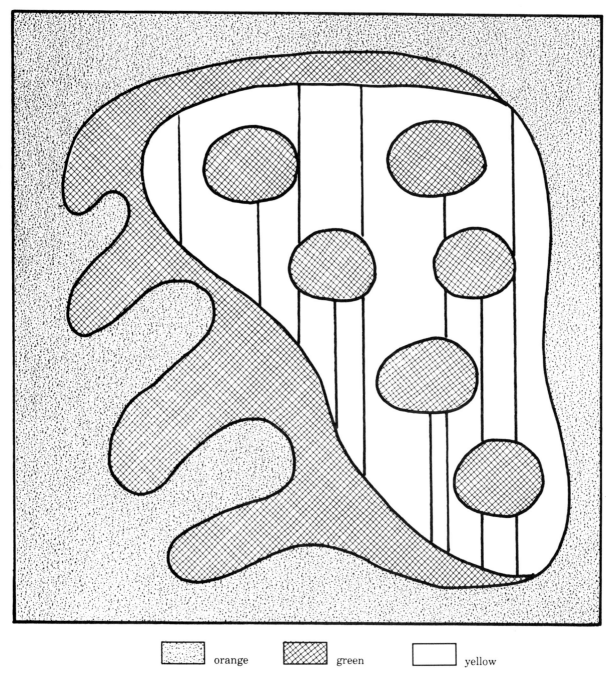

orange   green   yellow

Fig. 4.4 Pattern for reverse appliqué technique.

Fig. 4.5 Program 79, used to stitch stamens.

stitch several times to build up a ridge. Then I straight-stitched at each side of the satin stitches. This ridge could also be accomplished by stitching over a thick cord.

The flowers need stamens and these can be made in two different ways. First, you could simply use Program 79 to stitch the stamens (Fig. 4.5). Another way of doing them would be to put the fringe foot on the machine and zigzag over the foot to make fuzzy stamens. The latter way would give you a little more texture.

If you have a very complicated design with many layers, you may want to plan ahead when you are doing appliqué and combine layering with conventional appliqué. In this case, you could cut out the entire area of green, leaving the yellow area, and then add the flowers separately. This design, however, is simple enough to do as a true reverse appliqué

Blind hemming

A second way to attach appliqués to a background is with the blind hemstitch. Use the edging foot or blind-stitch foot. Prepare the appliqué according to Method E (see Fig. 4.3) and use monofilament thread on the top.

The blindstitch program on the machine cannot be narrowed down to less than 2.0 and, while this is usually sufficient for a relatively invisible blindstitch appliqué, I sometimes like to use either a "P" program or an "M" program.

The "P" program given in Fig. 4.6 is very short and easy to put in the machine. If you are unfamiliar with entering "P" program, check your instruction book.

The "M" program was given for the greeting card project. If you have not re-

moved it from memory, you can recall it now. Stitch around the appliqué, letting the straight stitches fall just outside the appliqué, with the bite of the widest stitch catching the edge. Remember, too, each of these created programs can be flipped over with your mirror key, should you be more comfortable working on the other side of the appliqué with stitches going in the other direction. You can write an "M" program so the machine will give the look you want. Do you want a wider bite? Then set the width on Program 10 to a higher number, and move the needle position further to the right on Program 01. These changes must be made before entering in the "M" memory, but on your "P" memory program, you can play around with the length and width to your heart's content. The length of the stitch determines the closeness of those two stitches that go up and back, holding the appliqué in place. Find the right length by doing a sample. Use this method of appliqué to attach patch pockets and to couch down heavy threads and cords. Monofilament is used on the top because it is almost invisible, but because of the nature of the stitch, you can use thread matching the background fabric with equally good results. .

If you change the monofilament to a thread that will contrast with the fabric, your regular blind hemstitch Program 17 — or Program 78 — will give you the look of buttonholing by hand.

A line of blind hemstitching is used in the greeting card project in Lesson 4 (Fig. 3.9).

Straight stitching

To apply fabric with a straight edge-stitch, you will place the appliqué on the background as you did for blind hemming (if you are working with non-wovens like suedes or felt, don't press the edges under). Use the blind-stitch foot #3. Set the straight stitch Program 00 at a 1.5 length.

With the presser foot in place on the fab-

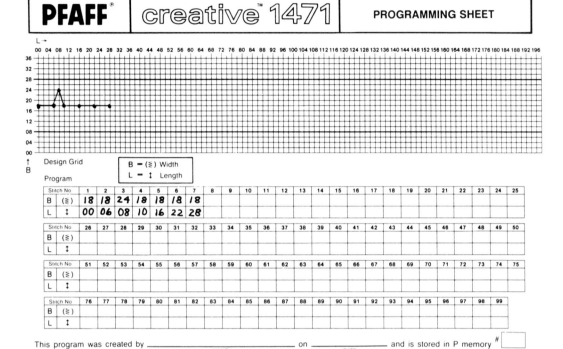

L →

Stitch No	1	2	3	4	5	6	7	8	9	10	11	12	13	14	15	16	17	18	19	20	21	22	23	24	25
B (≋)	18	18	24	18	18	18	18																		
L ↕	00	06	08	10	16	22	28																		

Stitch No	26	27	28	29	30	31	32	33	34	35	36	37	38	39	40	41	42	43	44	45	46	47	48	49	50
B (≋)																									
L ↕																									

Stitch No	51	52	53	54	55	56	57	58	59	60	61	62	63	64	65	66	67	68	69	70	71	72	73	74	75
B (≋)																									
L ↕																									

Stitch No	76	77	78	79	80	81	82	83	84	85	86	87	88	89	90	91	92	93	94	95	96	97	98	99
B (≋)																								
L ↕																								

Design Grid
Program

B = (≋) Width
L = ↕ Length

This program was created by _____ on _____ and is stored in P memory # _____
NAME   DATE

Fig. 4.6 "P" program for blind hem appliqué.

ric, move the red guide on the foot so the stitches fall slightly within the appliqué. Stitch around the motif.

Project
Tote Bag Square (Edge-Stitch Appliqué)

This tote bag square (Fig. 4.7) uses straight stitching on felt. Because there are several layers of felt used, it gives the appearance of a quilted design.

Program: 00
Stitch length: 1.5
Needle: #80/12

Feed dogs: up
Dual feed: engaged
Presser foot: Blindstitch foot #3
Tension: *top*, normal; *bobbin*, normal
Fabric suggestion: 9″ (22.9cm) squares of felt, one each of white, yellow, dark green, Christmas red, royal blue, and purple
Thread: monofilament (optional); regular sewing or machine embroidery thread to match
Accessories: fusible webbing, Teflon pressing sheet, tracing paper, white chalk pencil
Stabilizer: tear-away

Press fusible webbing behind each piece of felt, except white, which will be the background onto which you will appliqué

65

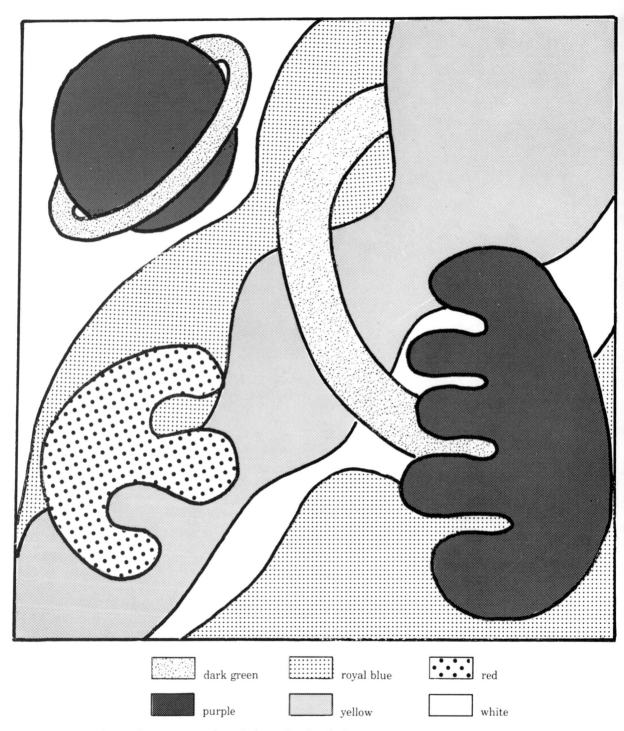

	dark green		royal blue		red
	purple		yellow		white

Fig. 4.7 Design for tote bag square, edge-stitch appliqué technique.

Fig. 4.8 Pattern for tote square. Use the fusible webbing method to attach tree shapes and circles to the background fabric, then stitch evenly spaced lines of straight stitching to hold them.

dark green　　　light green　　　yellow　　　turquoise

orange　　　red

the other fabrics. Within the 9″ (22.9cm) white square, draw a square 6¾″ (17.1cm).

Transfer the design in Fig. 4.7 to tracing paper. Cut apart and place the patterns on the felt pieces. Cut out felt shapes. Arrange your design within the 6¾″ square. First place the royal blue and yellow pieces on the background. On top of this, arrange the purple and green sections of the pattern, slipping the circular-shaped green pieces under the larger parts of the design.

Press in place, then stitch the edges with matching thread as closely as you can, or if you don't enjoy using your needle threader, you can use monofilament. Add quilting lines on the yellow section.

Place the red sections according to the pattern and press, then stitch. Finish the square as described in Chapter 12.

Project
Tote Bag Square
(Straight Stitch)

The next sample also uses straight stitches to hold appliqués in place, but is otherwise quite different. I used yellow, orange and two shades of green fabric on this one and layered several of the designs. The background is red.

Program: 0.0
Stitch length: 1.5
Needle: #90/14
Feed dogs: up
Presser foot: ordinary #0
Dual feed: engaged
Tension: *top*, normal; *bobbin*, normal
Fabric suggestion: light or medium-weight cottons in yellow, orange, two greens, for appliqué shapes; 10″ (25.4cm) red square for background
Thread: red machine embroidery on top; sewing thread the same color on bobbin
Accessories: fusible webbing; Teflon pressing sheet; washable marker; tracing paper, pencil
Stabilizer: freezer paper

Apply fusible webbing to all fabrics except the red background square, using the Teflon pressing sheet. Trace the appliqués from Fig. 4.8. Complete the large circles, even though they are partially covered by other pieces. Complete the branches on the tree shapes, also. Cut out each appliqué, using the pattern as your guide, and place on the background, sliding branches and circles over and under as shown. When arranged, press in place using Method B for fusible webbing.

With the water-erasable marker, draw lines from top to bottom every ¼″ (6.4mm) across the square. Starting at the top right corner, straight stitch to the bottom on the first line. Turn and stitch back, bottom to top, on the next line. Continue across the square. You may, if you prefer closer lines, stitch between the drawn lines.

Instead of row after row of straight stitches to hold appliqués in place, try satin stitches or use a double needle. Also try couching down metallics and thick cords. Finish the square as described in Chapter 12.

Cording edges

Corded edges give appliqués and decorative patches a neat, exact finish. The single cording foot will enable you to guide the cord easily, although you will also have good results with the appliqué foot.

When finishing patches, sew the corded edges in two passes. Place the patch over typing paper or tear-away stabilizer. You'll need two pieces—one for each pass—and they must be large enough to extend past the edge of the patch.

On the first pass, apply the cord, sewing at a narrower stitch width, and with stitch length slightly longer than the final pass.

The final stitching is done with a close satin stitch, the needle stitching down in the fabric on one side of the cord, but stitching off the cord and fabric on the other side. Leave enough cord at the beginning and end to poke to the back and work into the stitches. Use a needle with a large eye to do this by hand. Or, when you reach the end of the first pass, cut the cord to slightly overlap the start. If you can cut it on an angle, the join will not be noticeable when the second pass is completed.

It is not necessary to cover the entire cord if the cord itself is decorative or is a color that adds to the effect you wish to achieve. When I had to appliqué dozens of velveteen crosses to a woolen ecclesiastical garment, I used a velour cord and an open zigzag, and sewed with a thread the color of the velour. When finished, the velour edges looked like an extension of the velveteen.

Lesson 11. Appliquéing with feed dogs lowered

In this lesson, the appliqués are sewn in place freely; sometimes edges are not completely covered.

Set up your machine by lowering the feed dogs, using either a hoop or ironed-on freezer paper, and loosening the top tension slightly.

Blurring

What is blurring? Apply a fabric to another by starting to stitch within the appliqué. Then, following the shape of the appliqué, stitch around and around it, extending the stitching out into the background fabric. It's difficult to tell where one begins and the other leaves off. That is called blurring.

Although the sample here uses transparent fabrics, blurring can be done with any type of fabric. I chose to combine blurring with sheers and overlays to show you how to create pictures that look like watercolors. Thread color is usually the same as the appliqué, but never limit yourself. Use other colors as well.

When working with transparent fabrics, use pins to hold the appliqués in place. If possible, hold both in a hoop while sewing. Attach one layer at a time, sewing a straight stitch around the appliqué and

then cutting back to the stitching. Blur the edges. Then stretch the next transparent fabric in the hoop, stitch and cut away excess, then blur the edges.

To blur edges, find any point inside the appliqué. Stitch round and round, in ever-widening circles, until the edge of the appliqué is reached. But don't stop. Keep stitching past the edge and into the back-

Fig. 4.9 Blurring the edges of appliqués.

69

ground. Three transparent circles applied in this way, one overlapping the next, the third overlapping the others, makes a good sample (Fig. 4.9). Possibilities will grow from this one idea: try many colors, overlapping them to make other colors; give depth to a picture by overlapping so that the color becomes more intense as the layers are built up, and recedes where only one layer is used.

Project
Flower of Sheers and Overlays

Use this floral piece as a pillow top or slip it into your notebook. To do the flower sample (Fig. 4.10), set up the machine.

Program: 00; then 89
Needle: #80/12
Feed dogs: lowered
Presser foot: darning foot
Dual feed: disengaged
Tension: *top*, slightly loosened; *bobbin*, normal
Fabric suggestion: 10″ (25.4cm) square medium-weight white fabric for the background; ¼ yard (22.9cm) green transparent fabric; ⅛ yard (11.4cm) pink transparent fabric; 12″ (30.5cm) square off-white bridal veiling
Threads: machine embroidery in yellow, green, and pink
Accessories: 7″ (17.8cm) spring hoop (optional)
Stabilizer: tear-away stabilizer with hoop, or iron-on freezer paper without hoop

Use the circle and leaf shape to make the patterns. Cut out several dozen 1″ (2.5cm) circles in pink transparent fabric. Also cut the same number of 2″ (5.1cm) long leaf shapes from green transparent fabric. Pat-

Fig. 4.10 Use bridal veiling to hold small pieces of appliqué fabric in place.

terns are provided in Fig. 4.11. You may not use all of these petals and leaves: It will depend upon how much they are overlapped and how large an area you're covering with the design. If using freezer paper, iron it to the background fabric.

Arrange and overlap the leaves in a circle on the background fabric, points toward the center. Plan so they will fit within the hoop, (if you have chosen to work with one) keeping the leaves at least an inch (2.5cm) inside. If the presser foot gets too close to the edge, it will be difficult to sew around the appliqués without hitting the darning foot on the hoop.

Lay down the circles of color for the flower head, starting in the middle of the leaves. New colors pop out for the leaves

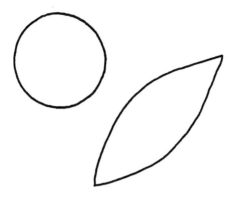

Fig. 4.11 Patterns for the flower design.

when you start and stop. It starts with the needle position in the left. Start in the center of the flower and when the program is complete, it will have built up a nubby "seed" (see Fig. 3.2). Anchor the threads again. Lift the presser foot and move to another place. Do another seed. There's no need to clip threads until all the seeds are completed. Keep building up the nubs and moving your needle from one place to the next until the flower center is to your liking. Then clip the threads between the zigzag areas.

Change the top thread back to green. Re-

and petals as you overlap, arrange and rearrange. Leave the center of the flower open. Don't pin down any of these small pieces.

After completing the arrangement of the sheers and overlays, cover with the piece of bridal veil to help hold them all in place. Pin the veiling down in several places near the center of the flower and at the edges of the fabric. If working with a hoop, lift your piece carefully from the table and place it in the hoop. Slip stabilizer under it.

Start by sewing around the petals of the flower. Use pink thread on the top, green thread on the bobbin. Stitch the petals very freely. Bring the stitching out past them, or inside, or make stitched circles between them. Stitch circles within circles.

Then change the top thread to green. Stitch around the leaves in the same free-flowing way. Go up the centers and down, stitching in veins on some and leaving others without.

Now only the center is left to stitch. Change the top thread to yellow and select Program 89, with a stitch width of 4.0. This is the button attaching stitch, which will automatically anchor your threads

Fig. 4.12 This is part of a design that has been appliquéd to a tote bag, using free-machining to hold the appliqués in place.

turn to Program 00. Sew around the seeds. Go from one to another until all are outlined. When the picture is complete, take it out of the hoop if you used one. Most of the stabilizer will drop away; the rest can be pulled off (or left on, since it won't show).

The bridal veil can be left as is. However, I often clip out areas to create color changes.

Scribbling

Scribbling is like darning over appliqués, but you will use both straight and zigzag stitches. It's a good way to lay in big areas of color without having to cover the areas with heavy embroidery.

The appliqué picture in Fig. 4.12 was placed on the outside of a tote bag. Use the

Fig. 4.13 Use these patterns to create one element of the design shown in Fig. 4.12.

patterns in Fig. 4.13 as a guide, enlarging or reducing to fit your purpose.

Program: 10
Stitch width: varies
Needle: #90/14
Feed dogs: lowered
Presser foot: darning foot #6
Dual feed: disengaged
Tension: *top,* slightly loosened; *bobbin,* normal
Fabric suggestion: medium-weight cotton
Thread: machine embroidery on top; sewing or darning thread on bobbin
Accessories: glue stick
Stabilizer: ironed-on freezer paper

Apply the appliqués with a dab of glue stick and begin to stitch the edges down freely with either a straight or a zigzag stitch. Sew freely over the entire appliqué first to anchor it before embroidering the designs. Stitch inside and over the edges of the appliqués. If you can live with raw edges, then don't be too particular about covering them exactly. Here is a good place to blur edges. Add to the design by laying in different colors with the same free machining. Add as much stitching as you wish, but don't cover the entire appliqué, as that would defeat the purpose. Let most of the color show through. It's like sketching with colored pencils.

Stitching Carrickmacross

Carrickmacross is an Irish lace made with appliqués of batiste. Tiny pops, or eyelets, are embroidered in the fine hexagonal net which is used as the ground, and it has a picot edge. If hand done, this type of lace is very fragile, but our machine version is both beautiful and sturdy (Fig. 4.14).

Project Carrickmacross Doily

Instead of batiste, we'll use organdy. I've used a polyester for the veiling, so my fabric will be the same. It will be white on white, typical of Carrickmacross lace.

Stitch width: 0
Stitch length: 0
Needle: #80
Feed dogs: lowered
Presser foot: darning foot #6
Tension: *top,* slightly loosened; *bobbin,* normal
Fabric suggestion: white polyester organdy; fine white polyester hexagonal veiling
Thread: white cotton machine embroidery thread and white cordonnet (optional)

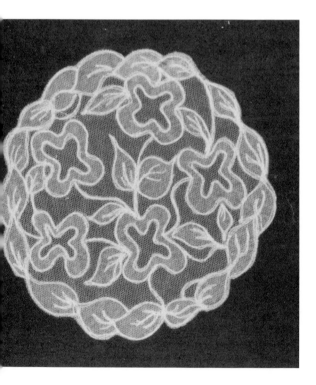

Fig. 4.14 Appliquéd lace (Carrickmacross), is made quickly using organdy and fine hexagonal net.

Accessories: 7″ (17.8cm) spring hoop; water-
   erasable pen
Stabilizer: water-soluble

Copy the design in Fig. 4.15 onto the organdy, using a water-erasable pen. Slip the
net underneath the organdy and put them
both into a spring hoop. If possible, always
use a hoop large enough so you can do the
entire design without having to move the
fabric and net.

Set up your machine for free embroidery. Anchor threads and stitch on the
lines around each motif at least three
times. It may be necessary to stitch a
fourth pass on some, but make it look consistent: Don't leave some lines with one
pass, others with four. Plot the course of
the needle ahead of time so there won't be
too many stops and starts.
   When the design is finished, take it out
of the hoop and cut out all the areas that

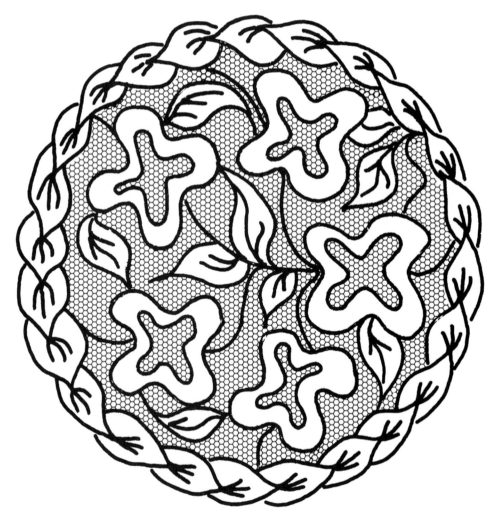

Fig. 4.15 The pattern for appliquéd lace.

are to be free of organdy. Use sharp, fine-pointed scissors. It helps to lift areas away from the net with the point of a seam ripper and then clip.

Should you cut the net, don't panic. Put it back under the needle and stitch a few lines of straight stitching over the cut, blending it into the other stitches already there. It will look like it was meant to be there all the time.

When that is completed and looks great, decide whether to go on or to stop while you're ahead. You may go one step further, as real Carrickmacross lace always has a picot edge and small eyelets in the net, as shown in Fig. 4.16.

To stitch the eyelets, mark some places, such as the middles of the flowers, that you think need pops. Stitch freely around those tiny spots. Then go back and poke holes in the centers with a darning needle. Set the stitch width to 2.0, and slowly (use the moderate speed setting on your machine if available), almost hand-walk the stitching from center to outside with the zigzag. Stitch twice, turn the hoop a hair, stitch 2 more times, turn the hoop, stitch again, all around the pop.

Hand-worked Carrickmacross lace has a

cord couched down around the appliqués to hold them in place. To do this by machine, stitch around the appliqués only once before cutting back. Do not trim around the outside edge. Put the piece back in the hoop upside down. Use cordonnet or pearl cotton in the bobbin.

Before beginning to outline the appliqués, dip the needle down and bring the cord up to the top. Hold both threads to one side as you take several stitches along the design. In other words, don't anchor the cord, as is usually done with thread. Later go back and work the threads into the stitches on the backside of the design.

Picots around the edge should be left until the rest of the stitching is completed.

Cut back to the edge. Use two layers of water-soluble stabilizer. The topside of the appliqué should be pinned against the stabilizer. Put all this into the hoop. First stitch the cord around the leaves at the inside edge. Then, with a water-erasable pen, mark small dots every 1/8" (3.2mm) along the edge to use as a guide for the picots. Stitch in by following the edge and making small loops at each mark. Take it out of the hoop and wash the stabilizer and blue pen marks out of the fabric.

What we've made is a small doily but, if you're like me, you are not big on small doilies. This is a fast technique, so think big. Try it for the edge of a bridal veil or for the bodice and puffed sleeves of the wedding dress itself. Now that's what I call a long-cut, but definitely worth it.

Fig. 4.16 Eyelets and picots in Carrickmacross.

Layering transparent fabrics

Shadow work is my favorite. I love the painterly effects of combining colors and toning down with whites. It's done using sheers and overlays. In the picture made in the following project, the color does not come from a colored cotton fabric layered between organdies; instead, these flowers are created only from transparent fabrics.

Project
Shadow Work
Picture

In this project, I switch from feed dogs up to feed dogs lowered or covered, but most of the stitching is done freely, so I've put it in this lesson. This design (Fig. 4.17) will give you an idea of what can be done with only white, mauve and green organza.

Program: 10
Stitch width: 0.0–4.0
Stitch length: varies
Needle: #70/10
Feed dogs: up, lowered
Presser foot: appliqué, fancy stitch foot #2, or darning foot #6

Tension: *top,* slightly loosened; *bobbin,* normal
Fabric: white, mauve, and green organza
Thread: green machine embroidery
Accessories: spring hoop; water-erasable marker
Stabilizer: water-soluble

Place the white organza over the design (Fig. 4.18) and trace it off with a water-erasable marker. Layer two mauves behind each flower on the white organza and pin them in place. Put this in a hoop.

With the machine set for free machining at a width of 0.0, without anchoring the threads, straight stitch around the flowers twice. Lift the needle and go to the flower centers. Stitch twice around each center, also: The lines should be next to each other, not on top of each other. Cut back to the stitching around the outside edge, but not too close.

Place the green organza behind the leaf areas and stitch in place with two lines of stitching. Cut back to the stitching at the edges.

Set up your machine for normal sewing. Put feed dogs up and use the appliqué foot. Use stitch width 2.0, stitch length 0.35, or a setting that will produce a smooth satin stitch. Sew around the flowers and leaves. Be careful: sew too closely and the stitches will cut the fabric.

From the front of your picture, cut the white organza from one flower, the white and one mauve layer from another. Turn the hoop over. Cut out one layer of mauve from the back on another. Or from the back, cut out both layers of color, leaving only the white organdy and the flower center intact. Can you imagine the combinations and shades of mauve you can create?

The large leaf is divided into four sections. In the first section, cut out the top white layer and place a layer of green be-

Fig. 4.17 Layers of transparent fabrics give a painterly effect to shadow work.

Fig. 4.18 Shadow work design.

hind the remaining green layer to darken it. In the second area, cut out the white and leave just green. In the third, place white behind the section to make it three layers. The fourth is left as is, the white in front of the green.

Once you have finished the flowers and leaves, go back to the flower centers and blur them out by stitching spirals from the centers out to the edges. Or start at the edges and travel to the outside of the flowers. Leave some flowers with only the first stitching around the center.

Satin stitches should be sewn through at least two layers of fabric. Ordinarily, we'd add stabilizer, but tear-away could leave specks in the fabric that might show through. To prevent this, use green organza as a backing for the stems. The lines are satin stitched, then the stabilizing organza is cut back to the stitching.

Finish up with straight stitching. Set up again for free machining by lowering the feed dogs and putting on the darning foot. Using water-soluble stabilizer behind the fabric, set the machine at a stitch width of 0.0, to sew in the accent lines.

If one of the fabrics has pulled away from the satin stitches, don't give up. Layer a piece of transparent fabric underneath and stitch it on. Then cut away the original one. Or put a piece of organza underneath, use straight stitching or zigzags to sew in some lines, and pretend you wanted it that way. On the flowers, too: If by mistake you cut through two layers instead of one, leave it or layer something behind it. Sometimes blurring out more lines of stitching will attach and hide any mistakes.

Keep the stitching light and airy, with no wide satin stitches. There should be more fabric showing than stitching. When finished, wash out the stabilizer and pen marks.

This type of shadow work is quite fragile and I suggest using it for pictures or window hangings, rather than for clothing.

Project
Stitching Three-Dimensional Appliqués

One of the prettiest dresses I've ever seen was at a fraternity dance back when we thought we had to wear yards of tulle and gobs of ruffles. This dress was a beautiful white organdy exception. Over the entire skirt were scattered lavender and peach pansy appliqués of organdy. They were attached only at the centers. It was a plain dress except for this scattering of flowers.

Detached appliqués do not have to have a heavy satin stitch edge, and I think you'll agree that straight stitching on fine fabric is easier and more beautiful. After all, that was a long time ago and I've never forgotten that dress.

Program: 00; then 89
Stitch length: 0.0
Needle position: center
Needle: #60 or #70
Feed dogs: lowered
Presser foot: darning foot #6 or no presser foot; fringe foot (optional)
Tension: *top,* loosened; *bobbin,* normal
Fabric suggestion: mauve and green organdy
Thread: machine embroidery thread to match
Accessories: spring hoop; water-erasable marker
Stabilizer: water-soluble type

Place a layer of water-soluble stabilizer between two layers of mauve organdy. Clip this into the spring hoop. Draw the design in Fig. 4.19 on it with a water-erasable marker. You will copy the petal design twice. The small sample is done in pieces and combined later (Fig. 4.20).

Set the machine on moderate speed for accuracy. Stitch three times around the

Fig. 4.19 Three-dimensional appliqué design.

edges with a straight stitch. Lines should be close together but not on top of each other. Use a colored thread that matches or is a shade darker than the fabric. Cut out the petals close to the stitching, but not too close.

The leaves should be worked in the same way on green organdy. Stitch only straight stitches as you follow the pattern. Go into the centers and stitch the veins as well. Cut out the leaves.

Place the flower petals on top of each other — stagger them so the petals underneath are not hidden by the top layer. Place this over the leaves and stitch them together with mauve thread by following the stitching in the center of the petals. You may go a step further and fringe the center. Using the tailor tacking foot, green

thread, and Program 89, stitch in several places in the center of the flower. Finish by holding the flower under the faucet and rinsing out some, but not all, of the stabilizer. Shape the flower and leaves carefully and let them dry. They will be stiff, as if heavily starched, and will retain their shapes. How can you use these three-dimension appliqués? Add a band of them to a bodice of Carrickmacross lace. Make an utterly fake corsage or a flowered hat. Add the flower to a cord for a necklace.

Helpful Hints for Appliqué

An appliqué will bubble only rarely. If you are scrupulous about using the dual feed for your preliminary stitching, it won't happen at all. Anyone can goof and

Fig. 4.20 Pattern pieces for floral 3-D appliqué.

forget to engage it at times, and if that happens, here are some suggestions for salvaging your project.

If an appliqué bubbles, fix it by taking it out of the hoop and nicking the base fabric beneath the appliqué, which will then allow the base to lay flat.

Or slit the back a bit and fill the appliqué area with cotton. This is called trapunto. Hand whip the slit closed. Machine stitch on top of the appliqué to add to the design and hold the batting in place.

Another way to keep appliqué puckers from showing is to hide them by hand or machine embroidering over the appliqué.

When layering net, there is sometimes a moiré look to it that spoils the effect of your picture. To eliminate it, change the direction of one of the layers.

Don't limit yourself to fabric appliqués; thread appliqués are also effective. Work spider webs in another fabric, cut them out, and apply.

Work lace in space inside a small ring. Apply it to a background by free machining all around the inside edge of the ring. Then cut the ring from the lace.

Check out Lesson 6 on beads, baubles, and shishas.

Do pulled and drawn threads with the machine on one fabric and attach them to another background.

80

CHAPTER **5**

Stitching Across Open Spaces

People have been stitching in space for a hundred years; you can, too. However, if you are nervous about doing it, stitching on water-soluble stabilizer usually produces the same effects with even better results. Water-soluble stabilizer is so thin and pliable that placing multiple layers of it in a hoop, along with fabric, is no problem. Another reason I am sold on it is that, once the design is drawn on the stabilizer, it can be stitched exactly, as if stitching on fabric. That isn't possible when actually stitching in space. I use it for cutwork because it holds the cut edges in place while I stitch them and sometimes I use it on both sides of the fabric to give it even more stability.

I use stabilizer when stitching in rings, too. It keeps threads in place until they are anchored. There is no problem with slip-ping, as often happens when stitching in space. Practice on water-soluble stabilizer, and when you are comfortable with it, graduate to open space and try that. There are occasions for both techniques.

This chapter includes cutwork, stitching in rings, creating needlelace, and stitching both Battenberg and Alençon laces. Hemstitching is included, as well. Be sure to keep all your samples in your notebook. You may not use an idea today or tomorrow, but maybe next year you'll refer back to your notebook and find just what you're looking for to make a special gift, or welcome a new baby. My notebook is especially valuable when I want to find machine settings for a technique I haven't used in weeks. No matter how well you know your machine, you can't remember every detail of a method you've tried.

Lesson 12. Cutwork and eyelets

Cutwork

Cutwork is the forerunner of all needlemade laces. It was common as early as the sixteenth century. In handmade cutwork, part of the background fabric is cut away and threads are stretched from one side of the open area to the other. Bars of buttonhole stitches are worked over the stretched threads and the cut edges. Cutwork can be done on most sewing machines, using satin stitches in place of buttonhole stitches.

Project
Cutwork
Needlecase

When I wanted to do a cutwork project on the machine without dedicating my life to a large, time-consuming sailor collar or tablecloth, I found that the needlecase in Fig. 5.1 was exactly the right size. The single design can be used as a repeat pattern and it can be combined with embroidery, appliqué or shadow work.

I traced the pattern (Fig. 5.2) on paper two different times. On one pattern I add-

ed lines where I wanted the thread bars, called "brides," to be.

Before you begin this or any project, practice, using the same fabric, needle and threads, stitch settings and stabilizers you will use on your finished piece. For this design, I practiced turning corners and satin stitching curves, as well as filling spaces with thread bars.

Cutwork is not usually backed by anything, but on this needlecase you can see that it is a necessity.

Program: 10
Stitch width: 0–2.0
Stitch length: 0.35
Needle: #80/12
Needle stop: down
Feed dogs: up or lowered
Presser foot: darning foot #6, fancy stitch
    foot #2
Dual feed: disengaged
Tension: *top*, slightly loosened; *bobbin*, normal
Fabric suggestion: closely woven linen or
    kettlecloth
Thread: machine embroidery
Accessories: spring hoop; tracing paper;
    small, sharp embroidery scissors; pencil, water-erasable marker, and permanent white marker
Stabilizer: water-soluble

Place the pattern without the thread bars on the back of the fabric and slip them both into a hoop. The topside of the fabric will be against the machine. Lower the feed dogs and take the presser foot off. Straight stitch around the outlines of the design two times with the same thread you'll use for the satin stitching. (Do not stitch the bars at this time.)

Take the fabric out of the hoop and peel off the pattern. Cut out the larger area. Put a piece of stabilizer over the topside

Fig. 5.1 The cutwork design on this needlecase can be used once, or as a repeat pattern.

82

Fig. 5.2 Cutwork pattern to copy.

and one underneath the fabric, and place all three layers in the hoop. Slip the second pattern under the hoop. With a permanent white marker, trace the bars on the top stabilizer. Put the pattern aside until later.

With stitch width set to 0.0, freely stitch in the bars. Do the long, middle branching line first. Anchor the thread at the top by sewing in one place a few stitches, make a pass from top to bottom and then back again. As you sew from the bottom on that second pass, stitch the branches out and back as well.

Increase stitch width to 1.5. Stitch the first pass from top to bottom, moving the hoop quite quickly (remember the branches). Then, stitch back up from the

bottom: This time move your hoop slowly. The stitches will be closer together. Remember, you control this by how fast you move the hoop. The stitches will look like satin stitches in space. Anchor each branch by sewing at 0.0 width into the fabric just beyond the stay-stitching. Zigzag to the top and anchor the thread.

Stitch the short bars at each side next. Anchor the threads at the top of the first bar, just beyond the two rows of straight stitching. Sew straight stitches across to the other side, anchor the threads again, and come back on the same line. Then begin zigzagging back across these threads with a 1.5 stitch width. When you reach the other side, stop, reduce the width to

83

0.0 and follow the stay-stitch line to the next bar position. Sew across, back, and then zigzag as you did the first one. Complete all the brides on each side.

Cut out all three smaller shapes that are left in the design. Try to do this without cutting through the stabilizer on the back, but if you clip it, you can always slide another piece of stabilizer underneath. Put another piece of stabilizer on top and place all layers in the hoop. Using your pattern again behind the hoop, draw the bars on the stabilizer. Proceed with these branched bars as you did with the large cutout.

When you have finished all the bars, change the machine settings. Raise the feed dogs and set the machine on stitch width 2.0. Use the fancy stitch foot. Begin sewing at the point of the heart. Anchor the threads and proceed clockwise. As you travel around the curves, stitch very slowly, your machine set on moderate speed. To fill in the curves smoothly, stop with the needle down on the right side, lift the presser-foot lever, pivot the hoop, lower the presser foot, and stitch again. Repeat several times when negotiating curves.

Satin stitch around each cutout. Carefully pull away the stabilizer and rinse out

Fig. 5.3 Eyelet stitch, made with Program 88.

any remaining pieces. Press the embroidery from the back.

Eyelets

I've used eyelets in my embroideries, clumping them together for a center of interest, and one of my teachers uses them to decorate lovely bed linens.

In Chapter 1, you will find information about the eyelet plate, and in Chapter 11 there is a project using decorative stitches with the eyelet plate. In addition to what we can do with this extra accessory we also have Program 88, which is a true eyelet stitch. This program can be used singly, in a row, or combined with other stitch programs. It is not used with the eyelet plate, and the centers need to be removed after stitching. Do invest in a small punch to remove the fabric centers from these eyelets after stitching (Fig. 5.3). These punches can be purchased at a hobby or craft store which sells supplies for leathercraft.

Lesson 13. Free-machined needlelace

The terms *cutwork, lacy spiderwebs,* and *openwork* all describe a machine stitchery technique far removed from darning holes in socks or shredded elbows. But, like darning, they do entail stitching across open spaces.

Program: 00
Needle: #80/12
Feed dogs: lowered
Presser foot: darning foot #6 or no presser foot
Dual feed: disengaged

Tension: *top,* normal; *bobbin,* normal
Fabric suggestions: any weight
Thread: one color, machine embroidery or polyester
Accessories: 6" (15.2cm) wrapped wooden hoop; water-soluble stabilizer (optional)

Openwork is done in a hoop with the fabric stretched tightly. Place the hoop, fabric side down, on the machine bed. Draw a circle on the fabric: Circles are easier to control than the squares, crescents and paisley shapes you may want to try later.

Start stitching at the edge of the circle by bringing the bobbin thread to the top. Anchor the threads by sewing a few stitches in one spot. Guide the hoop slowly as you stitch around the circle three times (Fig. 5.4A). Take the hoop off the machine and, without removing the fabric from it, cut out the circle close to the stitches. If you have opted to use water-soluble stabilizer, now is the time to slip it into the hoop under your fabric. Replace the hoop and secure the threads once again at the edge of the hole.

Now you will begin to lay in a network of spokelike threads across the space. To do this, begin by stitching across from one side of the hole to the other side. Move the hoop slowly, but run the machine moderately fast to strengthen and put a tighter twist on the spoke. When your needle enters the fabric again, move along the circle to another spot, secure threads, and sew directly across the hole again. Continue in this manner until you have as many spokes as you wish. On the last pass, go up to the center and backstitch right at the center of the wheel to strengthen the web. Starting at that backstitch, fill in the spokes by sewing in ever-widening circles around the center until the "button" is the size you wish it to be (Fig. 5.4B). Sew a few stitches into the button to lock the thread in place and again move to the outside to anchor the threads and complete that spoke.

Would you like a lacier filling? Sew one backstitch over each spoke after crossing it as you stitch around the center. This keeps the threads from slipping to the center. Travel around and around in wider circles till you reach the edge of the hole (Fig. 5.4C).

Although there are as many ways to finish off the edges of the spaces as there are ways to fill them with stitches, one of the softest looks is accomplished by straight stitching from the edge of the hole, out past it and back again, moving the hoop

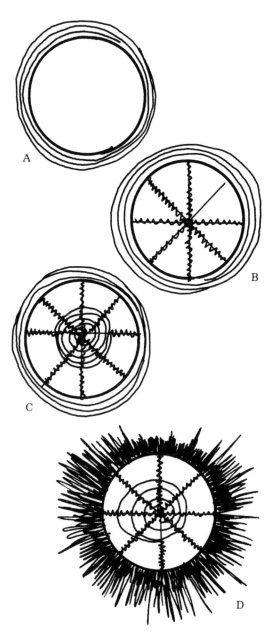

Fig. 5.4 Making needlelace. A. First sew around a circle three times. B. Cut out the center, embroider across the hole, creating spokes. C. Add circles of stitches around the center. D. Stitch radiating lines over the edge, into the fabric.

back and forth as if stitching sun rays. You can also use the widest zigzag and accomplish the same rays. Or, satin stitch around the edge and combine that with other embroidery. These are only a few ideas; try some of your own.

If you have used stabilizer, place your embroidery under a faucet and wash it out when your work is completed.

Create your own samples by placing a piece of medium-weight cotton in a hoop and drawing several circles on it. Stitch around one circle three times. Cut out the center. Stitch a spider web in the hole and finish it off on the edges. Go to the next circle and stitch both the center and the edges in a different way from your first sample. Then do another and another until you have many needlelace samples for your notebook. If you're pleased with the result and want to show it off, back with another fabric and use as a tote bag square.

Lesson 14. Battenberg lace

Battenberg lace was popular in the late 1800s. Straight, machine-made tape was shaped into a design and basted to stiff paper. Then the open spaces were filled with bars and embroidery stitches, which held the tape in shape. After the stitchery was completed, the paper was removed and the Battenberg lace could be used to decorate dresses, curtains or linens.

Project
Small Lace
Sample

This lesson will teach you how to make one small piece of Battenberg (Fig. 5.5). From there, you can go on to bigger projects, but let's see if you like Battenberg lacemaking by machine.

There is a variety of white, off-white, black, gold, and silver Battenberg tape to choose from. It's available by mail-order (see Sources of Supplies) and from some needlework shops.

Should you create your own design, choose a tape that doesn't overpower the pattern. The one I used is ½" (12.7mm) wide. On the sides of the tape is a thread

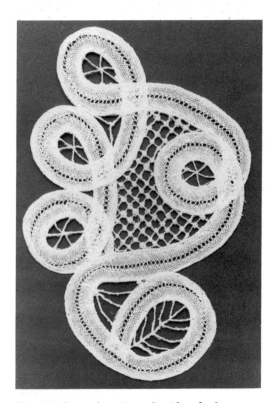

Fig. 5.5 Battenberg is embroidered after narrow tape has been shaped into a design.

that is thicker than the others. Pull gently to curve the tape into the shape you want.

Place a piece of water-soluble stabilizer over the design in Fig. 5.6 and trace the outline with a white permanent marking pen. Place this on a porous surface, such as a cord board or ceiling tile, as you will be able to pin into these boards. After starting out pinning, however, I switched to a glue stick, and found that this actually worked

Fig. 5.6 Battenberg lace pattern.

much better. Pull the heavy threads on the design to shape the tape, gluing or pinning as you go.

As you pull these threads, you will find you are faced with the problem of what to do with the little loops of thread that you pull. I have handled these in several different ways on some of my Battenberg projects. Preferably, work them down to a point in the pattern where you can tuck them under another edge of the tape. Sometimes, however, this is not possible, and it may be necessary to clip them, tie a tiny knot, and conceal the ends of the thread along the edge of the tape. This is where the glue stick comes in handy again.

Ends of the tape should be tucked under the design. Using a dab of Fray-Check will prevent them from raveling. Hand-baste the design with wash-away basting thread. Set up your machine.

Program: 10
Stitch width: 0 − 0 to 1.5
Needle: #90/14
Feed dogs: lowered
Presser foot: darning foot #6 or no foot
Tension: *top*, normal; *bobbin*, normal
Thread: wash-away basting thread; #50 (ecru) or white machine embroidery
Accessories: 7″ (17.8cm) spring hoop; water-erasable pen and white permanent marker; ecru or white Battenberg tape; glue stick; dressmaker's pins
Stabilizer: water-soluble, doubled, large enough for hoop

Put a *second* layer of water-soluble stabilizer over the tape and first layer of stabilizer. Place all in a spring hoop and, with the machine set for free stitching and a stitch width of 1.5, go around all the edges of the design. When you come to a place where the tape crosses *over* another section, continue with the zigzag stitch. If the section of tape is crossing *under* another part, change the stitch width to 0.0 and carefully straight-stitch across. This will

secure all the edges and make the lace strong without overpowering the design. At any point where the edges of the tapes are touching, such as the area between the three loops, be sure that your zigzag stitch catches both edges.

After you have stitched around the tape, remove your work from the spring hoop and cut away only the top layer of stabilizer from the centers. Draw in the stitching lines with the white permanent marker. You may extend them by drawing dots on the tape with a water-erasable pen. These dots can be used for reference if for some reason you find it necessary to cut away your filler threads and redo an area.

The larger, open center section (Fig. 5.7A) was finished first. Secure your thread on the edge of the tape by taking a few short straight stitches. Straight-stitch across the area, following the lines on the stabilizer. Set the machine for a narrow 1.5 zigzag and go over each straight stitch line one time. If you move your hoop slowly, the zigzag stitch will cover the lines smoothly and evenly. After you have covered the lines from one direction, go over the lines that cross, making a little spiral of thread at each intersection.

The smaller circles (Fig. 5.7B) are all filled in with intersecting lines. Again, use a straight stitch to cross, then overcast them with the narrow zigzag stitch.

The triangular area between two of the circles (Fig. 5.7C) is worked as follows: Start at one of the corners and straight stitch to the center of the area. Then turn slightly, and stitch to another corner. Secure the thread in the tape with a stitch, and stitch back to the center. Stitch to the third corner, back to the center and then to the corner where you started. Change the stitch width to 1.5 and overcast the straight-stitch lines.

The smaller triangle in Fig. 5.7D is stitched in a similar way. Start at the sharpest point of the curve and stitch directly across. Stitch back to the starting

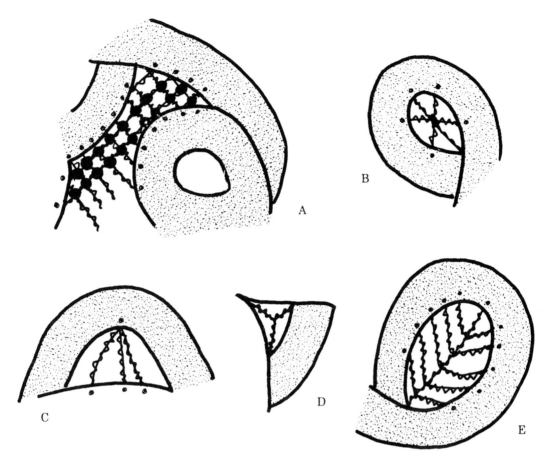

Fig. 5.7 Details of Battenberg design. **A.**
Large center section, stitch detail. **B.** *Small
loops.* **C.** *Lower triangle.* **D.** *Upper triangle.*
E. *Leaf shape.*

point, then equidistant on each side of the
center line, and overcast.

The leaf shape (Fig. 5.7E) is stitched by
making the center line first. Then as you
start back, make each one of the ribs by
stitching from the center line to the edge of
the tape and back to complete five ribs on
each side. These are overcast to finish As a

final finish, all the tape edges around areas
that are filled in are zigzagged with the
narrow 1.5 stitch width.

Tear away the surplus stabilizer from
around the outside edges and rinse out the
remainder. Press the lace between two
pieces of toweling.

Lesson 15. Hemstitching

Hemstitching is used on garments and table linens whenever a delicate, feminine look is desired. The technique looks complicated and difficult, but it is surprisingly easy to accomplish using both double- and single-winged needles.

Before you begin to stitch the bonnet, practice on two layers of cotton organdy.

Set up your machine.

Program: 10
Stitch width: 0.0 to no wider than the throat plate opening when using a double needle (usually 4.0)
Stitch length: varies
Needle: single and double hemstitching needles; double needles to match sizes of pintuck feet
Feed dogs: up
Twin needle key: engaged
Presser foot: fancy stitch foot #2
Dual feed: disengaged
Tension: *top*, normal; *bobbin*, normal
Fabric: crisp fabric, such as organdy or linen
Thread: cotton machine embroidery

You will not be able to use your automatic needle threader with the single and double hemstitch and double needles. When threading, place a spool of thread on each pin with a suitably sized unwinding collar. Bring both threads through the guides simultaneously, following the directional arrows. At the tension discs, the threads should each pass on different sides. They will be together until you reach the two little guides above the needle, where they will separate before threading through the eye. Remember to always thread your machine with the presser foot up.

Try hemstitching as described in your manual. Start with the single-winged needle and use Program 10. Stitch a row of hemstitching. At the end of the first run, leave the needle in the hole at left, turn and return, poking into the same holes as

on the first run. You can also use Program 15, which is a triple zigzag. Because it takes extra stitches in each hole, it is prettier (Fig. 5.8).

You can make an all-over design, covering a large area with hemstitches. This is usually worked on the bias, then appliquéd to something else.

Programs 75 through 79 are specifically designed for use with the hemstitch needle, and you will find other decorative stitches that adapt themselves to this useful accessory (Fig. 5.8).

Now practice with the double hemstitch needle. Set up your machine in this way:

Program: 10
Stitch width: 1.5
Stitch length: 1.5
Feed dogs: up
Twin needle key: engaged
Presser foot: fancy stitch foot #2

Make one pass, ending to the left. Lift the presser foot, turn the fabric and stitch the second pass.

Try this blind hemstitch.

Program: 17
Stitch width: 2.0
Stitch length: 1.5
Feed dogs: up
Presser foot: fancy stitch foot #2

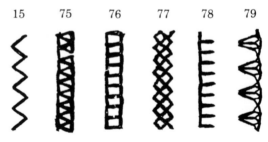

Fig. 5.8 Six programs designed for use with hemstitch needle.

Turn your hemstitching into shadow work as well. Cut back the piece of organdy underneath, clipping out both sides of the double fabric on either side of the blind hemstitches.

Project
Infant's Bonnet

I've combined hemstitching with built-in stitches and double needles to make the infant's bonnet shown in Fig. 5.9. Also included is a line of ribbon sewing. This can be made in the time it would take you to shop for a baby gift.

Nora Lou Kampe of LaGrange, Illinois, made this bonnet using embroidered eyelet fabric with a scalloped border—a way to make a baby gift in no more than an hour's time. I used her bonnet idea, but took the long-cut and embroidered the bonnet myself; it fits a newborn and you could make one for a christening. A gown can be done in the same hemstitching technique.

The finished bonnet is 13″ × 5¾″ (33.0cm × 14.6cm). Add to both width and length if you're adapting it for an older baby.

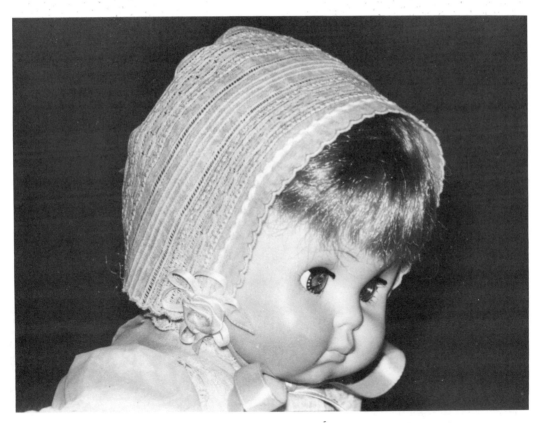

Fig. 5.9 Hemstitching, pintucking, and embroidery decorate the organdy bonnet for an infant or a doll.

Program: 00; 61; 77; other decorative stitch
    programs
Stitch width: varies
Stitch length: varies
Twin needle key: engaged
Needle: 1.6mm twin needle; single and dou-
    ble hemstitching needles
Feed dogs: up
Presser foot: fancy stitch foot #2; 5-groove
    cording foot
Tension: *top,* normal; *bobbin,* normal
Fabric suggestion: white cotton organdy
Thread: light-blue, fine machine-embroidery
    thread; #5 light-blue pearl cotton; white
    cordonnet
Other supplies: pearl bead (optional); 1/8"
    (3.2mm) double-faced satin ribbon, ap-
    proximately 1 yard (91.4cm); 1/4"
    (6.4mm) double-faced satin ribbon, 1/2
    yard (45.7cm); 1/2" (12.7mm) double-
    faced satin ribbon, approximately 1 1/2
    yards (1.4m)

Begin with two pieces of organdy, each
18" × 9" (45.7cm × 22.9cm). Start with a
much larger area than you need; the excess
fabric can be cut off later for your notebook.

Wash and iron the organdy. Mark the
top fabric lengthwise, using a water-erasable marker. Start by marking lines from
the front edge 1" (2.5cm) apart (Fig. 5.10).

Use a T-square for accuracy. Draw six
lines. Then mark a line 1/2" (12.7mm) from
the last line, and another 1/2" (12.7mm)
from that one; 7" × 13" (17.8cm ×
33.0cm) is marked. Pin the two pieces of
fabric together at the top of the lines.

Once you have learned how to hemstitch, the decoration is up to you. The following is only a suggestion: Thread the
double-wing needle with light-blue thread.
The first line of blind hemstitches are
stitched 1" (2.5cm) from the front edge.
Use the blue line as your guide and stitch
on top of it. When you reach the end, turn
and go back, cutting into the same hole you
stitched on the first run. Sew slowly. If the
needle does not hit exactly in the right
place, stop and move the fabric by one or
two threads. Continue.

Spread the fabric apart. The pintucking
is done between the blue lines on the top
piece only.

Change to the 1.6mm double needle and
straight stitch Program 00. Use the 5-
groove cording foot, light-blue #5 pearl
cotton, feed dogs up, stitch length 1.5.
Thread the hole in the throat plate with
pearl cotton.

There are three lines of pintucking, so
stitch the first line exactly in the middle,
between the blue marker lines. Stitch the

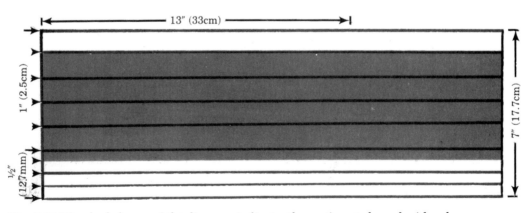

Fig. 5.10 The shaded area of the diagram indicates the portions to be embroidered.

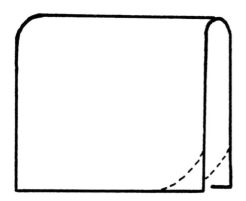

Fig. 5.11 When stitching is completed, fold the rectangle in half and round off the front corners, as shown.

others on either side of this one, using the grooves in the pintuck foot as guides.

If you wish, stitch all four groups of pintucks between the blue lines at one time, then go back, take the pearl cotton out of the throat plate, change to the hemstitching needle, and continue to hemstitch on the blue lines with the blind hemstitch. Remember, when you pintuck, work on one layer of fabric, but hemstitch on both layers.

Complete 4½″ (11.4cm) of the bonnet (shaded area on Fig. 5.10) by filling in the empty spaces between the hemstitched blind hem pattern and the pintucks. Use the open effect of the single-wing needle,

sewing in a straight line, and Program 77, just as it is in the machine.

Should you still want more decoration, use a built-in stitch of your choice. Sew down the sides of the lines of blind hemstitches. When you have decorated the fabric enough, mark around the edge of the bonnet rectangle with a vanishing marker.

Fold the bonnet rectangle in half (Fig. 5.11). The fold will be the top of the bonnet. Pin the fabric together, matching decorative stitches so it is exact. With your marker, round off the front corners where the rosettes will be sewn (see Fig. 5.11). Open up.

Change to the scallop design, Program 61, to stitch the front edge and the sides of the bonnet. Use the fancy stitch foot #2, size #80 needle, stitch width 6.0, stitch length 0.35, and pattern length of 12. Do a sample first.

Thread cordonnet or pearl cotton through the hole in the throat plate. Swing out your accessory tray which forms the bed extension, enough to allow the cord to feed under the tray and then through the slot under the needleplate. This assures that you will not inadvertently hold down the cord and keep it from feeding freely as you cover it with stitches. When the scallops are completed, clip fabric back from the edge to the stitching, but not so close that you cut the scallops. Put the surplus pieces in your notebook.

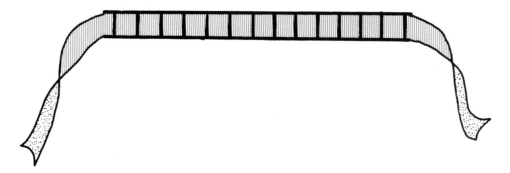

Fig. 5.12 Ribbon couched down using Program 76.

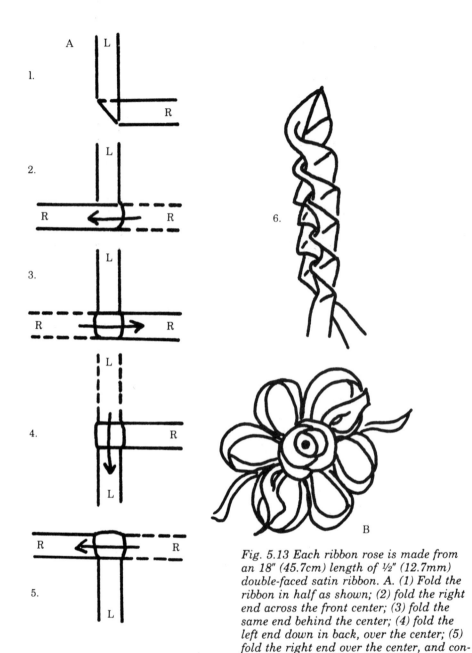

Fig. 5.13 Each ribbon rose is made from an 18" (45.7cm) length of ½" (12.7mm) double-faced satin ribbon. A. (1) Fold the ribbon in half as shown; (2) fold the right end across the front center; (3) fold the same end behind the center; (4) fold the left end down in back, over the center; (5) fold the right end over the center, and continue folding over the center until there are 30 folds between your fingers; (6) holding the last fold between your thumb and forefinger, release the rest of the ribbon, then pull on the ribbon end under the last fold to create the rose. B. By hand, stitch from the back to the center and back again to keep the rose from unwinding. Leave ½" (12.7mm) ends and cut each on a slant. Hold the loops in place with a small ribbon rose or tie small bows at the centers.

Use Program 00, with a stitch length of 6.0. Use the fancy stitch foot #2 with tension turned up to 9. Place the bonnet front on the bed of the machine. The ribbon will be stitched from underneath, ½" (12.7mm) from the front edge. When you finish stitching, pull out 8" (20.3cm) of ribbon and cut off.

Another way of applying ribbon is to use Program 76, and simply couch it down. At full width of 6.0, you can use the ⅛" (3.2mm) ribbon and it will look like you've spent hours weaving it under the stitches (Fig. 5.12).

Cut two ½" (12.7mm) satin ribbons, each 12" (30.5cm) long, for the bonnet ties. Attach at the rounded corners under the ⅛" (3.2mm) ribbon, using Program 89.

Make six loops from the 8" (20.3cm) of ⅛" (3.2mm) ribbon. Tack them by hand at the center on top of the ribbon ties. Make ribbon roses as shown in Fig. 5.13A, or tiny bows from the ½" (12.7mm) ribbon and attach these over the loops by hand (Fig. 5.13B). Use double thread. Poke the needle up from the inside of the bonnet, through the ribbon ties, loops, and the center of the flower and a pearl bead. Then poke the needle back through the flower, loops, ribbon tie and bonnet. Do this several times. It's not necessary to go through the bead each time. Anchor the thread underneath.

Thread 18" (45.7cm) of ¼" (6.3mm) ribbon through the back casing on the bonnet and pull up to tie into a bow at the back (Fig. 5.14). Cut off at the length you prefer. There you have it—a priceless gift.

Fig. 5.14 Pull on each end of the back ribbon and tie into a bow to shape the crown of the bonnet.

Stitch down on the line ½" (12.7mm) from the edge (back of bonnet) and stitch another ½" (12.7mm) from that line. Fold the back under ½" (12.7mm), then again another ½" (12.7mm). Stitch across the first fold to make the ribbon casing.

Next, wind the bobbin with ⅛" (3.2mm) double-faced satin ribbon. Tape the end onto the bobbin and begin winding by hand. Finish by winding slowly on the machine. Don't thread it through the spring when full. Instead, bypass the tension spring. Insert the bobbin into the machine and bring the ribbon to the top. Pull out at least 8" (20.3cm) of ribbon before beginning to sew.

Lesson 16. Stitching in rings

Stitching in rings is like making needlelace (Fig. 5.15). Instead of fabric surrounding a space, in this lesson the thread is attached to narrow gold rings. I selected rings about 2½" (6.4cm) in diameter as an appropriate size for tree ornaments. See Sources of Supplies for ordering these rings.

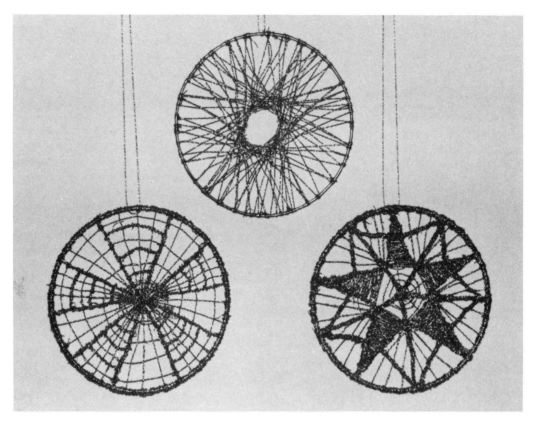

Fig. 5.15 Christmas ornaments stitched in gold rings.

Project
Christmas
Ornaments

A stabilizer isn't always needed when you sew in space, but it will depend upon your machine. I used to make these Christmas ornaments without a stabilizer and it worked beautifully. But with water-soluble stabilizer underneath, you can stitch more intricate designs, and the thread will stay in one place, as if you were stitching on fabric.

Set up your machine.

Program: 00
Stitch length: 0
Needle: #90/14
Feed dogs: lowered
Presser foot: bare needle
Dual feed: disengaged
Tension: *top,* slightly loosened; *bobbin,* normal
Thread: gold metallic on top and bobbin
Accessories: 2½" (6.4cm) gold ring; 7" (17.8cm) spring hoop; permanent white marker
Stabilizer: water-soluble

Double the stabilizer and put it into the hoop. Place the gold ring in the center.

96

Draw a design in the ring.

Dip the needle down at the side of the ring and bring the bobbin thread to the top. Hold the threads to one side. Anchor the ring by hand-walking the needle from the outside to the inside of it. Stitch from one side to the other several times. Hold onto the ring and stitch across to the other side. The chain of stitches will be tighter if you sew fast but move the hoop slowly. Anchor the thread on the other side by sewing over and back on the ring as you did at first.

Work back across and anchor on the other side. Keep doing this until you have laid in the spokes of the design. Remember, with water-soluble stabilizer you can change direction when stitching in open spaces. After the last anchoring stitches, go back into the ring and finish the piece. It can be symmetrical or not. I feel that the lighter the look, the better. Stitching it too thickly will be a detraction, but you may want to zigzag over threads, as in cutwork, to add variety to the design.

Anchor the last stitches and take the ring out of the hoop. Cut back the stabilizer, then dissolve it by holding the ring under running water. Hang it from your Christmas tree with a cord.

Lesson 17. Making Alençon lace

Alençon lace took its name from the French town. The lace was developed there and was so expensive it was rarely seen, except in shops with a wealthy clientele, where it was sold as yardage and used as trimming for lingerie, dresses, and household items.

On the fine, mesh net background is a heavy design, so closely woven it is almost clothlike. Characteristic of Alençon lace is the heavy thread that outlines the design.

Project
Alençon Pincushion

Our Alençon is made on a single layer of bridal veiling. The design is freely embroidered by machine, then outlined with pearl cotton or cordonnet (Fig. 5.16).

Program: 00; 60 or 61
Stitch length: 0
Needle: #80
Feed dogs: lowered

Fig. 5.16 Alençon lace pincushion.

Presser feet: darning foot #6 and fancy stitch foot #2

Tension: *top*, slightly loosened; *bobbin*, normal

Fabric suggestion: bridal veil, 36″ × 5″ (91.4cm × 12.7cm); pink satin, 4½″ × 11″ (11.4cm × 28.0cm)

Thread: #100 or #120 fine white sewing thread; #8 pearl cotton or cordonnet on bobbin to match

Accessories: 7″ (17.8cm) spring hoop; permanent white marker; 2 cups of sawdust

Stabilizer: tear-away and water-soluble

Prepare a sample of your stitching to be sure it looks like you want it to. I like a slight bubbly look to the pearl cotton, but you may want a tighter or even looser stitch. If so, tighten or loosen the top tension.

Put the water-soluble stabilizer in the hoop. Place it over the design and copy it with the permanent marker (Fig. 5.17). Then place the veiling over the stabilizer in the hoop.

Thread with fine thread in the top and bobbin. Bring the bobbin thread to the top and hold both threads to one side. After stitching a few stitches, clip these ends off. I don't anchor the threads as they will be sewn in anyway. Outline the design first with straight stitches.

When completed, go back and stitch in the petals and leaves. Sew a line next to the outline, then another within that and another, and so on until you have filled it in. If some of the lines overlap, don't despair, as this will happen. Just try to keep from building up heavy stitching lines.

It's not necessary to cut the thread as

Fig. 5.17 Lace pincushion design.

you complete one section and start another. Loosen the top thread by lifting up on the presser foot and turning the handwheel if necessary. Slowly pull or push the hoop to the next place. There's no need to bring up the bobbin thread again, as long as it is still connected to the fabric.

When finished stitching, go back and clip threads between motifs. Bring long threads to the back to be clipped and dotted with a drop of Fray-Check. Use tweezers to pull out loose threads on the back.

Change the bobbin to the one containing pearl cotton. Take the veiling out of the hoop and turn it over. The topside of the lace will be underneath. Double check the tensions by sewing on another piece of veiling in another hoop. The pearl cotton should lay flat underneath without pulling; yet it should not be so loose it looks loopy.

Dip the needle into the veil and bring the pearl to the top. Hold it to one side as you begin: Don't anchor it. Outline the design. It is very important to keep from going over lines too many times. You want it to be thick, but not ugly.

When you complete outlining, cut off the pearl cotton, bringing any long ends to the back. Work those under a few stitches on back by hand and clip them off. Put your lace, still in the hoop, under the faucet to wash out the stabilizer.

Measure the top of the pincushion. The finished size will be 4″ × 5″ (10.2cm × 12.7cm) so add ½″ (12.7mm) to each measurement; 4½″ × 5½″ (11.4cm × 14.0cm). Cut two pieces of pink satin this size. Stitch the lace to one of the rectangles. Seam allowance is ¼″ (6.3mm).

Cut a piece of veiling 36″ (91.4cm) long (twice the perimeter of the pincushion), and 5″ (12.7cm) wide. Cut a piece of tear-away stabilizer the same length and 2″ (5.1cm) wide. Pin the cut edges of the veiling together to hold it in place. Slip tear-away under the fold. Set your machine to Program 60 or 61. Raise the feed dogs.

With the right edge of the embroidery foot placed just within the edge of the fold, stitch width 6.0, length at 0.35 and pattern length at 12, sew down the length of the veiling and cut back to the stitching. Wash out the stabilizer.

To gather the ruffle, zigzag over cordonnet (see Lesson 4). Stitch the length of the cut edges (stitch length 2, stitch width 1.5). Use the cord to gather the ruffle.

Join the two ends of the ruffle by placing one end over the other and matching the beginning of one scallop with the end of the other. Using Program 10, with a 2 stitch width, and 0.35 length, satin stitch down the width of the piece of veiling. Cut back to the line of stitching on both sides.

Gather the ruffle, placing the seam at a corner. Corners should be heavily gathered to make sure they lay beautifully when completed. Distribute the ruffles around the edge of the pincushion. Remember that the embroidered edge will be toward the *center* of the pincushion. Stitch in place. It's not necessary to remove the cordonnet.

The last step is to sew the back of the pincushion to the lace. Place right sides together, and work all the net ruffles inside as you pin around the edge.

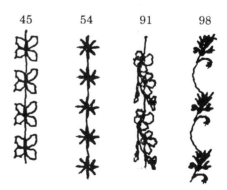

Fig. 5.18 Programs useful in lacemaking.

Sew within the stitching line on front. Leave a large enough opening so you can turn the pincushion to the outside. When turned, fill it very tightly with sawdust (or use another filler, if you prefer). Stitch the opening shut by hand.

Do you like making lace? Try other variations by using built-in programs such as 45, 54, 91 or 98 (Fig. 5.18), satin-stitch star flowers, or bands of intertwined cordonnet at the edges.

CHAPTER 6

Drawing Threads Out of Your Fabric

■ **Lesson 18. Needleweaving**

To create an area of free, lacy openwork called needleweaving, first draw threads out of a fabric, then stitch over the remaining threads. On this long-cut, I used exactly the same color thread on the top and bobbin as that of the dress; I'm constantly being asked how it was stitched. The solution to the mystery follows.

Lesson 18. Needleweaving

Because needleweaving is worked in a straight line, I chose to decorate the sleeves of a summer dress (Fig. 6.1). I knew this dress would be washed many times, so I chose a polyester sewing thread for durability. I matched it perfectly, both spool and bobbin, with the fabric.

First do a small sample of needleweaving for your notebook. The openwork is 1" (2.5cm) wide. Pull out a horizontal thread at the top and the bottom where the openwork will be. Straight stitch across those lines. Then pull out the horizontal or weft threads in that space.

Project
Openwork
on Sleeves

You will machine stitch over the vertical or warp threads, drawing them together as you zigzag (Fig. 6.2).

Program: 10
Stitch width: 0.0 – 4.0
Stitch length: 0.0 – 0.5
Needle: #80
Feed dogs: lowered, up
Presser foot: fancy stitch foot #2; darning foot #6 or no presser foot
Dual feed: disengaged
Tension: *top*, normal, loosened; *bobbin*, normal
Fabric suggestion: loosely woven
Thread: Metrosene polyester
Stabilizer: tear-away, or construction paper to match thread; water-soluble (optional)

Take off the regular presser foot and use a bare needle or darning foot. Try working without a hoop on this project. The stitching goes fast and a hoop would only slow you down. You may stitch with water-soluble stabilizer behind your work, but that is optional. Prepare your machine for embroidery by lowering the feed dogs. Be sure the presser bar is down in the notch before you start to stitch. Dip the needle down and bring the bobbin thread to the top. An-

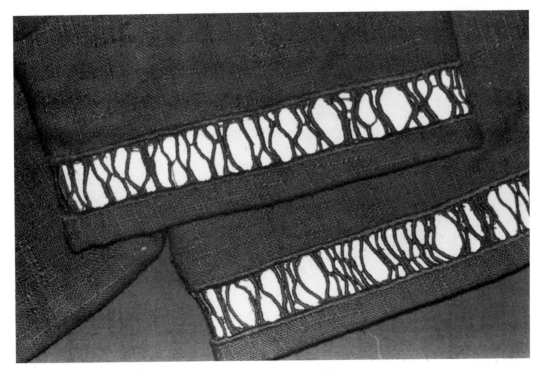

Fig. 6.1 Needleweaving decorates the sleeves on a summer dress.

chor the threads. Set the machine on stitch width 4 and normal tension.

Using both hands, grasp the top and bottom of the fabric between your fingers, stretching it slightly as you stitch. Keep the fabric as close as you can to the needleplate, and keep tension on the warp threads.

Begin to move from just below the stitched line at the bottom to just over the stitched line on top. Move the fabric slowly, but sew at a comfortable speed, catching several warp threads together as you zigzag to the top.

When you reach the top, move sideways to the next several warp threads and begin stitching those together. About halfway down, move the fabric to the side and catch a few stitches into the previous group of zigzagged threads. Then move back and continue to the bottom of the threads. Finish all the warp threads in the same manner, satin stitching up and down, while at the same time catching threads from the previous run in one or two places. This adds interest and strength to your openwork and is an integral part of your needleweaving.

After finishing, remove water-soluble stabilizer and pull the piece back into shape while damp. Press.

If you did not use stabilizer, then spray with water to enable you to pull it into shape. Press.

Draw two horizontal lines (one inch apart and as long as your needleweaving) across a piece of construction paper or tear-away stabilizer. Place your

Fig. 6.2 Pull out warp threads from the fabric and zigzag freely over the remaining wefts. Then finish the edges on each side with satin stitching.

needleweaving on top of this, using the drawn lines as guides to keep the open area straight.

Set up your machine for straight stitching with feed dogs up and the open embroidery foot on. Sew a line of straight stitches across the top and bottom on the same guidelines you stitched at the beginning. This will hold the needleweaving in place and stabilize it for the final stitching.

Set the machine to a wide zigzag 4.0, feed dogs still up, stitch length 0.35. Loosen tension slightly and satin stitch over those lines, covering the edges in two passes—the first narrower and more open than the second. This takes longer, but the results are more professional-looking. The stitching will fall just to one side of the fab-

ric and will catch the fabric on the other side to neatly finish the edge of the needlelace. Tear off the stabilizer and steam press the embroidery carefully.

If the stabilizer can still be seen behind the stitches, it may be possible to remove it by dampening it, then using a tweezers to remove it. Or use this trick: if you can find a permanent marker the same color as the thread, dab in the color where necessary.

Try needleweaving across the yoke or pocket of a blouse, or down the middle of sleeves, or combine two rows of this with lacy spiderweb circles scattered between.

If you don't like the see-through look, or if you want to add another color, back the open area with another fabric.

CHAPTER 7

Layering Fabrics: Quilting

I've always taken time to make handmade gifts for special people. But if I make a crib quilt, for example, I'd like to know that the baby won't be twice as long as the quilt by the time the gift is presented. If I'm sewing clothes, I'm realistic: I want the garment to be in style when the recipient opens the box.

So, although I love hand quilting and hand sewing, they often take too long. Machine quilting, on the other hand, is speedy and sturdy. You can use heavy fabrics like corduroy, as well as thick batts, and you will have no trouble stitching them together. If machine quilting is done properly, it can be as fine as handwork.

In this chapter I've included quilting with the feed dogs lowered and in place, trapunto, and Italian cording.

Remember several things when doing any type of quilting. The first is to preshrink all fabrics. I usually use cotton poly-ester blends for my quilts so they stay new-looking for a long time. Sheets are excellent backing materials. They come in a myriad of colors and prints, can be of excellent quality, and they won't have to be pieced. When I make a quilt, I use a sheet that is larger than the top.

I usually quilt with a polyester sewing thread. Most brands come in a wealth of colors. Should I want to emphasize the stitching line, I will double the thread. But when I sew on a patterned material or a fabric that changes color throughout, I choose a monofilament. I may or may not use monofilament on the bobbin, depending upon the samples I do first.

Using safety pins instead of hand basting is my favorite method of holding the fabrics and batt together before I quilt. I don't use dressmaker's pins because many of them fall out before the quilt is completed—and those that don't usually stab me.

Lesson 19. Quilting with feed dogs up

With the regular presser foot, always engage the dual feed when sewing lines of straight quilting stitches. It minimizes puckering on the backing fabric, as the top and bottom fabrics are fed through at the same speed with no slipping.

Before I had my Pfaff, I grasped the quilt in both hands and kept it taut as it fed through the machine. As I progressed, I stopped and looked underneath to be sure I had a smooth lining. I must admit I became an expert at sewing without puckers. It always took a lot longer, so I really appreciate the dual feed.

Can you imagine how fast you could make a quilt using striped fabric or a striped sheet for the top? Use the stripes as quilting lines. If you use stripes for garments, keep in mind that the more rows of quilting, the smaller the piece becomes. I either quilt the fabric first and then cut out the pattern, or I cut my pattern larger than necessary, do the quilting and then lay the pattern back on it when finished. I recut the pattern where necessary.

If you piece a quilt and decide to machine quilt it by using stitch-in-a-ditch, you may prefer using the blind hem foot #3, which has the little adjustable red guide. Use Program 00 and line up the guide with the needle. Stitch-in-a-ditch is done on top of the quilt by stitching in the seam lines (the ditches). With this presser foot, it is easy to stitch exactly in the ditch and because you can use the dual feed with this foot, your work will never pucker.

Project Tote Bag Square (Appliqué and Quilting)

This quilted sample can be used as a square for the tote bag in Chapter 12. It includes appliqué and satin stitches.

Program 00; 10
Stitch width: 0.0 – 3.0
Stitch length: 2.0 and 0.35
Feed dogs: up
Presser foot: ordinary sewing foot #0; fancy stitch foot #2
Dual feed: engaged and disengaged
Needle: #90/14 jeans needle
Tension: *top,* normal to −3+; *bobbin,* normal

Thread: cotton machine embroidery
Fabric: five 9″ (22.9cm) squares of royal blue, red, yellow, green, and purple; 10″ (25.4cm) square of fleece
Accessories: water-erasable marker; fusible webbing; ruler; Teflon pressing sheet; tracing paper and pencil
Stabilizer: iron-on freezer paper

Using the Teflon sheet, iron fusible webbing onto the back of each of the fabrics except blue. Blue is the background fabric on which the design will be placed.

Trace the design in Fig. 7.1 twice and lay one pattern aside until later. Cut one pattern apart. Place each piece of the pattern on the correct piece of fabric and draw around it with a water-erasable marker. *Hint:* Draw the two yellow pieces with ¼″ (6.4mm) seam allowances where they slip under the red and green fabrics instead of cutting to fit exactly. It will be easier to cover only one raw edge when you satin stitch over them.

Use the second tracing for placement. After you've put the fabrics in place, put the pattern on top of them and look at the design through the tracing paper to be sure it is arranged perfectly. Fuse the fabrics in place by pressing them with your iron. Also press freezer paper to the back of the blue fabric to stabilize your appliqué for stitching.

Satin stitch the edges using thread the same color as the edge you are stitching down. Select program 10 to do this. Use a stitch width no more than 3, and a length no more than 0.35. Use foot #2, and disengage the dual feed. Upper tension should be loosened to −3+ so you have a smooth satin stitch. Sew at a moderate speed and always turn with the needle in the fabric.

Place your appliqué on top of a piece of fleecy Pellon. Straight stitch (stitch width 0, stitch length 2, dual feed engaged, #00 presser foot, normal tension) on either side of the satin stitches, using matching thread colors. This not only quilts the

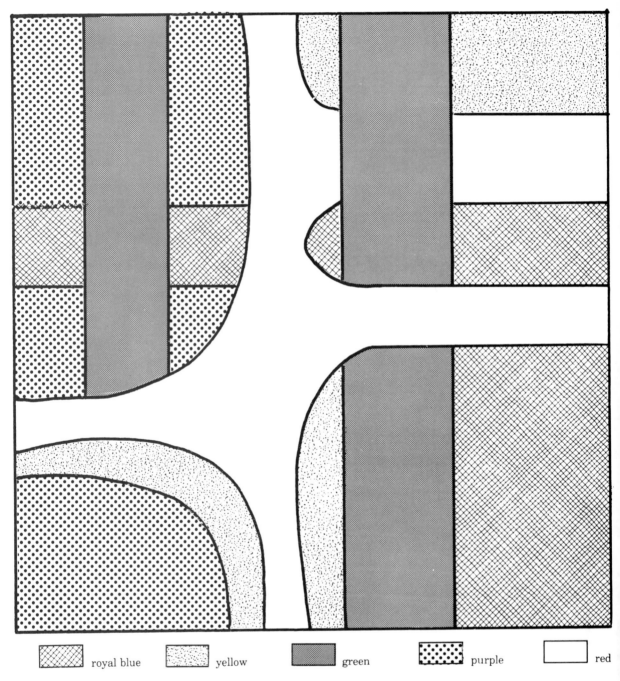

royal blue   yellow   green   purple   red

Fig. 7.1 Pattern for appliquéd and quilted tote bag square.

106

square, but it gives the satin stitches a clean finish. It is more decorative if you use a contrasting thread. Then back the square with a piece of fabric and finish it as described in Chapter 12.

If you want a puffy look on an appliqué quilt, don't fuse your appliqué pieces, as this flattens them out and no amount of washing will bring them back to life. Instead, use method A found in Chapter 4 to hold the appliqués firmly in place while you satin stitch them.

Lesson 20. Quilting with feed dogs lowered

As you can tell from the lesson title, this will be free-machine quilting. The machine setting will not control the length of the stitches; you will. If you move the fabric fast, the stitches will be longer than if you move it slowly. Not working in a hoop, you must use a darning foot to prevent skipped stitches. And no hoop means you must hold the fabric taut while stitching.

Program: 00
Needle: #90
Feed dogs: lowered
Presser foot: darning foot #6
Tension: *top*, slightly loosened; *bobbin*, normal
Fabric suggestion: medium-weight cotton; fleece or quilt batting
Thread: machine embroidery
Accessories: water-erasable marker

One of the easiest ways to learn free quilting and to practice control at the same time is to quilt around the motifs of a printed fabric as shown in Fig. 7.2. Even the underside looks terrific: you may like the looks of the lining better than the printed side. If so, it makes for a stunning reversible jacket.

When quilting any fabrics with feed dogs lowered, don't place the stitching lines too closely together, unless you want to emphasize the area that *isn't* stitched. Closely stitched, it will be too stiff and you'll lose the contrast of light and dark shadowing that makes this type of machining so effective.

Fig. 7.2 Cotton print, batting and velveteen are quilted together by stitching the butterfly design.

Lesson 21. Trapunto

In trapunto, two pieces of fabric are stitched together, following a design. Then the quilter selects the areas of the design to be stuffed with fiberfill. Usually trapunto is done from underneath the fabrics.

Layer two pieces of material together and use the felt flower design in Fig. 4.5 (Lesson 10). Transfer the design to the top fabric. Place both fabrics in a hoop. Stitch in the design, using machine embroidery thread the same color as the fabric, with your machine set up for free-machine embroidery or feed dogs up and embroidery foot on. Stitch in the design. Make small slits in the backing fabric behind the petals, leaves, or stamens—or all three. Add fiberfill, poking it in with a tool that is not sharply pointed. Whip stitch the slits closed by hand.

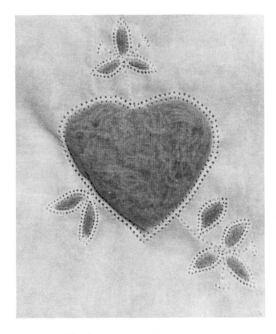

Fig. 7.3 Shadow trapunto heart.

You can trapunto from the top by appliquéing on top of a base fabric. Slip filling inside the appliqué before you've attached it all the way around. You may want to add stitches over the surface of the appliqué to hold the stuffing firmly and to embellish the design.

Project
Shadow Trapunto Heart

This project is called shadow trapunto. Instead of merely filling in a section of the design to give a raised effect, this design is done with organdy fabric so you can see the colorful yarns that have been used as stuffing (Fig. 7.3).

Program: 78; 79; 04
Stitch width: 3.0 and 2.0 on program 78; other programs as set
Stitch length: 3.0 and 2.0 on Program 78; other programs as set
Single pattern: engaged on Program 79 only
Mirror: Program 78 only
Needle: hemstitch needle
Needle stop: down on Program 78 only
Presser foot: fancy stitch foot #1
Dual feed: engaged
Feed dogs: raised
Tension: *top,* −3+; *bobbin,* normal
Fabric: white organdy
Thread: white machine embroidery, colors optional
Accessories: vanishing marker; bits of pink, blue and green acrylic yarn; embroidery scissors; hand sewing needle; yarn needle

Cut two pieces of organdy and, with a vanishing marker, draw the design in Fig. 7.4 on the top piece. Stitch around the heart shape with the Program 78 set on the longest and widest settings given, then change the settings to the smaller numbers and stitch around the leaf shapes.

When cornering with this particular stitch, you should be sure to use your tie-off key to complete the stitch program,

Fig. 7.4 Pattern for shadow trapunto.

then stitch a single program beyond the stitching line. In this way, when you turn the corner, you will stitch into the holes already made with no gap in the stitching at the point of the leaf or heart.

Use Program 79 to make the stamens of the flower, and connect them to the center of the flower with a few stitches of Program 04. The stems are also made with Program 04.

While white thread was used throughout for this design, it would also be pretty if colors were used on the heart, flower petals and leaves.

After stitching, slit the underneath layer of organdy just enough to poke in pink yarn cut into small pieces. Or use colored fiberfill. After stuffing the heart, whip the raw edges shut with a hand sewing needle and thread.

Because the flower petal and leaf shapes are small, you will probably find it more convenient to simply thread your green and blue yarns in a darning needle and pull the yarn through between the two layers of organdy, going back and forth three times to pad the shapes thoroughly.

The heart could be finished as a pillow top, if you like, or simply file it in your bulging notebook for future reference.

Lesson 22. Italian cording

Italian cording is often mistaken for trapunto. The difference is that the area to be stuffed in Italian cording will be the space between two stitching lines. Instead of using fiberfill, thread a cord of appropriate size through the double lines of stitching.

It's also possible to create the look of Italian cording in one pass of the machine, on one layer of fabric when stitching with a double needle. Thread gimp or pearl cotton through the needle plate of your machine and it will be caught between the lines of stitching by the bobbin thread.

Project
Tote Bag Square (Italian Cording)

This square (Fig. 7.5) was done using a single needle.

Program: 04
Stitch length: 3.0
Needle: #80 sharp

Feed dogs: up
Presser foot: ordinary sewing foot #0
Dual feed: engaged
Tension: *top*, normal; *bobbin*, normal
Fabric suggestions: 9″ (22.9cm) square lightweight cotton for top; stiffer cotton for backing
Thread: shiny rayon or machine embroidery cotton
Cord: appropriate-size acrylic yarn or cable cord
Accessories: hand-sewing needle; large-eyed hand-sewing tapestry needle to thread cord through the design; water-erasable marker

Draw the design in Fig. 7.5 on the fabric with a water-erasable marker, indicating where the lines will cross and which ones cross over, which under.

When you are stitching the lines, don't bother to anchor threads when the lines cross. Instead, touch your tie-off button to finish the stitch program. Then pull several inches of thread out of the needle. Hold the thread to one side. Skip over the inter-

110

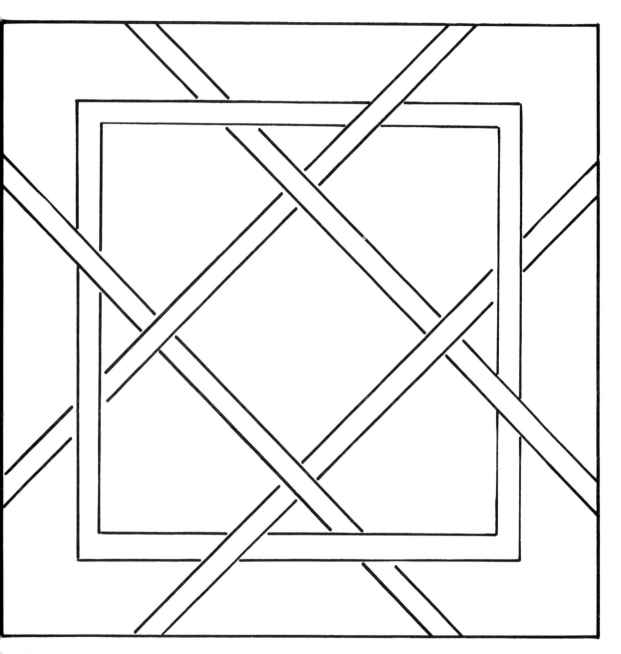

Fig. 7.5 Italian cording tote bag square.

section; then begin stitching again. When finished, go back and clip the threads in the middle. Thread up a sewing needle and poke all the top threads through to the back and work them in. Finish up by working the cord through the design by hand.

It's difficult to turn corners with cording and make those corners look sharp. Poke the needle out of the back fabric at a corner, and then back in again in the same place, leaving a small loop of the cord out in back.

When working with a double needle, turn corners in three steps. Stitch to the corner. Stop. Lower the needles so they are just grazing the fabric. Lift the presser foot. Half-turn the fabric. Lower the presser foot and turn the wheel by hand to make one stitch. Raise the needles and again bring the needle points down to barely touch the top of the fabric. Lift the presser foot again and complete the turn. Lower the presser foot and continue stitching.

Directions for finishing the square are in Chapter 12.

Look for inspirations for Italian cording in books on Celtic designs or bargello borders.

CHAPTER 8

Adding Interesting Seams to Your Fabric

- Lesson 23. French handsewing by machine
- Lesson 24. Seaming with feed dogs up and lowered

In previous chapters, the emphasis was on decorative stitchery. In Chapters 8 and 9, the focus is on sewing. The chapters are so closely related that at times they even overlap. Included in Chapters 8 and 9 are many of the sewing long-cuts I mentioned in the Preface and Chapter 1. But now, instead of decorating a garment by embroidering or appliquéing on it, you'll learn to make the garment unique by changing the seams, hems and edges.

Let's face it: seams are not always interesting. Most of them are hidden and it's not necessary that they do anything but hold two pieces of fabric together. On the other hand, seams can be the focal point of your creation. This chapter includes seams for the finest lace to the heaviest canvas — seams purely practical and those that combine decoration with practicality. Stitch up samples of all of them for your notebook. You'll discover that knowing your sewing machine is a joy.

The project in this chapter is a wedding handkerchief (Fig. 8.1). After learning how to accomplish French handsewing on the machine, work this project. It can also be used as a pillow top.

Lesson 23. French handsewing by machine

When I first heard about the type of clothing construction called French handsewing, I thought it was something new–until Marcia Strickland, a friend from Birmingham, Alabama, showed me her daughters' dresses. They were made of laces, with pintucks and embroidery, entredeaux and hemstitching, and looked like our family's christening gown. I knew French handsewing; I just hadn't been acquainted with the term. We'd always called it "sewing by hand" and I had agonized over it years ago, when I was sure I'd be struck blind by the tiny stitches before I made it through junior high school. It was hard for me to believe that I could accomplish the perfection of Marcia's clothing on my sewing machine (called "French handsewing by machine" or "French machine sewing").

It's possible to find lace and tucked blouses, skirts and dresses in any department store today. Because this feminine look is expensive in ready-to-wear, if you learn the following hand-sewing techniques by machine and sew them yourself, you will save money and have a lot of fun besides.

Fig. 8.1 French hand-sewn wedding handkerchief stitched on my Pfaff.

First, I had to learn basics before I could stitch collars or dresses. Marcia taught me that if I apply fabric to lace, one of the rules of French handsewing is that I must always have entredeaux between.

Entredeaux literally means "between two." It is purchased by the yard in fabric shops. The fabric on either side of the ladderlike strip down the center is trimmed off before it is attached. I also learned that the holes in entredeaux are never evenly spaced, no matter how expensive it is.

You can make your own entredeaux in the event you cannot find a source of supply. I use the hemstitch needle and Program 77 for a double row. For a single row, use the following M memory program.

Bring up an empty M memory; enter Program 54 once; enter Program 02 twice; touch repeat key to close program.

Program: M memory; 54-02-02
Needle: hemstitch
Feed dogs: up
Presser foot: fancy stitch #2

Dual feed: disengaged
Fabric suggestions: lightweight white cotton
    lawn or batiste or poly cotton blend, cut
    in strips
Thread: fine cotton machine embroidery,
    white
Accessories: ruler; vanishing marker; rotary
    cutter and mat

Cut strips of batiste 1″ (2.5cm) wide and, with vanishing marker and ruler, draw a line down the center. Stitch down the strip, following the line. When you are ready to use your entredeaux, trim away surplus fabric.

Marcia suggested size 100 pure cotton thread and #70 needle for sewing. She uses an extra-fine thread because the batiste fabric used is extremely lightweight, and stitches are visible when attaching lace and entredeaux or stitching pintucks. And she suggests using cotton thread for heirlooms because it will last a long time.

When handsewing, Marcia chooses cotton batiste because it is easier to roll and whip the edges of cotton. Polyester or cotton/polyester blends have minds of their own. It's hard to roll them as they keep unrolling while you try to whip them in place.

But French machine sewing can easily be done on blends, so I often choose a cotton/polyester for fabric (and thread), as it doesn't wrinkle like pure cotton.

I learned so much from Marcia, I filled a notebook with samples, ideas, and shortcuts. When you stitch up samples for your own notebook, if a technique can be done several ways, do them all and then decide which works best for you. The following techniques are all you need to learn for French machine sewing.

Sewing French seams

French seams are used on lightweight, transparent fabrics to finish the seams beautifully, disguising raw edges. They are

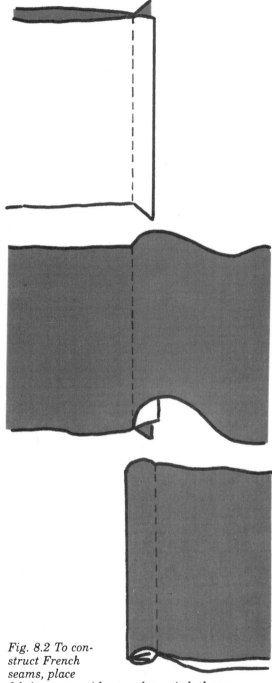

Fig. 8.2 To construct French seams, place fabrics wrong sides together, stitch the seam, trim to ⅛″ (3.2mm), then fold the fabric back over the seam allowance and stitch down outside the allowance.

115

also found on smocked garments as a fine finish.

The seams are accomplished in two different operations (Fig. 8.2). Begin with fabric pieces, wrong sides facing. Stitch the seam, using a #70 needle and fine sewing thread. Open and press seam to one side. Cut back the seam allowance evenly, to ⅛" (3.2mm). Turn the fabric back over the raw edges, press again (the seam will be at the edge), pin, and stitch again, enclosing the ⅛" (3.2mm) seam allowance.

Program 16 produces an exceptionally clean French seam.

Program: 16; 00
Stitch width: 3.0 on 16
Stitch length: 2.0
Needle: #70/10
Presser foot: fancy stitch foot #2
Dual feed: disengaged
Tension: *top*, −3+; *bobbin*, normal
Fabric: lightweight cotton or blend
Thread: lightweight cotton-wrapped or 100% polyester

Trim your fabric evenly to a ¼" (6mm) seam allowance and stitch allowing the needle to drop off the fabric on the right swings.

As you sew the seam on the first pass, the fabric is neatly rolled without an uneven edge. When the fabric is folded back over the seam allowance and straight stitched with Program 00, no maddening wispy threads poke out to ruin the perfect French seam.

Stitching rolled and whipped edges

Rolled and whipped edges are always used in conjunction with French handsewing because each piece of fabric must have a finished edge before it is attached to lace or to entredeaux. When working by machine, sometimes you can finish the edge at the same time you attach it to the lace. These edges can be worked several ways and everyone seems to have her own favorite.

Start right at the edge so even the first thread in the fabric will be rolled and whipped making sure the needle and bobbin threads are to the back. I like to use the ordinary sewing foot #0 with the dual feed. Again, the edge of the fabric is placed so the right swing goes off the edge.

Stitch, holding the threads from the top and bobbin and the fabric will roll very neatly right out to the end.

I like working a rolled and whipped edge with the fancy stitch foot #2 also, and I've used the same settings with the appliqué foot with the same excellent results.

Program: 16
Stitch width: 3
Stitch length: 2
Tension: *top*, normal; *bobbin*, normal
Fabric: batiste, work on wrong side
Presser foot: ordinary sewing foot #0 with dual feed, or fancy stitch foot #2 or appliqué foot without dual feed

Gathering rolled and whipped edges

Before you roll and whip, stitch (stitch length 2.5) along the edge of the fabric about ⅛" (3.2mm) in. Instead of anchoring your threads, leave several inches of thread at the beginning and end of the stitching. Starting at the top again, roll the edge with Program 16 set with a stitch width of 4.0. The straight stitching must not be caught in this modified zigzag (Fig. 8.3).

Hold the thread ends at the beginning of your line of straight stitching to keep them from slipping through as you gather. Pull on the top thread at the other end of the line of straight stitches and evenly distribute the ruffling (Fig. 8.3B).

Another way of doing it is to use the single cording foot and place tatting thread under the center groove. The machine will roll the fabric edge over the tatting thread,

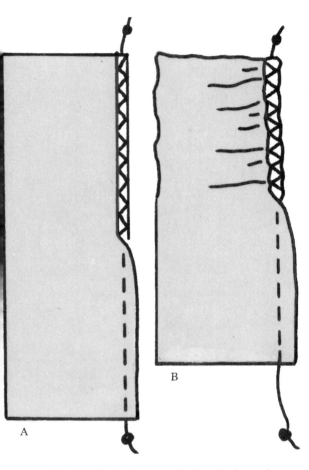

fabric. Pin the lace inside the lines. Machine straight stitch down both sides of the lace to hold it in place. Cut straight down the fabric behind the lace, allowing seam allowance on fabric. Fold the seam allowances back and press.

Then zigzag over the edges of the lace and the straight stitching to attach the lace and finish the edges simultaneously. Cut the seam allowances back to the stitching.

Apply scalloped lace as an insertion by placing it on the fabric and basting it down both sides. Cut down the fabric behind. Zigzag closely over the edge, following the scallop. Cut away the fabric underneath. This method can also be used for straight-edge insertion, but the join will not be as strong as folding back the seam allowance and stitching over the doubled fabric.

Joining scalloped lace

Find the most heavily patterned place in the design to join scalloped lace. Overlap two identical patterns, and stitch a fine zigzag (stitch width 1.5, stitch length 1.5) with feed dogs up. Follow the edge of the design as shown in Fig. 8.5. Trim back to the line of stitching.

Using entredeaux

Entredeaux is used between fabric and lace. Only the ladderlike strip of stitching down the center of the entredeaux is attached.

Program: 10
Stitch width: 2.0 to 3.0
Stitch length: 1.5
Needle: #70/10
Feed dogs: up
Presser foot: fancy stitch foot #2, or appliqué foot
Tension: *top*, normal; *bobbin*, normal
Fabric suggestions: batiste
Thread: #100

Fig. 8.3 Gathering a rolled and whipped edge. A. Sew a line of straight stitches along the edge of the fabric, then roll and whip over the line of stitching. B. Gather the material by pulling on the top thread from the line of straight stitches.

and fullness is easy to adjust because the heavier thread is less likely to break. Stitch width is also set at 4.0 for this technique. Tatting thread can be purchased at any needlework shop.

Applying insertion

Insertion is lace with two straight sides. It is easily applied by machine (Fig. 8.4). Draw two lines the width of the lace on the

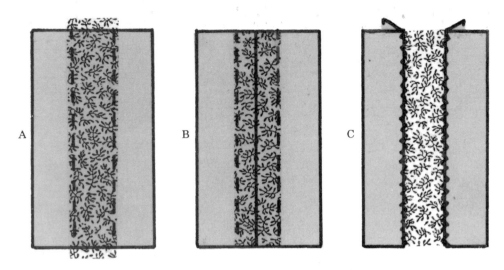

Fig. 8.4   A. Sew lace insert to fabric by straight stitching down each side of the lace. B. Cut through the fabric behind the lace from top to bottom. C. Turn back the seam allowances on both sides and zigzag down the edges of the insertion. Trim the seam allowances back to the stitching.

Measure the length of entredeaux you will need and cut off the fabric on only one side. Attach that side. Place the topside of the entredeaux to the topside of the rolled and whipped edge, the entredeaux on top, as shown at left in Fig. 8.7. Be sure the edges touch. Hand walk the machine through the first couple of stitches to be sure the needle is clearing the edge on the right side and falls into the holes of the

Fig. 8.5 Join two pieces of lace together by overlapping the design at each end, zigzagging the "seam," then cutting back the surplus lace to the stitches.

118

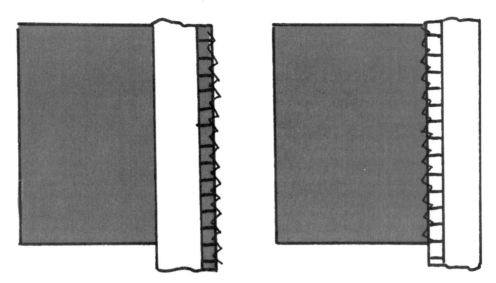

Fig. 8.6 To apply entredeaux to rolled and whipped edges, place it on the fabric, right sides together. Zigzag into each hole and off the edges. Then press open.

entredeaux on the left (Fig. 8.7). Don't worry if the needle skips a hole in the entredeaux once in awhile, because it won't show. If possible, sew with the machine set on moderate speed. When fin-

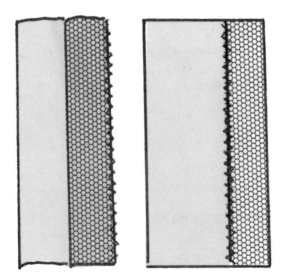

Fig. 8.7 Place insertion on top of a rolled and whipped edge; zigzag to attach. Press open.

ished, pull the entredeaux to the side away from the fabric and press (at right in Fig. 8.6). Repeat for the other side.

Gathering lace edging

There are several threads at the edges of lace. Use a pin to find the one that gathers the lace and then pull up the thread. Hold onto both ends of this thread, or you might pull it all the way through when gathering the lace. Evenly space the gathers.

Attaching straight-edged lace to rolled and whipped edges

Place the topside of the lace against the topside of the fabric (Fig. 8.7). Be sure the edges are even. Use a zigzag at a setting of stitch width 2.5 and length 1.5. The needle should stitch within the edges of lace and fabric on the left, and stitch off of them on the right swing (Fig. 8.8). Flatten out and press.

Attaching entredeaux
to lace insertion

Stitch width: 2.0 or adjust
Stitch length: 1.5 or adjust
Presser foot: fancy stitch foot #2
Dual feed: disengaged

Trim fabric from one side of the
entredeaux. With topsides up, place the
trimmed edge of the entredeaux up next to
the edge of the lace.

Zigzag the edges together so the needle
barely catches the lace and goes into each
hole of the entredeaux (Fig. 8.8). Start by
using a 2.0 stitch width and 1.5 stitch
length, but make adjustments in these figures if you find they are needed.

Sewing lace to lace

Program: 12
Stitch width: 2.5
Stitch length: 1.0
Presser foot: ordinary presser foot #0
Dual feed: engaged

Put the straight edges of the lace together so they are just touching. Stitch so the
center stitch made by the needle goes between the piece of lace. The machine will
zigzag first to the left and then to the right.
Use the center of the presser foot as a
guide. This is really easier than it sounds
and your pieces of lace are joined almost
invisibly.

Fagoting

There are times when we need different
detailing on a bodice, sleeve or skirt. It may
not be called for in the pattern, but it's a
way to make that garment our own, so we
choose to take a long-cut and add a creative
touch of our choosing to the original pattern.

Fagoting is one way to change a seam or
add one. With your machine, you need only
a tailor tacking foot, since it's like making
fringe.

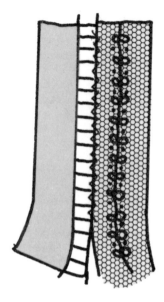

*Fig. 8.8 To attach
entredeaux to lace insertion,
place edges next to each other and zigzag together.*

Program: 10
Stitch width: 2.0
Stitch length: 0.35 to 0.5
Presser foot: fringe foot; fancy stitch foot #2
Stabilizer: water soluble or freezer paper

Make a sample first. Loosen the top tension on your machine to about 1 or 2.

Place two pieces of fabric together, with
right sides facing. Stitch along the seam
line using the fringe foot. When the line is
completed, pull the seam open to reveal the
stitches.

I like to press this so the fabric is nice
and flat with the stitches between the two
pieces well separated. Change to the fancy
stitch foot and put stabilizer underneath
your work. Choose a decorative stitch or
even straight stitch to sew each side of the
fabric close to the fold.

To make it extra wide, I sometimes do a
first row of satin stitches with the length
set at 0.5 and the width at 6. Let the right

120

Fig. 8.9 Wide fagoting for a braidlike effect.

swing of the needle go off the fold and into the space between the two pieces of fabric. Do the opposite side with the left swing of the needle going into the space. The slightly looser stitch length will enable you to overstitch the row of decorative stitch made with Program 63 or 65 without a ridgy, corduroy effect, which is unattractive.

Go even further with fagoting and bundle the stitches: Sew down the center of the openwork with Program 04.

Use fagoting above the hem of a skirt or around a sleeve or square collar.

Project
Wedding
Handkerchief

Many of the techniques you have learned for French machine sewing will be used to make the handkerchief (see Fig. 8.1). You will need: 5″ (12.7cm) square of fine batiste; ½″ (12.7mm) lace insertion; 1″ (2.5cm) beading; entredeaux; lace edging; ⅛″ (3.2mm) double-face satin ribbon, about 6 yards (5.5m); a ruler and water-erasable marker.

How to figure exact amounts of lace and entredeaux is included in the directions below; the width of your lace will determine the length you will need. Use a #70 needle and #100 sewing thread.

For the center of this handkerchief (Fig. 8.10), I rolled and whipped a 5″ (12.7cm)

square of batiste. Use the method you prefer. Entredeaux was added to the edges; do one side of entredeaux at a time, cut and overlap the openings of the entredeaux at the corners.

Stitch the beading (the lace with holes for threaded ribbon) and lace strip together before attaching them to the entredeaux. Together, the strip of lace is 1½″ (3.8cm) wide.

Estimate how much lace you'll need for your wedding handkerchief by first measuring around the center square of batiste and entredeaux; the example is approximately 20″ (50.8cm).

Double the width measurement of the strip of lace you've made when you stitched the beading to the lace insertion: 1½″ × 2 = 3″ (3.8cm × 2 = 7.6cm).

Multiply 3″ × 4 = 12″ (7.6cm × 4 = 30.5cm) to arrive at the number of inches (cm) needed for the corner miters.

Add the distance around the center square (20″ or 50.8cm) to the corner miters (12″ or 30.5cm). Exact measurement of the lace needed is 32″ (81.3cm). Add 2″ (5.1cm) more for safety.

Leave 2″ (5.1cm) of lace at the corner before you begin attaching lace to the entredeaux (Fig. 8.11A). Trim the entredeaux. Place the edge of the lace strip next to the entredeaux so the edges touch. Stitch along the first side, ending with needle down at the corner, extending the lace 1½″ (3.8cm) beyond the corner (this is the width measurement of the strip of lace I used). Raise the presser foot. Fold the lace back on itself by the same measurement,

121

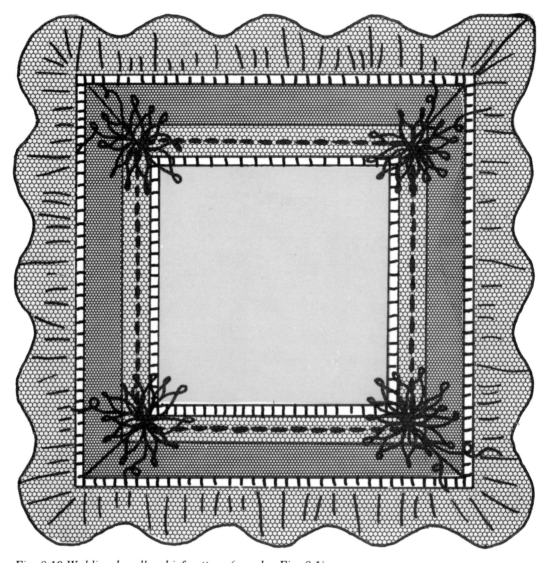

Fig. 8.10 Wedding handkerchief pattern (see also Fig. 8.1)

1½″ (3.8cm) or the width of your lace. Pin the lace together at the corner and then fold the lace so it will lie at the edge of the entredeaux on the next side you will stitch (Fig. 8.11B). Turn your work to continue stitching, and put the presser foot down. Hand-walk the first stitch to be sure it catches the lace. Continue stitching slowly to the next corner. Attach lace to the other sides as you did the first.

After the strip of lace has been attached, go back to each corner and fold the lace diagonally to miter it. Check carefully that the corners will lie flat. Pin each one. Mark

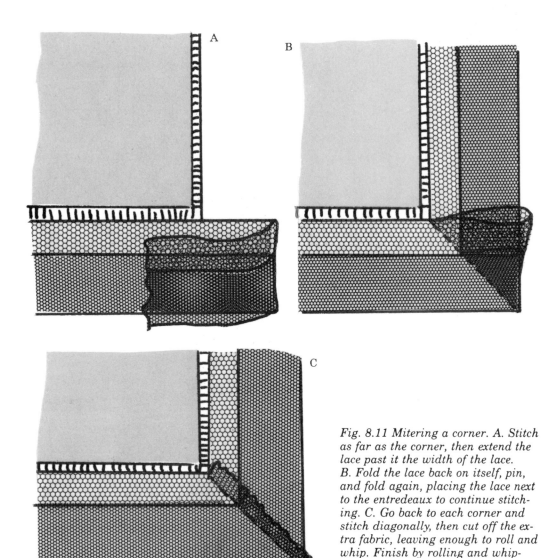

A   B

C

*Fig. 8.11 Mitering a corner. A. Stitch
as far as the corner, then extend the
lace past it the width of the lace.
B. Fold the lace back on itself, pin,
and fold again, placing the lace next
to the entredeaux to continue stitching. C. Go back to each corner and
stitch diagonally, then cut off the extra fabric, leaving enough to roll and
whip. Finish by rolling and whipping each corner.*

with a ruler and water-erasable pen where
the line of stitching will be (Fig. 8.11B).
Sew down the line with a straight stitch
before cutting back, leaving enough lace to
roll and whip by machine (Fig. 8.11C).

Attach entredeaux to the edge of the
lace, overlapping the holes of each piece at
the corners, as done previously.

Measure around the outside edge. Double this for the gathered lace measurement. Sew the ends of the lace together by
overlapping and at the same time, matching the designs top and bottom. Sew a narrow zigzag along the design and cut back to
the line. Place this seam in a corner.

Gather the lace edging by pulling the

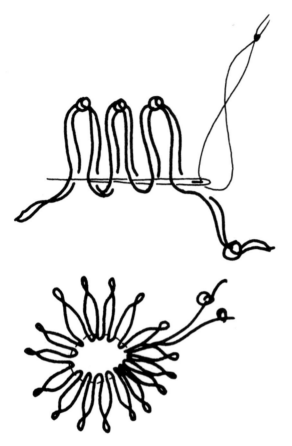

correct thread and attaching it to the entredeaux. Pin the gathered lace to the entredeaux first to adjust the gathers. Keep the corners of the lace ruffle quite full. Next, stitch the lace to the entredeaux. This can be done in two ways: (1) Place entredeaux on top of the gathered lace, topsides together. Line up the edges and proceed as if attaching the entredeaux to rolled and whipped edges; or (3) Place gathered lace next to the entredeaux, topsides up, and zigzag stitch as you did in "Attaching Entredeaux to Lace Insertion."

Thread ⅛" (3.2mm) double-faced satin ribbon through each of the four sides. Leave 3" (7.6cm) tails at each end. Tie overhand knots at the ends. Stitch the tails in place by hand to keep the ribbon in place.

Make rosettes for each corner (Fig. 8.12): First tie an overhand knot every 2½" (6.4cm) along a length of ribbon until you have 16 knots. Leave long ends. Use a double-threaded needle. Make loops on the needle by arranging the ribbon with knots at the top (Fig. 8.12). Sew back through all of the loops again. Pull up and attach the rosettes to the corners of the handkerchief. Tie knots at the ends of the ribbons.

Fig. 8.12 To make a rosette, tie overhand knots in the ribbon every 2½" (6.4cm). Fold the ribbon into loops with knots at the tops. Sew through each loop, then pull into a rosette.

Lesson 24. Seaming with feed dogs up and lowered

Using the felling foot

Why is this foot so infrequently used? After all, it sews seams that are used for strength and decoration, and that look good on both sides.

My reason is that I cannot use the dual feed with the felling foot, and with many fabrics, I like the results better if the seam is stitched with the ordinary foot #0 and the dual feed enployed.

But to truly know your Pfaff, you should know when to use the felling foot — or feet, in Pfaff's case. There are two widths of felling feet. The narrower, (4.5mm seam) is for shirt-weight material. If you want a wider seam for denim weights, then buy the wider felling foot for a 6.5mm seam.

To use the narrow felling foot, pin two pieces of fabric wrong sides together and stitch on the seam line. If you have a ⅝" (15.9mm) seam allowance, you will have to trim off the surplus fabric. This can be done before stitching, in which case the underneath fabric will project ⅛" (3.2mm) beyond the top piece (Fig. 8.13A). Stitch the first pass.

Iron the seam. Open up the fabric. Put it into the felling foot, folding the raw edge under the scroll. Pull gently away from the seam on both sides as you guide the seam through the presser foot for the second time. The second line of stitching finishes the raw edge and the seam so it will lie flat (Fig. 8.13C).

For a wider seam, let the bottom layer of fabric project ¼" (6.4mm) beyond the top piece.

If you use the ordinary presser foot #0 with the dual feed, I find it simpler to place wrong sides together, stitch with a ⅝" (15.9mm) seam allowance, and then trim. Press the seam allowance to the left. Trim away the underneath seam allowance, fold under the raw edge and press again.

If you are going around a curve, clip the upper seam allowance almost to the fold line. Stitch edge, using the dual feed, and it will turn under beautifully. For extra strength, use Program 04.

Sewing a lapped seam

Using the following method, the lapped seam looks a great deal like the flat felled seam, until you look at the wrong side of the fabric.

Program: 01
Stitch length: 2.5
Needle position: ϵ 2 and ϵ 6

Needle: #90 jeans needle
Feed dogs: up
Presser foot: blind hem #3
Dual feed: engaged
Tension: *top*, normal; *bobbin*, normal
Thread: polyester sewing thread
Fabric: denim or duck

Sew a ⅝" (15.9mm) seam, with right sides of fabric together; press the seam allowance to the left (Fig. 8.14A, B).

With fabric right side up, using the blind hem foot #3, move the red guide to the right as far as it will go. Place the red guide in the ditch or seam line, needle position to near left, at ϵ 2 position. Stitch.

For the second run, place the guide on the first stitched line, needle in ϵ 6 position, and sew a second line of stitches (Fig. 8.14C).

Of course, you can stitch lapped seams with just the ordinary sewing foot #0. It's possible to use the edge of this foot as a measure. Or, mark the stitching lines with water-erasable marker.

Seaming with a rolled hem foot

A neat seam for lightweight fabrics is one stitched with the rolled hem foot #7, and I've always referred to it as a mock French seam.

Place your fabrics right sides together, with the underneath fabric extending ⅛" (3.2mm); pin (Fig. 8.15A). Place it under the rolled hem foot and take a stitch in the bottom layer only. Pull out about 3" (7.6cm) of thread. Hold the needle and bobbin threads and use them to pull the fabric into the scroll of the hemmer. Stitch, rolling bottom layer over the top layer (Fig. 8.15B).

Another way of starting this seam would be to use the method discussed in Lesson 27, Chapter 9. Everyone has a personal preference, and sometimes one way will work when the other one doesn't.

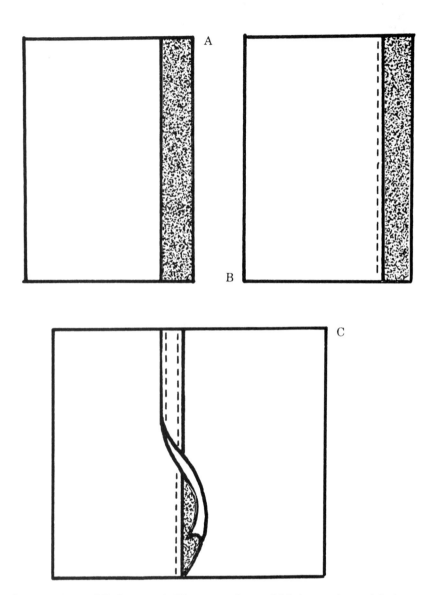

Fig. 8.13 Constructing a felled seam. A. Place two pieces of fabric together, with the underneath fabric extending beyond the top. B. Stitch the first pass with underneath fabric projecting. C. Open the fabric for the second pass, permitting foot to roll under raw edge.

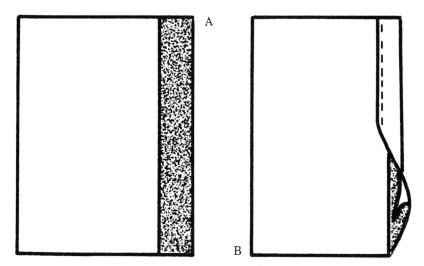

Fig. 8.14 Sewing a lapped seam. A. Seam two fabrics together. Fold the seam allowance to one side.
B. Stitch down the allowance from the right side.

Stitching over thread on knits

No more stretched-out seams on knits and jerseys when you use this method.

Program: 25 or 26
Stitch width: as programmed
Stitch length: as programmed
Needle: #80/12
Feed dogs: up
Presser foot: fancy stitch foot #1
Dual feed: engaged
Tension: *top,* normal; *bobbin,* normal
Thread: polyester sewing

Take a few stitches of the program and stop. Pull out enough needle thread to equal the length of the seam, holding it to the front. This is a double thread, so allow one thread to ride in the right groove under the foot and the other in the left groove. Lower the foot.

Lower the needle in the fabric and take a few more stitches. Now gently pull the

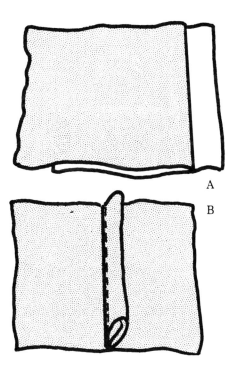

Fig. 8.15 Seaming with rolled hem foot #7. A. Underneath fabric extends ⅛" (3.2mm). B. Bottom fabric rolls over top edge.

127

threads as you stitch, to keep the fabric in shape.

Imitating hand-piecing on quilts

Here is a seam shown to me by a quilter. After stitching two quilt pieces together, run a narrow zigzag, Program 10, width 1.5, length 2.0, over this line of straight stitches (Fig. 8.16). When the seam is pressed open, it gives the impression of perfect hand piecing. Why not skip the first step of straight stitching? Because the two passes will make the quilt seams sturdier, and the line of straight stitching is an excellent guideline for the zigzagging.

Joining veiling with a scallop stitch

What kind of a seam can be used on veiling? In Lesson 17, a straight seam is stitched on Alençon lace, using a close zigzag stitch. A more decorative seam is stitched with the built-in scallop stitch,

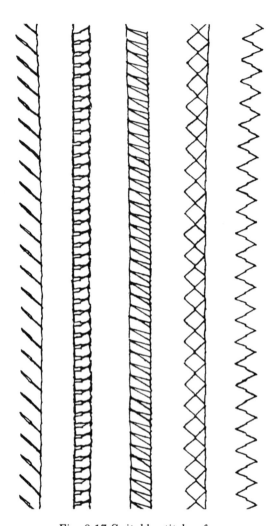

Fig. 8.17 Suitable stitches for topstitching sweatshirt seams.

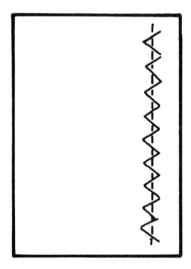

Fig. 8.16 To create the look of hand piecing, zigzag over a seam of straight stitches. Then press the seam open.

#61. Overlap the edges, stitch, then cut back excess material on each side to the scallop.

Using built-in stitches

Don't overlook the built-in stitches on your machine, particularly Programs 20 through 24.They can be sewn from the top of the fabric, using the ordinary sewing foot #0, with the dual feed for topstitching seams in sweatshirts (Fig. 8.17). If the stitches seem distorted due to fabric peculiarities, you can use the balance key. Using a sample of the same fabrics, use the keys (+ and −) to find the correct setting for a perfect decorative stitch.

Program 28 is still my favorite for inside seams on many knit fabrics. Programs 23, 25, 26 and 28 can all be used with the knit foot for neat seams which will look like they have been sewn on a serger. Trim away the surplus seam allowance if your pattern calls for ⅝″ (15.9mm) and stitch off the edge. Or you can stitch the seam first and then remove the extra fabric.

Built-in stitches can be sewn between two pieces of fabric to create an open, interesting seam. Program 12 is one that works beautifully, as do the herring bone #27 and feather stitch #29 (Fig. 8.18). The feather stitch is one of my favorites. I use it on quilt tops to stitch the layers together.

Try using Program 12 to join Ultrasuede scraps, similar to the method used for joining lace. Using the ordinary presser foot with the dual feed is important when working with Ultrasuede or leathers. You might try cutting the Ultrasuede scraps into squares or rectangles, and stitch the scraps together. Sew the horizontal seams first, then go back and sew the vertical seams. When the stitching is complete, place the pattern for whatever you are going to make over the Ultrasuede and cut off fabric projecting beyond the edges. After that, you can finish your project according to the directions.

27   29

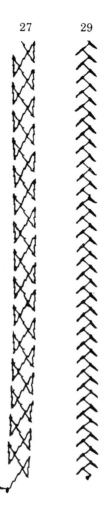

Fig. 8.18 Decorate and stitch a seam with either the herringbone or feather stitch.

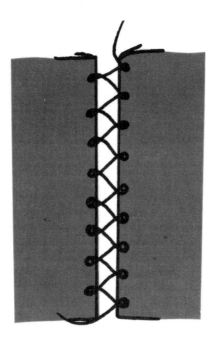

Fig. 8.19 Stitching a decorative seam using free machining.

Creating seams with feed dogs lowered

If you use a similar seam with fabric instead of Ultrasuede, fold under seam allowances at least ⅝" (15.9mm) and press. Move the two pieces of fabric about ⅛" (3.2mm) apart, topsides down. If the fabric is washable, you may want to slip water-soluble stabilizer under it and baste the fabric ⅛" apart. Use thick cord or pearl cotton in the bobbin. Lower the feed dogs and use the darning foot. Sew freely from one side of the fabric to the other, making loops as you enter and leave it (Fig. 8.19). When you finish, turn it over and stitch down along the folds again. Then cut back underneath to the stitching.

These techniques only scratch the surface of interesting seams for your fabric. The nice part about your Pfaff Creative is that, if you can think of a seam you would like to incorporate into your machine, all you need to do is draw it on your charting paper, write down the coordinates, and enter them. In the meantime, however there is no lack of beautiful and practical work you can do.

CHAPTER **9**

Adding Hems and Edges

I remember when "good clothes" didn't mean "clean jeans." There were puffed sleeves, sweetheart necklines — always braided, piped, or embroidered in some way. We wanted to dress like movie stars. Dresses were molded to them and then decorated creatively. Designers always took many long-cuts.

The more you know about your machine, the more inventive you can become: no more boring clothes! You may not think you'll ever use all the decorative hems and edgings in this chapter, but make samples for your notebook anyway. You may be surprised.

With the range of fabrics and styles now available, and the variety of effects we want to achieve, choosing the appropriate hem or edge is not always easy. Before sewing a hem or decorative edge on anything,

ask yourself these questions: What type of fabric? What type of garment? Who is the garment for? Will it be worn forever? How decorative is it to be?

I have my favorite ways to hem and finish edges. I've also learned hems and edges I will never do again. What makes the difference? Appearance, of course, and ease of stitching. I think I have tried every imaginable variation, and those that follow are the ones I prefer because they are useful and good-looking.

Stitch samples of each and put the results in your notebook for reference. Include your own favorites as well. Write the machine settings on each one, along with comments such as what fabrics work well, where you would use them, whether they were long-cuts with happy endings or more trouble than they were worth.

Lesson 25. Turning hems once

I used to cringe at the thought of hems turned only once — all those raw edges! But I have changed my way of thinking.

Using double needles on knits

My favorite hem for T-shirts and other casual knits is turned once and stitched in place with a double needle. The two stitching lines share one bobbin thread, giving the stitches the stretch they need, and encasing the raw edge.

Program: 00
Stitch length: 2.0
Needle: double, at least 2mm
Twin needle key: engaged
Tension: *top*, normal; *bobbin*, normal
Fabric: knit
Presser foot: ordinary sewing foot #0; fancy
    stitch foot #1 or 5-groove cording foot
Dual feed: engaged
Thread: polyester
Accessories: cording blade (optional)
Stabilizer: tear-away (optional)

It is simple to fold up the hem and sew with a double needle from the topside of the fabric.

When finished, trim the fabric back to the stitching underneath.

For a decorative corded hem, treat your double needle stitching as a corded tuck. Do not use the stabilizer, and put the cording foot on the machine without the dual feed. If you like, you can run a cord through the hole in the needleplate, but I prefer to use the cording blade so the fabric stays stretchy. Stitch three rows, using the groove in the foot as a spacing guide.

Program 13, with the width set at 3.5 and the stitch length set at 1.5 to 2.0, can be used for variation. Another gorgeous stitch when used as a double needle hem is Program 19; or, for dainty scallops, use Program 38 (Fig. 9.1).

Always be sure to have the twin needle key engaged when you use the double needle. You can use needles with up to 2mm spacing without concern.

Hemming with a double needle on sheers

Use a double needle for sheer fabrics, too. When a narrow hem would be neither suitable nor attractive, fold up a 4″

(10.2cm) hem on lightweight fabrics and sew across. Lightweight garments hang better with the weight of a deep hem and it's also more attractive when the hem of the underskirt isn't visible underneath.

Of course you can add more rows of stitching, evenly spaced from the first. Cut back to the top of the stitching.

Hemming with built-in stitches on front

The next hem for delicate fabrics is much the same, but uses a single needle and the built-in scallop stitch.

Program: 60 or 61
Stitch width: 3.0 to 6.0
Stitch length: 0.35
Pattern length: varies
Needle position: center
Presser foot: fancy stitch foot #2
Stabilizer: adding machine tape

To hem heavy, canvas-type fabrics, you can use Program 04 or 05, or if you prefer a zigzag stitch, use Program 15. Practice on a piece of the same fabric you will use for the finished article. Set up the machine for a triple zigzag or straight stitch.

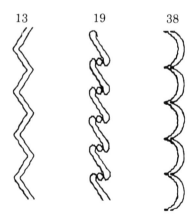

13   19   38

Fig. 9.1 Double needle program stitches used for decorative hems.

Program: 04, 05 or 15
Stitch width: varies
Stitch length: varies
Needle: #110 jeans
Presser foot: ordinary sewing foot #0
Dual feed: engaged

This is an extremely strong stitch. Use it for anything from deck furniture canvas to jeans.

Refer back to the stitch samples you did in Chapter 2. You may prefer other decorative built-in stitches to those mentioned here. Experiment with different fabrics and built-in stitches, keeping all your samples in your notebook.

Quilting a hem

Another single-fold hem can be done on heavy materials such as wool or velveteen. Use the ordinary sewing foot #0 with dual feed engaged. Allow about 8″ (20.3cm) for the hem of the skirt. Put light batting, such as flannel sheeting, inside and pin in place. Sew four or five rows of straight stitches, one line at a time, to quilt the hem (Fig. 9.2). Space the lines of stitching as you wish. Try quilting a long Christmas skirt or an evening skirt using metallic thread.

Or turn the skirt inside out and put pearl cotton on the bobbin to contrast with the skirt. The topside will be against the

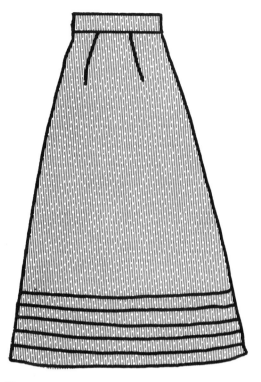

Fig. 9.2 Use light flannel between hem and skirt, then quilt the hem with lines of straight stitching.

bed of the machine. Stitch rows, then cut back to the last line of stitching. This can be done around sleeve bands or down jacket facings as well.

Lesson 26. Blind hemming

I remember when most of the hems I put in garments were blind hems worked by hand. Times have changed, but that doesn't mean I've given up blind hems. The only difference is that I do them more quickly now — by machine.

To begin the hem, decide first if you can live with a raw edge. If you can, then leave it as it is, but if you hate that unfinished edge, then attach a lace edging over it or use Program 18 instead of 17. You can also prefinish the edge with a decorative or utility stitch of your choice.

Turn up the hem 1½″ to 2″ (3.8cm to 5.1cm) and pin about every 4″ (10cm) around it, about an inch from the top. Because of the dual feed, the fabric will not slip or shift, but if you don't trust yourself, then try Tami Durand's method. Baste the hem by machine, using Program 00 with a stitch length of 6.0, ¼" from the edge of the turned-up hem (Fig. 9.3A). Fold back and proceed as you do with the pinned hem (Fig. 9.3B). When finished, pull out the basting. (If you use water-soluble basting thread, you can simply dampen the hem and it will disappear.)

Set your machine up.

Program: 17
Stitch width: 4.5
Stitch length: 2.5
Feed dogs: up
Presser foot: blindstitch #3
Dual feed: engaged
Tension: *top,* loosened; *bobbin,* normal
Thread: sewing
Accessories: dressmakers' pins

Fold the garment back on itself, leaving ¼" (6.4mm) of hem allowance at the edge to stitch on (Fig. 9.4A). Put the fold of the fabric against the left side of the red guide of the blind stitch foot. The first stitch of Program 17 is the stitch to the left, so you can easily move the red guide into position in order to catch only a thread or two of the fold. The straight stitch will be completely on the hem allowance. Check the settings on scrap fabric first to determine if the stitch width and length are correct for your fabric. Thick fabrics will require different settings than lightweight fabrics. Then, when you are ready to hem your garment, press the pattern start key to move the needle into first position.

I made a fine batiste bishop dress with yards of blind hemming, but the stitching pulled too tightly. Despite the fine thread, loosened tension, and a #60 needle, I didn't like the looks of it. The answer? I sewed from off the fabric. I folded the fabric back so the fold met the edge exactly. Then I stitched outside the fabric and the

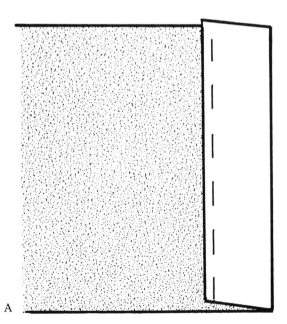
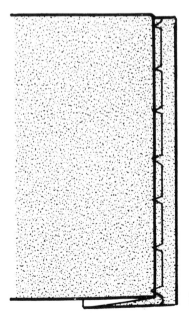

Fig. 9.3 Blind hemming. A. Hem turned up and basted. B. Final blind stitching.

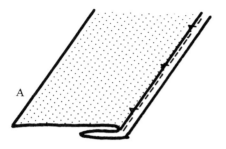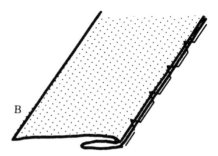

*Fig. 9.4 Blind hemming. A. Fold over the hem, then fold the skirt back, letting ⅛"
(3.2mm) show beyond the edge; stitch on the edge of the fabric. B. Or fold the garment
back even with the edge, and stitch off the fabric, the left swing stitching the fold.*

left bite held it together with no pulling (Fig. 9.4B). I've tried it on several heavier weights of fabric as well, and it works beautifully.

Still hesitant about stitching in space? Then place water-soluble stabilizer under your stitching.

One other tip: if you disengage the dual feed when going around the bias portion of an A-line skirt, the extra fabric on the hem allowance will ease in beautifully. Be sure to re-engage the dual feed when stitching the portion of the hem which is on the straight grain of the fabric.

Lesson 27. Sewing narrow hems

Probably the most unused accessories are the rolled hem feet. I think I know why: few stitchers ever take time to practice with them. They're great time savers, but I had to learn to use them, too. Now after yards of hem samples, I can't do without them.

Set up your machine, read the directions, and reread as you work. Before you begin to hem a garment with your rolled hemmer, cut back the seam allowances that have to be sewn over. Then learn to start the fabric. I hated starting a hem because of those first problem inches until I tried Gail Brown's method, which follows.

Straight stitching

The rolled hem foot #7, which you will find in your accessory box, is easy to use when learning because it is narrow enough

so the fabric does not have to be absolutely on grain. Also needed are lightweight cotton to hem and a 3" (7.6cm) square of tear-away stabilizer.

Overlap the piece of tear-away stabilizer with the fabric about ¼" (6.3mm) and sew them together. Start rolling the stabilizer into the scroll of the hemming foot. By the time the fabric is introduced into the hemmer, the hem is being sewn down starting on the first thread of the fabric.

Guide the fabric by holding it taut and lifting it slightly as it rolls through the foot. The edge of the fabric must be vertical. As long as you pay attention, guiding and holding the fabric correctly, the machine does the rest.

The 4mm rolled hem foot, which is an extra accessory, will not only make a wider rolled hem on light fabrics, but is also ideal for a narrow hem on heavy fabrics where you normally might not be able to do it neatly.

As I mentioned in Chapter 1, the back of the foot is cut out to accommodate the dual-feed mechanism. Recently, I had to shorten a full skirt made of heavy taffeta, and this helpful attachment did it quickly and easily. Many rolled hems develop a "bias twist" on the curves, but this foot eliminates the problem.

Sewing on lace

This method is simple and it does save time.

Program: 16
Stitch width: 4.0
Stitch length: 3.0
Presser foot: appliqué, or fancy stitch foot #2
Tension: *top,* −3+; *bobbin,* normal
Dual feed: disengaged
Fabric: lightweight cotton, lace edging
Thread: fine sewing thread to match

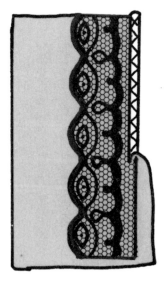

Fig. 9.5 Lace is attached with a finished edge in one step.

Place the lace on top of the fabric, topsides together, the edge of the lace ⅛" (6.3mm) from the edge of the fabric.

The fabric is usually placed to the right of the middle of the presser foot but practice first with the presser foot you choose. As you sew, it will roll and be whipped over the heading of the lace (Fig. 9.5).

I am particularly indebted to Theta Happ of Oklahoma City for telling me about the appliqué foot for this purpose.

See other methods of sewing lace to fabric in Lesson 25, "French handsewing."

Attaching scalloped lace

Apply scalloped lace to fabric, topsides up, by overlapping it to make a hem (Fig. 9.6). Let the fabric extend well past the curve on top of the lace. Baste lace to fabric. Zigzag along the edge, following the scallop. Cut back the fabric underneath to the stitching line.

Stitching shell edging

This is a good hem and edging for lingerie (Fig. 9.7). Or use it to decorate ribbon and tucks.

Set up your machine:

Program: 17
Stitch width: 6.0
Stitch length: 1.5
Pattern mirror key: engaged
Feed dogs: up
Presser foot: fancy stitch foot #2
Dual feed: disengaged

If you are going to cross a seam when hemming, then cut back the seam allowances that will be sewn over.

Fold the fabric under ½" (12.7mm) and place the folded edge to the right. Stitch, letting the right swing of the needle sew over the edge, creating the shell pattern. At the end, cut back to the stitching underneath.

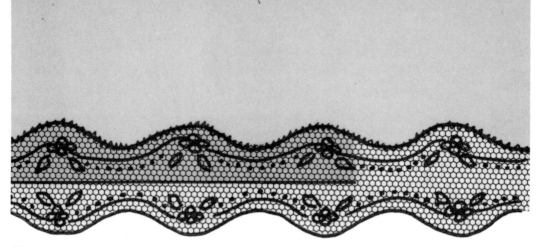

Fig. 9.6 Attach scalloped lace to fabric by overlapping it, zigzagging along the scalloped edge, then cutting the fabric back to the stitching line.

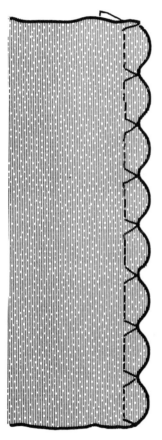

Fig. 9.7 A shell edge on tricot, stitched with the blind-hem stitch.

Roll and shell hemming

The rolled hem foot #7 not only makes a narrow, straight-stitch hem, but it also rolls and shells as shown in Fig. 9.8, if the machine is set on zigzag. Usually it's the finish of choice when hemming tricot, as it decorates and hems in one operation. It's impossible to turn square corners on these hems, so round off any corners before you begin to stitch. Because tricot rolls to one side, hem with the right side up. If you will stitch over a seam while hemming, first cut back the seam allowances you'll cross so the fabric will feed in without a problem. As the fabric is rolled into the foot, it will curl and be sewn into a narrow, puffy roll.

Stitch width: 4.0
Stitch length: 2.5
Feed dogs: up
Presser foot: rolled hem foot #7
Dual feed: disengaged

It's important to keep the fabric straight ahead of the presser foot and raise it a bit to keep it feeding easily. The needle goes into the fabric at the left, then off the edge of the fabric at the right.

137

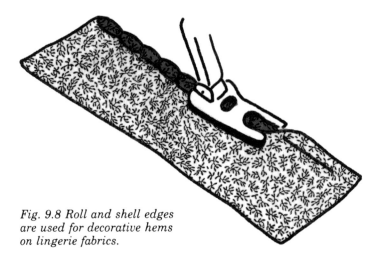

Fig. 9.8 Roll and shell edges are used for decorative hems on lingerie fabrics.

Lesson 28. Using bias tape

I must admit, I equate bias tape with the edges of Grandma's apron, but now that I can apply it so easily, I'm finding new ways to use it. I especially like it for toddlers' sunsuits and dresses.

This is the only method I use; what I like best about it is that the tape is sewn on almost invisibly. You don't need the bias binder accessory.

Program: 00
Stitch length: 2.5
Feed dogs: up
Presser foot: ordinary sewing foot #0 or blind stitch foot #3
Dual feed: engaged
Needle: #80/12
Thread: monofilament
Fabric: lightweight cotton, double-fold bias tape
Accessories: glue stick, pins

Look at the bias tape: One side is wider than the other. The wide side will be on the back of your work. Open the bias tape and place the narrow side on top, the cut edge of the tape along the cut edge of the fabric. If there is a ⅝″ (15.9mm) seam, cut it back to fit the width of the bias. Pin in place.

Depending upon the foot you use, either use the center slot of foot #0, or the red guide of the blind stitch foot as a guide, riding on the crease to ensure a perfect stitch-in-the-ditch. Stitch along the crease. Be sure to use the dual feed.

Fold the tape over the edge. I sometimes dab the underside with glue stick between tape and fabric. Pin if you wish, or baste by hand.

Press the bias and check that the underside of the bias extends slightly beyond the seam line on the topside.

From the topside, stitch in the ditch of the seam. Again, adjust the foot to enable you to sew exactly in the ditch. The stitching catches the edge of the bias underneath. I'm sure by this time you realize what a useful accessory the blind stitch foot can be, especially with the dual feed to eliminate all the feeding problems.

Lesson 29. Zigzagging a narrow edge

This is only one of several methods to produce a strong, finished hem or edge of tiny, tight zigzag stitches. Use it to finish ruffles, napkins and scarves.

Program: 10
Stitch width: 1.5
Stitch length: 0.5
Presser foot: fancy stitch foot #2
Dual feed: disengaged

Fold the fabric under about ½" (12.7mm) and guide the fold of the fabric exactly in the middle of the fancy stitch foot #2.

Stitch on the fabric with the left swing of the needle, the right swing stitching just off the right side of it (Fig. 9.9). After stitching is completed, cut the fabric back to the stitched edge, as partially done below.

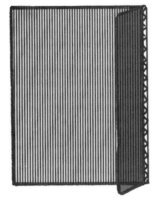
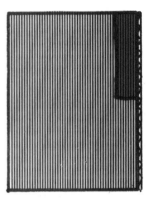

Fig. 9.9 From the top of the fabric, sew a narrow, close zigzag down the folded edge (left). Cut back the fabric underneath to the stitching line.

Lesson 30. Covering wire for shaped edges

In a bridal shop I saw yard goods that included nylon filament at the edges of chiffon and organdy ruffles. It was an attractive finish for the ruffles that can be applied to skirt and sleeve hems or across the drop-shoulders of wedding gowns and formal wear.

A case displayed dozens of headpieces using the same nylon filament to keep bows perky and ribbons from wilting. You are invited to create your own, combining filament and sheer fabrics, beads and silk flowers.

I could also see many Halloween costume possibilities here. Use the filament at the bottom edge of a long, filmy skirt or, if you want to make an angel costume, use heavy gauge filament for floppy wings.

Nylon filament is available by the yard at stores that sell bridal lace and fabrics. But I found that it is much easier to buy 25-pound-test fishing line in a sporting goods store. Cheaper, too. I've used both and I don't think there's a difference. There are different weights to fishing lines, which means they come in different thicknesses.

For super-thick costume fabric, you can use weed-trimmer line. It comes in a 50-foot length and the diameter to use is .05mm. Use a double-grooved foot such as fancy stitch foot #1. Use the same method to apply any of the nylon filament mentioned.

Program: 10, 11 or 16
Stitch width: 4.0
Stitch length: 1.0
Presser foot: fancy stitch foot #1
Dual feed: engaged

I've used appliqué and cording feet also. The settings will be different, so experiment with different stitch widths.

I placed the filament about ¼" (6.3mm) from the edge of the fabric (the needle should stitch off the edge of the material on the right swing). As you sew, the edge of the fabric will roll over and enclose the line (Fig. 9.10).

Milliner's wire or florist's wire is available already covered with thread. Both of these can be stitched into the edge of fabric in the same way as nylon filament. They both come in different gauges. Unlike the nylon edge, the wire can be bent into any shape you might want. Buy milliner's wire at bridal shops and florist's wire at craft shops. Make flower petals and leaves using wire.

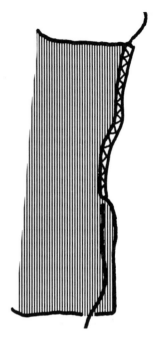

Fig. 9.10 Rolling fabric over nylon filament or wire creates a rigid, finished edge.

Lesson 31. Cording edges

Covering cords

Covered cord produces one of the finest, prettiest edges to use on table linens, on scarves, collars, wherever you want a delicate but very strong edge.

Program: 10
Stitch width: 2.0, then 4.0
Stitch length: 0.5
Presser foot: single cording foot
Dual feed: disengaged
Thread: machine-embroidery or sewing
   thread; #5 pearl cotton

Fold the fabric under about ½" (12.7mm) and press. Thread pearl cotton through the slot in the single cording foot. Place the slot at the edge of the fabric and stitch (Fig. 9.11). Cut back to the stitching underneath when it's completed.

To create a thicker edge, go back over the first line of stitching with the 7-groove cording foot. Place the edge you've completed in the slot to the left and another cord of pearl cotton between the toes of the presser foot to hold it in place. Change to stitch width 4.0.

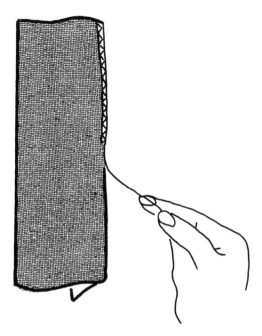

Fig. 9.11 Zigzagging over cord produces a strong corded edge.

If you use this method to finish the edge of a collar, you won't need to turn the collar. Instead, sew with wrong sides of upper and under collar together to eliminate the bulk of a turned-in seam allowance.

To make a delicate edging for a bridal veil, cord the edge.

Program: 10
Stitch width: 2.0
Stitch length: 0.5 to 0.7
Presser foot: single cording foot
Dual feed: disengaged
Thread: fine sewing thread to match veil; #8
    pearl cotton to match veil

Without folding the veiling, place it so the edge extends past the presser foot on the right. Slip #8 pearl cotton in the slot of the cording foot. Sew over the pearl. Cut back to the pearl for a fine finished edge. (Try a corded scallop stitch, too.)

Creating crocheted edges

This decorative edge is used to finish shirt plackets and collars. It's a delicate, lacelike finish that lends itself to feminine clothes and baby items.

Instead of threading pearl cotton or gimp through the presser foot, this time it is threaded up through the needle plate on the bed of the machine.

Program: 61
Stitch width: 4.0 to 6.0
Stitch length: 0.35
Program length: 10 or 12
Presser foot: fancy stitch foot #2
Dual feed: disengaged
Fabric: medium-weight cotton

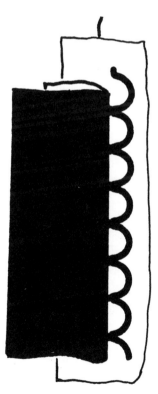

Fig. 9.12 Make a crocheted edge with the built-in scallop stitch.

Fig. 9.13 Memory combination 38, 03, 03
used as a decorative edging.

Thread: color to contrast with fabric; gimp or
#5 pearl cotton the same color as the
thread
Tension: top, −3+; bobbin, normal
Accessories: tear-away stabilizer or colored
paper to match thread

Use the fancy stitch foot #2 and pearl
cotton to do a corded edge using the scallop
stitch. Place stabilizer underneath and far
enough to the right to be under the stitches, as shown in Fig. 9.12. The fabric should
be doubled; the fold is placed to the left,
halfway between the center of the foot and
the line formed by the joining of the clear
plastic insert and the metal portion. Your
first stitch will catch the fabric at the edge.
The scallops will be off the edge onto the
stabilizer (Fig. 9.12). Carefully tear off the
stabilizer when you finish.

Try other decorative stitches at the
edges of fabrics. I like the small, decorative
combination formed by putting Programs
38, 02, 02 in memory and using it on the
edges of tucks, plackets or sleeves and to
decorate collars (9.13). Sew on the finished
or a folded edge of the fabric over water-
soluble stabilizer. When done with regular
sewing thread it is very dainty, or you can
use a heavier thread or cord in the bobbin.

Reshaping knits with elastic

Elastic can be used to keep stretchy
edges in shape, or to reshape them.

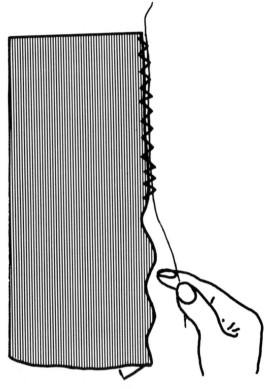

Fig. 9.14 Keep knits from stretching by
stitching in an elastic thread.

Program: 10
Stitch width: 2.0
Stitch length: 2.0
Presser foot: single cording foot

Thread the elastic through the slot in
the single cording foot. Keep the elastic at
the edge of the knit and sew down the fold
(Fig. 9.14).

Lesson 32. Making thread fringe

How many machine owners use a tailor-
tacking foot for tailor tacking? I can't find
one. Most of the time the tailor tacking

foot is used for fringing, fagoting, or for
sewing on buttons.

To make a fringed edge, you will need

two pieces of fabric. Both pieces will be folded under about ⅝″ (15.9mm), but one piece of fabric will be eliminated later.

Loosen the top tension.

Program: 10
Stitch width: 2.0
Stitch length: 0.35
Presser foot: fringe foot
Duel feed: disengaged
Tension: *top*, 0; *bobbin*, normal
Thread: machine-embroidery
Fabric: medium-weight cotton
Stabilizer: tear-away

Don't overlap, but butt the fabric folds next to each other. Hold them together as you sew down between them (Fig. 9.15A). Pull the bobbin thread out, then *very carefully* pull the fabrics apart, but leave them connected by the stitching (Fig. 9.15B). Care can make or break your work as the fringe wants to jump out of the fabric until you accomplish the next step.

Tighten the upper tension to normal setting between 4 and 5 and place a stabilizer under the fabric. You may also want to put a stabilizer on top of the fringe to keep it from catching on the presser foot. On the side that will retain the fringe, stitch a line of decorative stitches along the fold to keep the fringe in place. Carefully pull off the other piece of fabric (Fig. 9.15C, D)

If you look closely at the eyelashes of the denim doll in Fig. 3.17, you will see thread fringe. As you get to know your machine, you'll see more and more ways to use it to make the simplest tasks even simpler.

Another way of making a shorter fringe on the hem is to simply stitch along the hemline using the fringe foot. Draw a line on the hemline with a vanishing marker, open the fabric flat and stitch. Fold the hem allowance back and press.

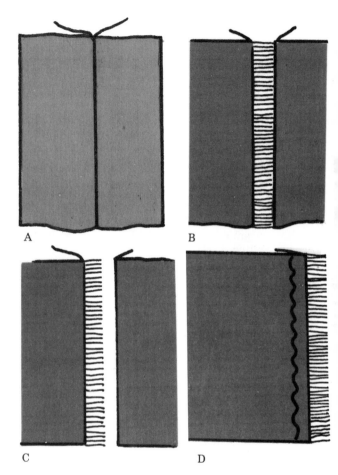

Fig. 9.15 Making thread fringe. A. Butt two pieces of fabric together. Stitch down between folds with zigzag stitches over the tailor-tacking foot. B. Open up the stitching and pull out the bobbin thread. C. Then pull off one side of fabric. D. Use a decorative stitch to sew along the fringed edge.

Remove the fringe foot and replace it with the ordinary foot #0. Engage the dual feed. Stitch close to the edge of the fabric, securing the thread fringes.

143

Lesson 33. Piping edges

Miniature piping is especially pretty and colorful on the edges of children's clothing. Use a #3 or #5 pearl cotton and a piece of bias fabric twice the width of the seam allowance. I may not use bias fabric at all. It seems to make little difference, and though held sacrilegious, you can save fabric by cutting on the straight, so try it for yourself. Or cover the pearl with purchased bias tape. Use either the 7-groove cording foot or the zipper foot #4, and Program 01. The cording feet have grooves in which to fit the covered pearl while stitching it, but the zipper foot will give you the greatest flexibility, as you can adjust the needle position to sew a little nearer to the cord on every pass. Further, with the zipper foot you can use your dual feed, which means you can make cording out of any any fabric without problems.

To cover thick cord for upholstery, use a bulky overlock foot. The wrapped cord fits into the groove of the overlock foot and feeds easily. Use Program 01 and move your needle position to either side of the cord.

Lesson 34. Topstitching

There is nothing richer-looking on a coat or suit than an even line of topstitching.

When you need a narrowly spaced double line, use a double needle with Program 05, which is especially nice on heavy fabrics. For topstitching Ultrasuede, I use a 90/14 stretch needle with two sewing threads and Program 00, eliminating the extra holes that Program 05 puts in the fabric. Buttonhole twist frays easily, and I don't like the way it sits on top of the fabric, so my preference is the double thread. Sew the second line of stitching in the same direction as the first.

When topstitching on lapels, the roll line indicates where the top threads will go to the underside. For this reason, if you use two threads on top, you must use two threads on the bobbin as well. Wind the bobbin with two threads at one time instead of using only one. Then treat the threads as if they were one.

Instead of anchoring threads, leave a long enough thread at the beginning and the end to work in later invisibly by hand.

Do experiment with Program 04, for a slightly different topstitch. With this program, you can use orange thread to stitch denim seams to duplicate the look of commercial topstitching on jeans.

I have also used both the single and double outline stitches on Programs 06 and 07 for very distinctive topstitching.

How can you keep topstitching straight? You have several choices. Use tape along the edge of the fabric and sew next to it. Or, use the blindstitch foot and reposition the red guide as needed.

If using lightweight material, set the machine for 10 − 12 stitches per inch (stitch length 2.5). If using medium-weight fabric, a longer stitch looks better. Stitch samples on scraps of the same material to see what stitch length setting you prefer.

I think there is hope for more decorative dressing. Have you noticed how Joan Crawford's clothes don't look so funny anymore?

CHAPTER **10**

Machine Tricks: Adding Threads to Threads

■ **Lesson 35. Making cord**
■ **Lesson 36. Making tassels**

For nine chapters, we've used fabric and thread for sewing and embroidering. I'll bet you know your sewing machine pretty well by now, but there's more: In this chapter, I'll show you how to make cords using your machine. Some will be used for practical purposes, such as belt loops and hangers for pendants, but we'll make other cords for decoration, bunching them together into tassels.

Lesson 35. Making cord

Twisting monk's cord

Monk's cord is made from several strands of thread or yarn held together and twisted to make a thick cord. The cord may be used in many ways—as a finish around pillows, as a handle for handbags, and as thick fringe in tassels.

On the machine, monk's cord is made using the bobbin winder. If the thread or yarn is small enough to go through the tiny hole on top, you may tie the cord on it. A better way is to tie dental floss—it doesn't slip—around the center of a thick cord, leaving long enough ends to seat the floss into the middle of the bobbin winder. Then you are able to wind monk's cord of any thickness.

If you are working alone, you will also be limited by the length of cord you can use and still reach the machine's foot pedal.

Fortunately for me, the retractable cord reaches halfway across my sewing room. Use a 2 yard (1.7m) length. Fold this in half, knot the two ends together, and slip a piece of dental floss through the end of the loop that is formed. The ends of the dental floss are then put through the center of the bobbin. Of course you can tie the cord onto the dental floss loop and work with one cord, not two. If you do work with one cord, tie a loop at the end of the cord to slip your finger through before you begin to twist the cord.

Next, push the bobbin down into place on the pin (Fig. 10.1). When clicked into place, the bobbin will hold the cord securely. Push the bobbin to the right to activate the winding mechanism and disengage the clutch knob. Put your index finger in the loop of cord at the other end and stretch

145

Fig. 10.1 Make monk's cord by slipping a doubled pearl cotton thread down inside the bobbin and activating the bobbin winder.

the cord to keep tension on it. Press the foot control.

Keep winding the cord until it is so tight the blood supply to your finger is threatened. Work your finger out of the loop and, still holding it tightly, find the middle of the cord with your other hand. Hold onto that spot while you place the loop from your finger over the thread holder pin, if it is close enough. Otherwise, keeping tension on the cord, bring both ends together and very carefully let it twist to make a monk's cord. Work down the twists with both hands to keep the cord smooth. At this point you will see that it is more successful if you work with a partner.

When the cord is twisted as tightly as it will go, take it out of the bobbin and off the thread-holder spool pin. Tie an overhand knot to hold the ends together until you actually use it.

I use this cord to make thick fringe for tassels, sometimes slipping washers, bells,

Fig. 10.2 Machine-made monk's cord is used to make this tassel.

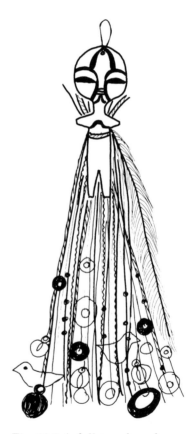

Fig. 10.3 A doll tassel made with monk's cord.

beads or a spacer to the middle of the cord after I have twisted it and before I double it and make the final twists (Figs. 10.2 and 10.3).

These quick cords can be used for belt loops, button loops, ties for clothing. Or twist up a batch to tie small packages.

Stitching belt and button loops

Belt loop cords can be made by pulling out the bobbin and top threads and folding them over to make about eight strands. Use Program 10, stitch width 4.0 and a stitch length of 1.5. You will use your regular presser foot with the dual feed. Hold the threads loosely, front and back at first, then the dual feed and lower feed dogs will pull the threads through as you stitch. You will only have to guide the threads.

Because you can select different stitch lengths, you can get different textural effects with your cord. These tiny cords work well for button loops and belt carriers, but I prefer them for decorative tassels and trims. They are especially attractive made with rayon machine embroidery thread. I clean off my bobbins by making cords when I've been overly enthusiastic about winding them fuller than necessary, and wind these cords on empty thread spools to save for future projects.

Two lengths can be combined and zig-zagged together for heavier cords, or they can be twisted on the bobbin winder for monk's cords.

The cords were used to finish the edge of one of my pendants, and several lengths were knotted together to make the "chain" (see color insert).

You can also zigzag over thicker cords and hold them together. If you add a contrasting thread color, you can make interesting tassels (see the next lesson).

Lesson 36. Making tassels

I'm drawn to tassels. I sketch them when I see them in museums or books, and I have a notebook full of ideas cut from magazines. I've labored over a few myself, using hand embroidery, even tiny macramé knots. Sometimes they look like fetish dolls—another weakness—and so I play them that way.

How can my sewing machine help me make tassels? First of all, I make monk's cord using the bobbin winder. I combine those with other cords, sometimes stringing beads or bells on them (Figs. 10.4 and 10.5).

I can also use a braiding foot or open embroidery foot to make colorful cord. Holding several pearl cotton cords together, I place them in the groove on the bottom of the presser foot and zigzag stitch over the pearl with a contrasting color. I choose a stitch width 4 to enclose the cords, and a stitch length 1 to let some of the cord show through.

Project
Tassel Collar

Several ways to make tassels by machine involve using water-soluble stabilizer. The first method is for a collar of stitched cords to wrap around the main tassel cords.

Program: 10
Stitch width: 4.0
Stitch length: 0.5
Needle: #80/12

cotton to match cord; many yards of string, thread or yarn for main part of tassel (the more yarn used, the plumper and more attractive the tassel), cut into 16″ (40.6cm) lengths

Thread: rayon embroidery to match rayon cord

Accessories: water-soluble stabilizer

Fig. 10.4 Monk's cord is used for the tassels at left *and* center. *A collar, stitched by machine, was used for the one at* right.

Presser foot: fancy stitch #2
Dual feed: disengaged
Feed dogs: up
Tension: top, normal; bobbin, normal
Cord: 16 yards (14.5m) rayon cord (available at fabric shops) for the collar; #5 pearl

Fig. 10.5 More tassels stitched by machine.

First fold the 16″ (40.6cm) lengths of yarn in half to find their centers. Use one yarn piece to tie the lengths together there. Knot tightly. Then tie an overhand knot with the ends of that cord to make a hanger for the tassel.

Cut six dozen 8″ (20.3cm) lengths of purchased rayon cord. Place a piece of water-soluble stabilizer on the bed of the machine and lay these cords next to each other across the stabilizer (in horizontal rows as you are looking at them). Starting ½″ (12.7mm) in from the right side, place a strand of #5 pearl cotton perpendicular to and crossing all the cords (Fig. 10.6). Satin stitch over the pearl cotton and the rayon cords. Sew down several more rows of pearl, lining up each pearl cord next to the one stitched before it. When completed, cut off the ½″ (12.7mm) rayon threads protruding from the top of the collar. Zigzag

over the edge, which will give the top a smooth finish.

Wrap the collar, inside-out, 1½″ (3.8cm) down from the fold of the tassel cords. Pin the collar tightly around the cords. Remove it from the tassel and machine stitch the ends of the collar together. Cut back to the stitching line and zigzag over the edge. Turn right side out, then pull the yarn tassel cords from the bottom through the collar to complete it. The collar should fit snugly.

You could embroider the same basic collar in an almost endless variety of ways for your tassel collection.

Project Covered Wire Tassel

Cover 18″ (45.7cm) of milliner's wire with stitches for the next tassel (Fig. 10.7).

Program: 10
Stitch width: 4.0
Stitch length: 0.5
Needle: #80/12
Feed dogs: up
Presser foot: fancy stitch #2 or appliqué
Tension: *top*, normal; *bobbin*, normal
Thread: rayon embroidery
Accessories: tweezers
Stabilizer: water-soluble (optional), cut into long strips 1″ (2.5cm) wide

Set up your machine and place water-soluble stabilizer under the wire if you wish. Sew over the wire. If the wire doesn't feed well, then use a longer length stitch and go over it twice. The milliner's wire is covered with thread and this keeps the rayon stitches from slipping.

Make 45 thick cords for the tassel by zigzagging over two 12″ (30.5cm) strands of #5 pearl cotton for each one. *Hint:* Stitch

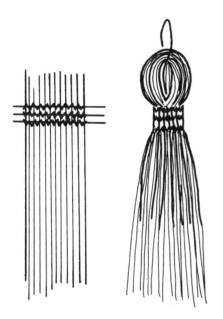

Fig. 10.6 Make a collar for the tassel by placing cords next to each other, then zigzagging over cords laid at right angles across them.

149

Fig. 10.7 Cover milliner's wire with stitches and twist the wire around cords to make a tassel.

ing linen, jute and monk's cords (see Fig. 10.3) all tied to a small African doll. I placed the bundle of cords on the bed of the machine, letting it extend 1″ (2.5cm) to the right of the presser foot and flattening it with my fingers to allow me to stitch over the cords. The machine was set up for free-

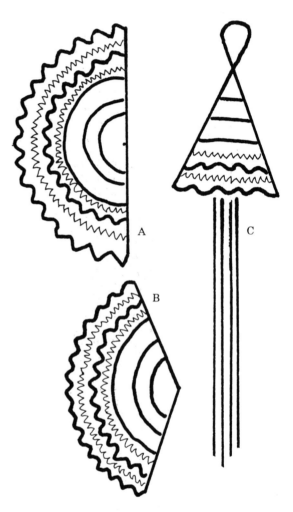

two 15-yard-long (14m-long) cords together and cut them into 12″ (30.5cm) pieces.

To use the wire for the tassel, first fold the 12″ (30.5cm) long cords in half. Slip an end of the wire through the fold, extending it past the cord 2″ (5.1cm). Bend the wire back 1″ (2.5cm) at the end and twist it around itself to make a loop for hanging (the loop will enclose the cords).

With the other end of the wire, wrap the tassel around and around till you reach halfway down the length of it. Hold the end of the wire with the tweezers. Wrap it around the point of the tweezers to make a decorative coil at the end (Fig. 10.7).

Project
Doll Tassel

The fertility doll tassel is a combination of several dozen 10″ (25.4cm) cords, includ-

Fig. 10.8 Making a machined tassel. A. Embroider a half-circle of felt. B. Cut a wedge from it, and sew up the sides to form a cone. C. The cone becomes the top of the tassel.

machining, with feed dogs lowered and a darning foot in place. Using the widest zig-zag, I stitched forward and back across the cords. When I finished, I spread glue from a glue stick across the stitching on one side of the bundle and placed this at the back of the doll, wrapping and tying it in place with a linen cord.

To decorate the tassel, I slipped a long feather under the linen wrapping cord, and strung some of the tassel cords with beads, brass bells and metal washers. Overhand knots held the objects in place at different heights on the cords. There's a hole in the top of the doll, so I added a loop of cord there to hang the tassel.

Project
Making
Two Tassel Tops
by Machine

For the following tassels shown in Fig. 10.8C and 10.9, the tops are made on the sewing machine. Put a 7″ (17.8cm) square of felt in a 5″ (12.7cm) spring hoop. Draw half a circle and embroider this using decorative, built-in machine stitches. Take it out of the hoop and cut out the half-circle (Fig. 10.8A). Cut out a wedge from the side of the half-circle (Fig. 10.8B). Fold the larger piece in half, topsides together. Straight stitch the cut edges. Turn to the right side.

Cut six tassel cords, each 18″ (45.7cm) in length, from rayon cord or machine-made monk's cord. Find the center and tie them together at the middle with a cord 8″ (20.3cm) long. Thread that cord through a large-eyed needle and push it up from inside through the top of the cone. Tie a knot at the end and hang the tassel.

The second tassel is also made of felt, with a machine-stitched top (Fig. 10.9).

Fig. 10.9 A tassel made of satin stitches on felt.

Program: 10
Stitch width: 6.0
Stitch length: varies
Needle: #90
Feed dogs: up
Presser foot: cording feet or fancy stitch foot #2
Tension: *top*, loosened; *bobbin*, normal

Fabric suggestion: 9″ (22.9cm) square of felt (tassel top will be completely covered with stitches)

Thread: rayon machine embroidery—I chose red, yellow and blue; #8 red pearl cotton; #5 blue pearl cotton (optional)

Accessories: 7″ (17.8cm) spring hoop, small bells, glue stick, fine-point marker

Stabilizer: tear-away

The finished size of the tassel top is 2″ × 2″ (5.1cm × 5.1cm). I worked with a 9″ (22.9cm) piece of felt so it would fit in the 7″ (17.8cm) spring hoop. This allows enough room for the presser foot without hitting the edge of the hoop, as you will stitch both sides of the tassel top—2″ × 4″ (5.1cm × 10.2cm) area—at once.

Trace the pattern from Fig. 10.9. Cut around the tracing and lay this on the felt. Draw around the pattern with a marker (it won't show when tassel is completed).

Begin by carefully stretching the felt in the hoop. Use the fancy stitch foot #2 for this top or use corded (#5 pearl cotton) satin stitches with a cording foot. Starting on the right side, place one line of close, smooth satin stitches. Add another row next to the first, and continue, changing colors as you wish. Now sew between the satin stitches, using a contrasting color and Program 04.

Cut out the stitched design; then cut it in half. Place wrong sides together.

Cut about five dozen lengths of pearl cotton, each 12″ (30.5cm) long. Fold them in half. Place the folds inside the felt pieces along the straight edge. Pin the felt together or use a dot of glue stick to hold everything in place as you stitch. Zigzag across the straight edge of the felt to keep the pearl cotton in place. Zigzag around the curve as well. Then go back with a satin stitch and stitch around it again with stitch width at the widest, stitch length 1/2. Add bells to each side and a hanger at the top. Clay or metal found objects also work well as ornaments.

I agree, making tassels is a nutty thing to do (but it's fun). Use them to decorate your tote bag, for key chains, zipper pulls, decorations on clothing, curtain tiebacks. I confess that I hang them all over my sewing room.

CHAPTER **11**

Decorative Stitches

by AUDREY GRIESE

- **Lesson 37. Using Existing Stitches**
- **Lesson 38. Using M Memories**
- **Lesson 39. Stitching Cross-Stitch, Blackwork, and Personally Designed Stitches**

Your Pfaff Creative 1471 has many stitch programs, with the potential for adding as many more as you can dream up. These created stitches can be permanently retained in the machine memory, if you will use them again and again, or file away the programming sheets for future use. In this chapter, I am going to fit in as many suggestions as space will permit in an effort to get your creative juices flowing, so that you, too, will *Know Your Pfaff.* I will be giving you ideas for using the machine's automatic stitches, as well as pointers for combining stitches in your M memories to create even more stitch programs. You will also be using your P memories to add new stitches of your own design.

I am sure that your original notebook is full to overflowing by this time; if you haven't already started a second volume, you may want to do so. A separate notebook for your own personal stitches is almost a necessity, as you will need it to keep track of all the settings, as well as samples of the results.

There will be some new projects for you to try, as well as additional tote bag squares. Some of the lessons will give you ideas which you will be able to use on ready-made garments.

Lesson 37. Using existing stitches

Making eyelets

The eyelet plate, mentioned earlier, is an accessory that works beautifully with some of the satin stitch programs in the machine, creating little eyelet flowers. The programs used here are 60, 61, 63, 65, 66 and 67 (Fig. 11.1), in addition to the regular satin stitch. These decorative eyelets are attractive on blouses and children's clothing.

Specific directions for setting up the machine are in both the Owner's Manual, which you can purchase from your dealer, and the instruction and idea book which comes with your machine. These decorative eyelets are fun to do.

For eyelets on soft fabrics, you will need

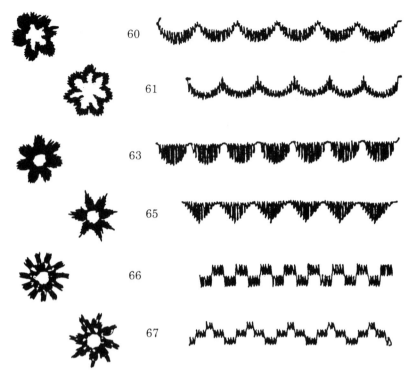

Fig. 11.1 Program stitches and sample flowers made with the eyelet plate.

to use a wooden embroidery hoop in order to hold the fabric firmly enough. Still, sometimes you may have to use a small spring-type hoop, especially if you are working on a ready-made garment. In this case, use water-soluble stabilizer underneath, putting it into the hoop, also.

Make eyelets in groups of three or five, add stems with Program 04, and a leaf or two with Program 83 (Fig. 11.2).

You can make your own eyelet trim using programs 60 and 61 as edgings, and cutting the surplus fabric away after you are through stitching. This is definitely a long-cut, but having an exact match on fabric and thread is well worth the extra work.

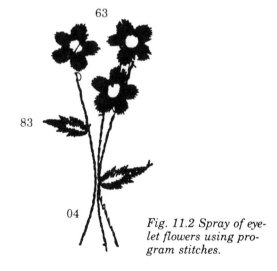

Fig. 11.2 Spray of eyelet flowers using program stitches.

154

Project
Vinyl Belt with Decorative Eyelets

Vinyl belting works nicely because it's stiff enough that you don't have to use an embroidery hoop. I chose this particular blue vinyl, shown in Fig. 11.3, because it was nicely finished with a faille backing.

I used an eyelet punch to make the holes. This accessory should be available at most hobby and craft stores. You could also use an awl or the point of your embroidery scissors. Clip out a tiny ⅛″ (3.2mm) circle wherever you wish to make a hole. Mine are spaced 1″ (2.5cm) apart along the exact center of the length of the belt. For the stitchery I chose leaf green for the stems and leaves, and white and yellow for the flowers. Select colors that will show up well on the belting you've chosen.

Program: 50
Stitch width: 6.0
Stitch length: 16

Needle: #90 jeans
Needle stop: up
Feed dogs: raised
Presser foot: fancy stitch #1
Dual feed: engaged
Single pattern: engaged
Tension: *top*, −3+; *bobbin*, normal
Fabric: vinyl belting, waistline measurement plus 6″ (15.2cm); buckle to match
Thread: rayon machine embroidery thread in green for leaves on top; cotton machine embroidery thread to match belt backing on bobbin
Accessories: edge guide #8

After punching the holes for your eyelets, place the center of the presser foot on the line formed by the row of holes. Attach the edge guide (accessory #8 in your attachment box), positioning it so that by guiding the edge of the belt along the guide, you will be able to stitch exactly down the center line.

Using the green thread, and starting ¼″ (6.4mm) from the first hole, stitch a single Program 50. Skip over the second hole, and repeat for the length of the belting.

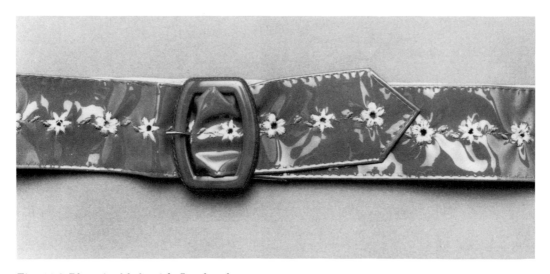

Fig. 11.3 Blue vinyl belt with floral eyelets.

Program: 63 and 65
Stitch width: 6.0
Pattern length: 10 on 63; 8 on 65
Feed dogs: lowered
Dual feed: disengaged
Presser foot: removed.
Accessories: eyelet plate

After stitching the leaves, remove the presser foot and shank, and snap on the eyelet plate. Lower the feed dogs. Push the nub of the eyelet plate through the first hole in the belting. Using white thread (or selected flower color) with Program 63, stitch five or six complete programs around the hole, manually turning the belting. The number of programs needed to form a flower will depend upon how fast and evenly you turn the belting. Do not turn it so fast that the satin stitches are distorted, but try to synchronize your machine speed with the speed you are turning your work. It will be easier than it sounds. Stitch a white flower around every other hole.

Change to yellow thread and Program 65. Stitch seven or eight complete program patterns around the remaining holes.

If you are using a prong-type buckle, you will have to finish one end of your belt as shown in Figure 11.4. Trim one end of the belt so it is perfectly even, then turn under the corners as shown to form a point. Stitch the folds with thread to match the vinyl, and trim the surplus if desired. Put the buckle on the other end of the belt, according to the directions on the packaging.

Medallion embroideries

I love to select a stitch program, press the single pattern key and the needle-down key, then make cute little medallion embroideries by stitching either in a square or octagon. If you have a good eye for angles, you can stitch triangular shapes, hexagons and pentagons, too.

Take a piece of plain fabric and divide it into 1½″ (3.8cm) squares. Then make sam-

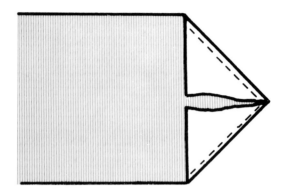

Fig. 11.4 Fold over the ends at point of belt and stitch.

ples of all the stitch programs in the machine stitched in squares or other geometric shapes.

Program: personal choice
Stitch width: as preset, narrow or widen
Stitch length: as preset, shorten or lengthen
Pattern length: as preset, shorten or lengthen
Single pattern: engaged
Needle: #80/12
Needle stop: down
Presser foot: fancy stitch #2
Dual feed: disengaged
Feed dogs: up
Tension: *top*, −3+; *bobbin*, normal
Fabric: plain color woven for practice; variety of fabrics for use
Thread: machine embroidery top and bottom
Stabilizer: freezer paper

Stitch a single pattern and, with the needle down in the fabric, turn 90°, and stitch another single pattern. Continue until you have stitched all four sides of your square (Fig. 11.5). You will be surprised at the variety of designs, even with the utility stitches. Some, obviously, are going to work better as octagons (fourth row, Fig. 11.5). Also try pivoting in the opposite direction with each pattern. Some will work in only one direction, or will be the same, regardless of which direction you turn.

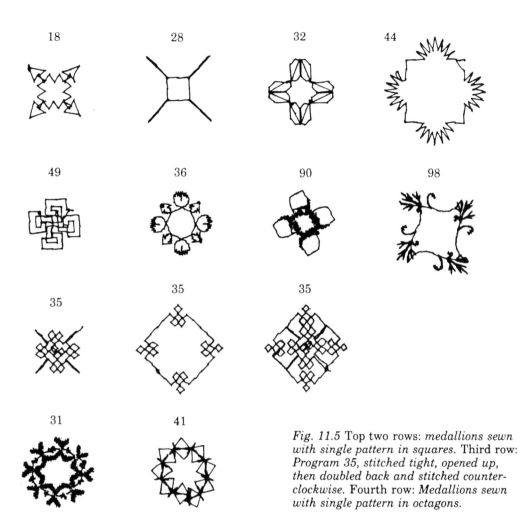

18 28 32 44

49 36 90 98

35 35 35

31 41

Fig. 11.5 Top two rows: *medallions sewn with single pattern in squares.* Third row: *Program 35, stitched tight, opened up, then doubled back and stitched counterclockwise.* Fourth row: *Medallions sewn with single pattern in octagons.*

Keep notes, as it is easy to get carried away with this. Suddenly you find you have a lot of cute little spot embroideries and you won't be able to remember how you got them. It is fun to experiment.

After doing some of the squares, I doubled back after completing the fourth side, stitching in the opposite direction and creating even more interesting designs (see Program 35 in third row, Fig. 11.5).

Use these medallions on fabric buttons or pendants (see Chapter 2), a tote bag square, or scattered over a scarf or sweatshirt.

Project
Infant's Socks

While this project (Fig. 11.6) doesn't necessarily use medallion stitchery, you could use it on larger sizes. Any fancy stitch on your machine will work equally

Fig. 11.6 Baby socks with a single motif.

well. While you might think this is a good opportunity to make use of the open arm, this created a design around the sock and I wanted a vertical, not a horizontal, motif. I found an easy way to get what I wanted: I turned the sock wrong-side-out after marking a stitching line down the side where I wanted the decoration. Use the vanishing marker and make a line from about ¼" (6.4mm) to ½" (12.7mm) above the heel to the bottom of the cuff.

The sock fabric tends to distort the stitches, so stabilizer is required; however, you do not want to use any more than is absolutely necessary. Too large a piece of stabilizer is only difficult to put in place and handle. Cut a short strip of tear-away stabilizer ½" (12.7mm) wide times the length of your marked line plus 1" (2.5cm). Pull the top of the sock open to expose the line you have marked and slip the stabilizer under the area you are going to stitch.

Program: 91, or your choice
Stitch width: 6.0
Stitch length: 20

Needle: #80/12
Feed dogs: raised
Dual feed: disengaged
Presser foot: fancy stitch foot #2
Needle stop: down
Single pattern key: engaged
Tension: *top*, −3+; *bobbin*, normal
Fabric: cotton or cotton/polyester blend socks
Thread: rayon machine embroidery thread, top and bottom
Stabilizer: tear-away

Stitch a single pattern, following your line. Because you are using the single pattern key, the machine will pause between each program, enabling you to rearrange your stitching area. This is difficult to do while continuously stitching.

While I used Program 91 with pastel thread, there are many others that I found worked equally well. A single Program 97 was just the right size for the peanut-sized anklets I bought for my newest granddaughter.

Flower stitchery

One of the things that sold me on my first Pfaff was its pattern elongator, which changes the length of the tapered satin stitches and other decorative satin stitches without losing the density of the stitch. This feature opens up a whole new realm of stitching possibilities. With the Creative, I can also change the width of these stitches.

If you did not make samples of single programs with various types of thread back in the first chapter, be sure to do it now. Draw a line across the top of your fabric and, starting with the shortest possible length for Programs 60 through 65, plus 82, 84 and 85, stitch a single program starting exactly on the line every time (Fig. 11.7). After stitching each program, you will be changing only the pattern length, not the stitch width or stitch length. Make

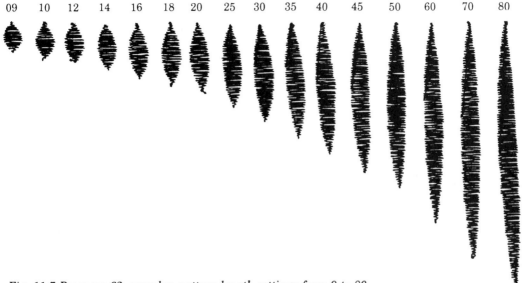

| 09 | 10 | 12 | 14 | 16 | 18 | 20 | 25 | 30 | 35 | 40 | 45 | 50 | 60 | 70 | 80 |

Fig. 11.7 Program 62, sampler, pattern length settings from 9 to 80.

a separate sampler for each individual program.

You will refer often to these samplers, which show you exactly how long any given program will be for the length you need to do floral stitcheries or other designs.

Fig. 11.8 A program takes on a new appearance if fabric is turned to stitch gentle curves.

Even though the pattern-length indicator on the machine tells us the length in millimeters, it is always better to have an actual sample in front of you. Then the computer makes an exact setting easy when you are ready to stitch.

Different weights of thread may necessitate changing the stitch length, which may change the pattern length, so make your sampler with the thread you normally use for machine embroidery, whether it is cotton or rayon. Better yet, make a sampler for different weights of thread.

Now try stitching some of the longer pattern lengths in gentle curves (Fig. 11.8). You will see how this changes the appearance of the stitches and how, by freeing yourself from straight lines, you will be able to add creativity to your design.

Practice to see how sharp a curve you can stitch without distorting the pattern or stitches. You can also fool the eye into thinking it is seeing a curve when it is actually seeing a series of straight lines (Fig. 11.9). Do this by choosing a shorter pro-

159

Fig. 11.9 Turn fabric after each single program to give the appearance of curves.

gram, single pattern key, needle down, and simply turning the fabric slightly after each program is stitched.

To stitch realistic-looking flowers which are neat and unpuckered, start at the center of the flower and stitch toward the outside. Do not be afraid to use plenty of tearaway or freezer paper as a stabilizer. I have embroidered floral designs on all kinds of fabric, from Quiana knits to georgette to stone-washed denim, using the automatic stitches and letting the machine do all the work.

Before computers, we had to use the ornamental ball stitch for petals and leaves alike, but now we have lovely leaf pro-

Fig. 11.10 Unbalanced leaf on a stem.

grams on the machine (Programs 80, 81 and 83). Again, make a sampler so you can actually see what size leaf you are going to use before you stitch. Now use your balance key to deliberately throw them a bit off one way or the other. Many times the off-balance shape lessens the rigidity of the embroidery, making it look more natural (Fig. 11.10).

Project
Tote Bag Square
(Floral Stitchery)

This is a favorite design, one that I have used on many different items (see back cover for color photo). It requires only a single program for the satin-stitch portions, with the addition of a few straight stitches to complete the design.

Be sure when transferring the design that you draw only single lines (Fig. 11.11). The machine will take care of the tapering. All you will need to do is change the program length as indicated on the pattern, with a minor adjustment in width for one segment, and follow the marked lines. Always start at the center of the design and stitch outward. Use an extra layer or two of stabilizer under the center, where all the stitches come together.

You will use your M memories for the stamens. You need not program all of the straight stitches—simply enter Program 00 once at the corrected stitch length of 1.5, as indicated on the pattern. Program 85 will also be entered in a memory, reduced in size and pattern length.

Program: 62 (85 and 00 entered in separate memories)
Stitch width: 6.0, unless otherwise indicated
Stitch length: 0.35, or as indicated on pattern
Pattern length: as indicated
Pattern start: as indicated

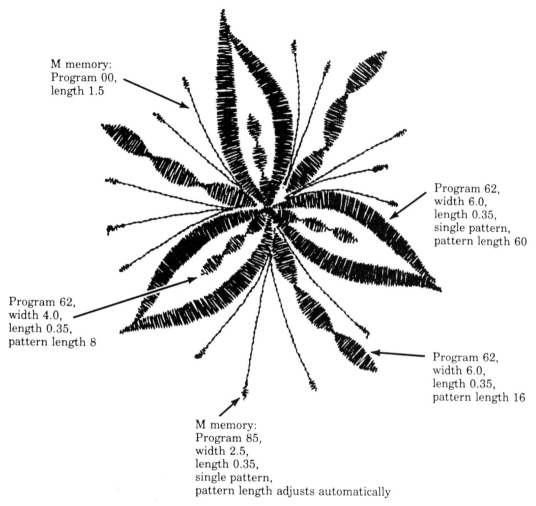

M memory:
Program 00,
length 1.5

Program 62,
width 6.0,
length 0.35,
single pattern,
pattern length 60

Program 62,
width 4.0,
length 0.35,
pattern length 8

Program 62,
width 6.0,
length 0.35,
pattern length 16

M memory:
Program 85,
width 2.5,
length 0.35,
single pattern,
pattern length adjusts automatically

Fig. 11.11 Pattern for freeform flower tote square (see back cover for color photo).

Needle: #80/12
Needle stop: up
Presser foot: fancy stitch foot #2
Feed dogs: raised
Dual feed: disengaged
Tension: *top,* − 3 + ; *bobbin,* normal
Fabric: 9″ (22.9cm) square of orange duck or
  similar heavy fabric
Thread: machine embroidery thread in red,
  green and yellow

Accessories: tracing paper, dressmaker's
  carbon, vanishing marker, dry ballpoint
  pen
Stabilizer: tear-away or freezer paper

Trace your design, then center it over
the square of fabric. Slip the dressmaker's
carbon under the tracing and, with the dry
ballpoint pen, trace the lines of the petals,
the center lines of the petals, and the long

flowing lines between each petal. Do not trace the lines of the stamens. These are freely drawn with the vanishing marker.

Starting at the center and with yellow machine embroidery thread top and bottom, stitch the outlines of the petals using Program 62 with a program length of 60, curving your line of stitching. Change your thread color to green and pattern length to 16, then stitch the flowing lines between the petals. Change the pattern length to 8 and width to 4.0, and with red thread stitch the center lines of the petal shapes.

If you haven't already entered the shortened straight stitch in one of your memories, do so now, and in another memory enter Program 85, which has been reduced to a pattern width of 2.0 and length of 4.0.

Stitch the stamens with red thread, starting at the center and using your straight stitch memory program. You will note that because this stitch is in memory, it will have a little extra stitch between each programmed one, which will give it an interesting texture. After stitching the stamen, change to the memory in which you have entered Program 85 and, with the single pattern key engaged, add the little end to the stamen. Do the remainder of the stamens the same way, always starting at the center and working to the outside.

Finish the tote bag square according to the directions given in Chapter 12.

Lesson 38. Using M memories

As you become familiar with your machine, you will constantly be thinking of different ways to use the memory features, in practical as well as decorative ways.

For example, the memory is used with the cross-stitch programs to create beautiful designs, but I also use the memory to keep track of frequently used stitch settings which are different from those in the machine. I like to use a very narrow zigzag stitch for one of my pet projects, so I keep it in the memory instead of selecting settings every time I want to use it.

You will also be able to create totally new and different stitches by combining the programmable straight stitches with other programs. We have touched on some of these stitches in previous chapters—e.g., the stitch for making entredeaux in the lesson on French handsewing by machine.

One of my favorite stitches is Program 19 and this, with the programmable straight stitches, forward and reverse, and the decentered-needle straight stitches, can be built into a whole repertoire of decorative stitches (Fig. 11.12).

The simplest is entering Program 19, and then mirroring it and entering it a second time (Fig. 11.12B). Another is to enter Program 19, then enter Program 02 two times (Fig. 11.12C). Now enter 19, 02 three times, 19 mirrored, and 00 twice: still another stitch (Fig. 11.12D).

This goes on and on. Be sure you make a careful note of any stitch you "invent," because with endless possibilities, you will not be able to remember them all.

All of the stitches that I have given you had the programs entered without any change of length or width. When you override the computer settings with the length and width keys, you create more variations.

In an earlier chapter, I mentioned Program 37 and showed its versatility (Figs. 2.2 and 2.3). One of the stitches was created by reducing Program 37 to a width of 3.0, and combining it with Program 02 en-

A   B   C   D

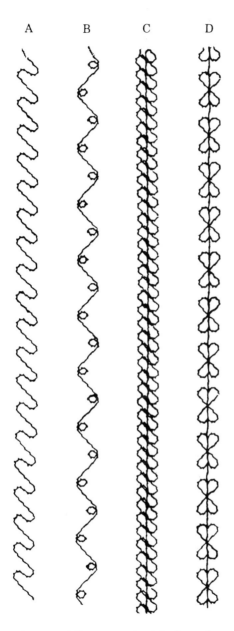

tered twice, then Program 37 again, reduced in width and mirrored, followed by Program 00. Because I still had this in the machine, I used it to trim a ready-made hooded sweatshirt for one of my grandchildren (Fig. 11.13). It was fun to do, and the possibilities for decorative stitchery on sweatshirts are endless. A number of my ideas are shown in Fig. 11.14 to get you started.

Monogramming with script letters

This is really fun. Leave secret messages for your family, put dainty monograms on your undies, stitch out your favorite recipe for a friend, and create all sorts of interesting items. I like to use my memory with the alphabet for craft items. With the Creative I can program an entire poem into the memories, and produce many duplicate items with that particular verse on them.

Fig. 11.12 Program 19 variations. A. Preset Program 19. B. Variation by simple mirroring. C. Addition of programmable reverse stitch. D. Program 19 with programmable reverse stitches, mirroring, and programmable forward stitches.

Fig. 11.13 Variations of Program 37 used to decorate a ready-made sweatshirt.

Fig. 11.14 Decorative stitches follow necklines, raglan seams, pockets, are stitched vertically or horizontally.

Your Pfaff instruction book offers very clear instructions for programming the alphabet, and I suggest reading it thoroughly.

Up to 373 letters and figures can be stored in your memories, as many as 249 in one memory alone. If you put that many in one memory, you must deduct the 249 from the 373, the balance of which can be put in other memories. It is not unlike picking apples and having 373 apples to divide between 16 baskets. A single basket will hold only so much fruit, but you don't have to fill it. How you divide your apples between the baskets is up to you, and so it is with your available memories and stitch programs.

You will note that a + . symbol appears in front of the letter "A." This indicates that this is the script alphabet. A − symbol in front of your letter indicates block letters. You will use the block letters a lot more than the script. Between these two alphabets you will see a number appear with a dot in front of it (.1). This indicates the figures or numerals that you can program, should you wish to write an address, stitch a birthday card, or stitch the quantities in your favorite recipe.

For punctuation, the hyphen and period are built into the machine. In addition, the machine indicates a flat line, which is the space symbol used between the individual words. Let's start with a simple monogram. For practice you can dig out all your long-sleeve shirts and blouses and put the monogram on the cuff. For this practice we will use the + .A symbol.

Program: + .A
Stitch width: as preset
Stitch length: not applicable
Single pattern: engaged
Needle: #80/12
Presser foot: fancy stitch foot #2
Dual feed: disengaged
Feed dogs: up
Tension: *top*, − 3 + ; *bobbin*, normal

Fig. 11.15 L.J.W. monogram in script.

Fabric: woven plain color for practice
Thread: machine embroidery
Stabilizer: freezer wrap if needed

Because this is a monogram, we will want periods after each initial. These instructions, therefore, are a bit different, because we will be using speed dots, rather than going back each time to the period that is found in the alphabet.

The monogram that I am going to enter is "L.J.W." (Fig. 11.15), the initials of my daughter. Of course you will enter your own letters.

1. Find an empty M memory and press the program key
2. Select the + .A program. Use the + or − key on the right to locate the letter "L."
3. Press the program key to enter this letter.
4. Press the program key a second time, hold it in and, at the same time, press the + key on the left side. You will see that the second "L" that had appeared is replaced by a dot.
5. Locate the letter "J," enter it, and repeat step 4.
6. Locate the letter "W," enter it, and repeat step 4.
7. Press the repeat key to close the program and prepare the machine for stitching.

At this point, you will engage your single pattern key and stitch your sample.

Programming with block letters

Do not put a period after block letters if you are writing something out, such as your name and address or a phrase. In the block letter alphabet, the machine puts in a dot the same way on the display screen, which shows as a space symbol. For this reason, when you put a period at the end of a sentence, it is best that you actually go to that punctuation mark and enter it. The dashes will be fine when you stitch off and they become dots, but if you use your display for review, the dashes could be confusing.

If you are going to align the left side of your message or verse, then you only need mark a vertical starting line in addition to the horizontal lines on which you will stitch the programs. More often, we want to center a name or a phrase.

To center, enter the phrase in a memory, stitch a sample, and find the center of the phrase. Then find the center of the line on which it is to be stitched. With your ruler, measure the length from the beginning of the phrase to the center line, and mark that measurement on the stitching line to the left of the center line.

Program: −A
Stitch width: as preset
Stitch length: not applicable
Single pattern: engaged
Needle; #80/12
Presser foot: fancy stitch foot #2
Dual feed: disengaged
Feed dogs: up
Tension: *top*, −3 + ; *bobbin*, normal
Fabric: plain color woven fabric for practice
Thread: machine embroidery in contrasting color
Accessories: vanishing marker, ruler
Stabilizer: freezer paper

Select an empty M memory and press the program key. Now bring up the −A program. The phrase that I am going to enter is CUTE KID.

Find the letter C and enter it. Then find the letter U, then T, then E. Now go back to the letter "A," and press the right-hand minus key two times. Your program screen

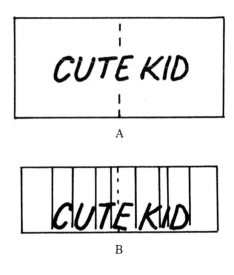

Fig. 11.16 A. CUTE KID centered and stitched. B. Mark center of phrase and clip fabric. C. Match center mark of curve on background fabric with center of phrase. Mark placement for final stitching.

will now show two dashes: − −. The right-hand dash represents the space. Enter the space, and continue with the second word of the phrase. Touch the repeat key and stitch the sample (Fig. 11.20).

To center letters on a curve, first stitch the letters on a piece of fabric and cut the fabric across at the bottom of the letters (Fig. 11.16A). Measure and mark the center of the phrase.

Then clip from top to almost bottom between each letter (Fig. 11.16B).

On the background fabric, draw a curve

and mark the center with a vanishing marker.

Match the center mark on the curve with the center of your phrase. Fan out the letters around the curve and mark the placement for your final stitching (Fig. 11.16C).

Project Irish Blessing Stitchery

I love making these stitcheries for gifts. Sometimes I make a small wallhanging, or frame it as a picture. Others I have put in wooden hoops and decorated with lace or ribbon (Fig. 11.17).

Program: − A
Stitch width: as preset
Single pattern: engaged
Needle: #80/12
Presser foot: fancy stitch foot #2
Dual feed: disengaged
Feed dogs: up
Tension: *top*, − 3 + ; *bobbin*, normal
Single pattern: engaged
Fabric: woven white linen, two pieces, 12″ (30.5cm) square
Thread: Kelly-green machine embroidery cotton or rayon
Accessories: ruler; vanishing or water-erasable marker; 9″ (22.9cm) wooden hoop, or larger if preferred; pregathered lace to go around hoop; green satin ribbon to go around hoop, plus sufficient for bow and hanger

Enter the words of the Irish Blessing in the memories. You will need seven empty memories, and I suggest that you clear out everything in your M memories to make room for this.

in M1 enter: MAY THE ROAD RISE TO MEET YOU

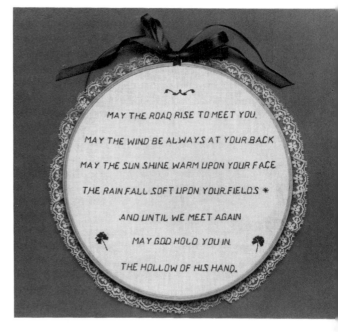

Fig. 11.17 Irish blessing stitchery.

in M2 enter: MAY THE WIND BE ALWAYS AT YOUR BACK
in M3 enter: MAY THE SUN SHINE WARM UPON YOUR FACE
in M4 enter: THE RAIN FALL SOFT UPON YOUR FIELDS
in M5 enter: AND UNTIL WE MEET AGAIN
in M6 enter: MAY GOD HOLD YOU IN
in M7 enter: THE HOLLOW OF HIS HAND

Iron the freezer paper to the back of your squares of fabric. On one square of fabric, draw seven lines 1″ (2.5cm) apart. This will be your practice piece and the one which you will measure to find the center of your lines. Stitch off your programs, one on each line.

On the second piece of stabilized fabric, draw a vertical line down the center. Draw seven parallel lines horizontally. Measure the length of each stitched program and divide it in half. I am not giving you exact measurements because each machine is different. When you have the length of the line divided in half, measure that distance from the vertical center line, and mark it with your marker. This is your starting point for that particular line or program.

You can measure all your lines at once, before you are ready to stitch. I strongly recommend stitching another practice sample to check out your math before going to the finished article. Math is not my strong point and a fraction of an inch error can throw the whole thing out of whack. After you have your measurements, all you have to do is press M1, stitch the first line, press M2, stitch the second, and so forth.

What happens if you cannot divide fractions? People like me, who have trouble balancing a checkbook, can rescue a project without having to spend hours picking out a misplaced line: simply add a little decorative program before or after the errant line.

To complete the embroidery on your Irish Blessing, select Program 99, stitch a single program on your sample fabric, and measure the length. Divide it in half, and stitch it centered 1″ (2.5cm) above the first line. You can add some shamrocks before and after the sixth line. These are made just like medallion stitchery, using Program 84, except that only three sides are stitched, and a stem is stitched out from the center using Program 04.

To complete your Irish Blessing, clip all the little connecting threads between the letters and words. The letters are individually tied off, and if you clip the threads before pulling off the stabilizer in back, that will pull any little loose ends through to the back.

Center your embroidery in the hoop, and trim off the surplus fabric. Leave just enough to fold to the inside of the hoop where it can be glued. Glue the pregathered lace to the back of the hoop, and glue the green ribbon around the outside of the hoop. Refer back to the infant's bonnet instructions in Chapter 5 for instructions for making ribbon roses and bows.

Lesson 39: Stitching cross-stitch, blackwork, and personally designed stitches

Your Pfaff Creative has two different sizes of single cross-stitches in two different needle positions, as well as the ability to mirror them and create a third needle position. In addition, you have a double row of cross-stitch, and a diagonal cross-stitch.

Your instruction book shows many interesting designs for decorative cross-stitch borders. Let's take an easy example of using the M memories with the cross-stitch to create a border pattern.

Program 70 is in the left-needle position. Pattern mirror will place this stitch in the right-needle position, and by using the M memory, you can create a design such as shown in Fig. 11.18A and B. By combining Program 70 with program 71 — or 70 and 70 mirrored with 71 — you can create the designs shown in Figure 11.18C and D.

Project Mock Ski Sweater

These patterns can be stitched in rows on a ready-made sweatshirt for a ski sweater look, a good gift for boys or men (Fig. 11.19).

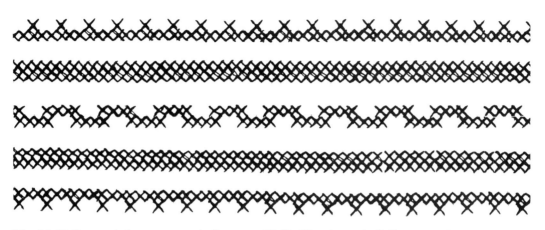

Fig. 11.18 Cross-stitch programs. A. Program 70. B. 70, mirrored. C. Programs 70 and 71 combined. D. 70 + 70, mirrored with 71.

Program: 70, 71
Stitch width: 3.0
Stitch length: 3.0
Needle: #80/12
Presser foot: fancy stitch foot #2
Dual feed: disengaged
Feed dogs: up
Tension: *top,* −3+; *bobbin,* normal
Fabric: ready-made sweatshirt in bright color
Thread: machine embroidery thread in contrasting color
Accessories: vanishing or water-erasable marker; ruler
Stabilizer: freezer paper

In one empty M memory, enter Program 70 twice, then 71 one time. Touch the repeat key to close the program. In a second empty M memory, enter Program 70 two times, 71 one time, 70 mirrored two times, and 71 again. Press the repeat key to close the program.

Lay the sweatshirt on a flat surface, and measure 1″ (2.5cm) down from the sleeves on the underarm seams. Be sure to mark both the front and back of the garment. With the ruler, draw a line across the front and across the back. Draw a second line across the front and back 2″ (5.1cm) above the band.

Fig. 11.19 Mock ski sweater uses cross-stitch programs or a purchased sweatshirt.

169

Stitch the lower line nearest the band with the first program, being sure that the freezer paper is under the line of stitching. Mirror this program and stitch the top line across the chest and across the back.

Using the width of the presser foot as a guide, keep the right side of the foot against the line of cross-stitches you just made, and stitch a single row of Program 71. Using the same spacing, stitch the second memory program parallel to the row of double cross-stitches. Return to Program 71 and stitch parallel to the memory program just done, using the edge of the foot as a guide. Bring up the first memory program. Do not mirror it, but stitch parallel to the last row of stitching.

Again lay the sweatshirt on a flat surface. Divide the unstitched area between the decorative border and the lower row of stitches into equal divisions and draw parallel lines across the front and the back. Make a small dot every 2″ (5.1cm) on the first line, marking all the way around the sweatshirt. On the second line, mark dots every 2″ (5.1cm) but make them in the alternate inch spaces (Fig. 11.20). At each of these markings, make a single cross-stitch, Program 70. Clip the threads, remove the stabilizer, and you have your "ski sweater."

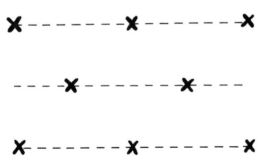

Fig. 11.20 Diagram of single cross-stitch marking.

Developing cross-stitch combinations

Programs 73 and 74 are smaller cross stitches. Program 73 is also a left-needle position, which can be mirrored to the right. Program 74 is a centered-needle position to fill in the gap, and by combining these programs, you can create another border design (Fig. 11.21).

As you may have noticed when doing the sweatshirt project, once you have entered a chosen sequence in your M memory, you can mirror the entire memory, so that for a complicated border pattern, you need only enter one-half of the design. Figure 11.22 shows a sample of a border which has been mirrored. When stitching a border such as this, it is important that you commence stitching each row on exactly the same starting line. Draw your stitching line, then a starting line at right angles. The red lines on fancy stitch foot #2 are a big help in placing the needle exactly on your starting line.

The programs for this particular border are given below. Be sure to use the freezer paper as stabilizer ironed onto the wrong side of the fabric. The machine is set up the same as for the sweatshirt project, except that I would suggest a woven fabric. You will need to use three memories to complete this design.

M memory #1: 70M–71–70M
M memory #2: 70M–70M–70–70M–70–
    70M–70–70M–71–71–71–70–71–
    71–71–70M–70–70M–70–70M–70
M memory #3: 70M–70M–70–70M–70–
    70M–71–71–71–70–70M–70–70M–
    70–71–71–71–70M–70–70M–70

Using the first memory and following your stitching line exactly with the center of the presser foot, stitch the first row of the design.

Skip a space of 3mm, or the width of a single cross-stitch. Select the second memory. Lower the needle into the starting

Fig. 11.21 Cross-stitch using Programs 73 and 74, with 73 mirrored.

line, as with the first program, and begin to stitch the second program.

The third memory program is stitched so that the cross-stitches are barely touching the previous row. Using a smooth fabric with the ironed-on freezer paper helps with accuracy, but it is crucial that you check frequently to see that your pattern is lining up properly. If you find that you are getting a thread or two off, stop and correct it, so that the problem is not compounded later. This is the most difficult part.

Rest periods are important when you are doing a complicated cross-stitch design, so stop, have a cup of coffee or soft drink, and relax. Get your eyes uncrossed, too.

When you come back to your machine, mirror Program 3 and stitch again, with the crosses just touching those in the previous row. Then mirror Program 2 and stitch with the crosses just touching the previous row.

Mirror Program 1, and remember to again skip the 3mm space when you stitch.

I admit this program is a real challenge, but if you enjoy a long-cut, this is it.

Creating blackwork stitchery

Like cross-stitch, blackwork is another type of counted-thread embroidery. In fact, cross-stitching is sometimes incorporated as part of blackwork stitches. The counted-thread stitches are made over a given area of the design, with each portion a slightly different pattern. The areas are then outlined to define and separate them. In traditional blackwork, gold thread was sometimes used to highlight the various portions of the design.

Blackwork by hand uses hundreds of different stitch arrangements and patterns, but because they are counted, it is easy to duplicate this type of work on a sewing machine with its accurate stitches.

Take a piece of smooth, evenly woven white or cream fabric, and divide it into 1½″ (6.4cm) squares. Select a decorative stitch program such as 30, 31, or 49, and stitch a short row in one of the squares. Stitch a second row adjacent to the first, so that the stitches touch (Fig. 11.23). You will see how an interesting pattern develops, as these stitches are arranged and stitched close together. Try a different

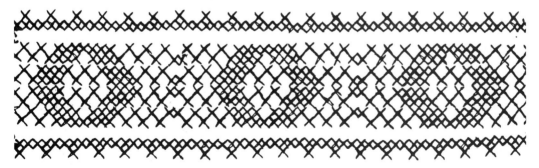

Fig. 11.22 Elaborate cross-stitch border design is challenging but fun.

171

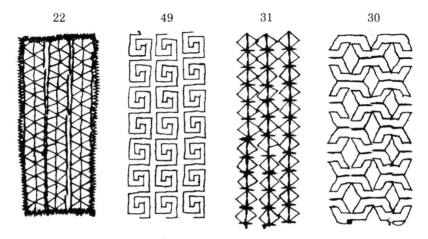

| 22 | 49 | 31 | 30 |

Fig. 11.23 Four programs, stitched close together with rows touching, can be developed into blackwork patterns.

stitch program in each of the squares. Be sure to use your tie-off key to end the program and your pattern start key to begin it, so these short programs are accurate.

You may find that certain stitches can be altered, redefined or recreated, put in the M memory and used for blackwork designs, or you may want to create some of your own stitches using the P programs.

After you have filled your squares, select either a very narrow satin stitch to cover the straight lines or, better yet, use program 06 or 07, the outline stitches.

Project
Blackwork Tote Bag Square

This blackwork design of your Pfaff will make a most interesting conversation piece (see color insert).

Draw the design in Fig. 11.24 on linen-like fabric, or any fairly smooth, evenly woven fabric. The heavy outlines separate the various blocks of stitchery. Arrows show you which direction to stitch.

Programs: 04, 06, 10, 30, 31, 33, 51, 84; plus special programs specified on pattern
Stitch width: as specified
Stitch length: as specified
Single pattern button: where required
Mirror: where specified
Pattern start: use at beginning of each line
Needle: #90/14
Needle stop: up or down, as required
Presser foot: fancy stitch foot #2
Dual feed: disengaged
Feed dogs: up
Tension: *top,* 3 for machine embroidery thread, 1–2 for metallic thread; *bobbin,* normal
Fabric: 9″ (22.9cm) square of smooth even-weave in white or cream
Thread: *top,* black machine embroidery, and gold metallic or yellow machine embroidery; *bobbin,* black or yellow machine embroidery
Accessories: water-erasable marker; ruler; embroidery scissors
Stabilizer: freezer wrap, or tear-away if required

Enter the special programs for hexagon mesh and brick walk (Figs. 11.25 and 26).

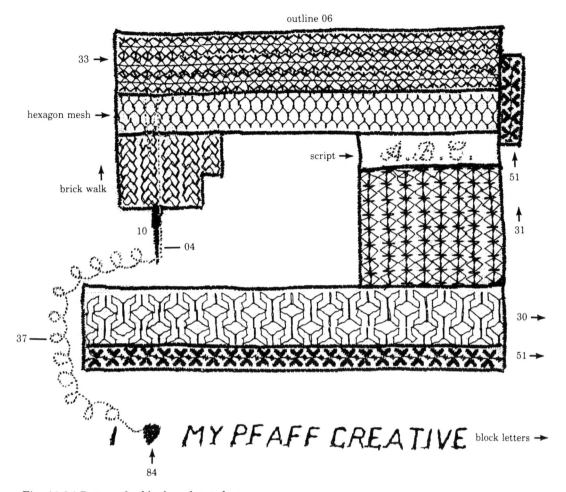

Fig. 11.24 Pattern for blackwork tote bag square.

You may wish to substitute a stitch program already in the machine.

Stitch the various programs, as indicated on the pattern, then outline all the sections with Program 06, length reduced to 1.5.

The needle image is stitched with Program 10 zigzag, with a starting width of 3.0 and a stitch length of 0.35. After stitching the upper part, reduce the stitch width to 1.5, and gradually taper to 0 while sewing.

Make the single block letter "I" with black thread, then skip over to the rest of the phrase, which you can put in one of the M memories. You should allow about 1″ (2.5cm) between the "I" and the "MY." The latter phrase "MY PFAFF CREATIVE" is not centered. Carefully clip the little threads between the letters, and tug the bobbin threads lightly to pull the loose ends to the back.

If you are troubled by little bits of black lint after doing this, wind some Scotch

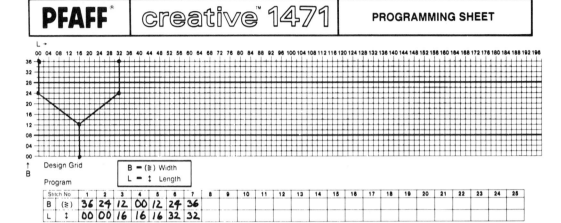

L →

00 04 08 12 16 20 24 28 32 36 40 44 48 52 56 60 64 68 72 76 80 84 88 92 96 100 104 108 112 116 120 124 128 132 136 140 144 148 152 156 160 164 168 172 176 180 184 188 192 196

Design Grid

B = (≷) Width
L = ↕ Length

Program

Stitch No	1	2	3	4	5	6	7	8	9	10	11	12	13	14	15	16	17	18	19	20	21	22	23	24	25
B (≷)	36	24	12	00	12	24	36																		
L ↕	00	00	16	16	16	32	32																		

Stitch No	26	27	28	29	30	31	32	33	34	35	36	37	38	39	40	41	42	43	44	45	46	47	48	49	50
B (≷)																									
L ↕																									

Stitch No	51	52	53	54	55	56	57	58	59	60	61	62	63	64	65	66	67	68	69	70	71	72	73	74	75
B (≷)																									
L ↕																									

Stitch No	76	77	78	79	80	81	82	83	84	85	86	87	88	89	90	91	92	93	94	95	96	97	98	99	
B (≷)																									
L ↕																									

This program was created by _____ on _____ and is stored in P memory # [   ]
NAME   DATE

Fig. 11.25 Hexagon mesh program for blackwork square.

tape around your fingers and gently brush the area. The sticky tape will pick up the lint and leave your white fabric nice and clean.

The balance of the design should be stitched with either metallic gold thread or bright yellow thread. Use Program 04 to stitch the thread, pivoting with the need-down button engaged. Be sure that you complete the entire sequence of this program when you pivot, so your line doesn't take off in some direction of its own. After crossing the "needle," change to Program 37, with a length of 6.0, and stitch to the area left between the words "I" and "MY." Change to Program 84, and stitch the heart.

I used a very fine German metallic gold thread which is a single filament, different from most metallics. I had it for many years, a gift from a friend who was unable to use it in her machine (not a Pfaff). I do not know if the thread is available any longer, but you should be able to substitute either Madeira or Kanagawa (see Sources of Supply).

If you are unable to find metallic threads, or are dissatisfied with the appearance of what you have, you can substitute a bright yellow machine embroidery thread of the same weight as the black.

Sometimes, with a design that has uneven or irregular lines, it may be easier to cover an entire piece of fabric with your chosen blackwork stitch, and then cut out the pattern piece and appliqué it to a similar background fabric. As a general rule, however, the satin stitches around the edge become overpowering, so the preferred way is to work directly on the fabric

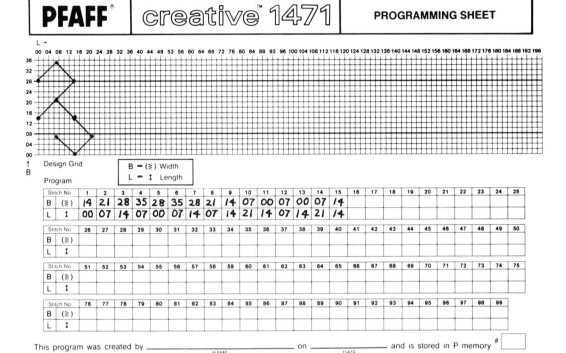

L→

Stitch No	1	2	3	4	5	6	7	8	9	10	11	12	13	14	15	16	17	18	19	20	21	22	23	24	25
B (≶)	14	21	28	35	28	35	28	21	14	07	00	07	00	07	14										
L ↕	00	07	14	07	00	07	14	07	14	21	14	07	14	21	14										

Stitch No	26	27	28	29	30	31	32	33	34	35	36	37	38	39	40	41	42	43	44	45	46	47	48	49	50
B (≶)																									
L ↕																									

Stitch No	51	52	53	54	55	56	57	58	59	60	61	62	63	64	65	66	67	68	69	70	71	72	73	74	75
B (≶)																									
L ↕																									

Stitch No	76	77	78	79	80	81	82	83	84	85	86	87	88	89	90	91	92	93	94	95	96	97	98	99	
B (≶)																									
L ↕																									

Design Grid — B = (≶) Width — L = ↕ Length — Program

This program was created by _____ NAME _____ on _____ DATE _____ and is stored in P memory # [ ]

Fig. 11.26 Brick walk program for blackwork square. On some fabrics, it may be necessary to change stitch length to 2.5 and balance to +2.

and use the outline stitches to define the area.

Creating personal stitch designs

I readily admit I am saving the best for last. My favorite amusement is doodling up new stitch designs for my Pfaff Creative 1471. I have written programs for about fifty stitches, and keep at least ten of them in the machine at all times, both practical and simply pretty ones. This still leaves many empty memories for seasonal stitches, such as Christmas designs, or for trying out new ideas.

Best of all, if you have a Pfaff Creative, no other sewing machine in the world can claim an exclusive stitch, because you will be able to duplicate it if you want it!

My teddy bear (Fig. 11.27, detail) has been popular with my students and everyone else who's seen him, whether they sew or not. The bear is a double program. After you have punched in the coordinates using two separate P memories, you bring up the first P program and stitch his front side, using single pattern and needle down; then bring up the second P program, pivot and stitch his back.

Program: enter special programs in Figs. 11.28 and 11.29
Stitch width: as machine computed
Stitch length: as machine computed
Single pattern button: engaged
Needle: #80/12
Needle stop: down

175

 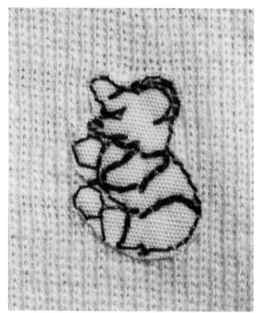

Fig. 11.27 Chelsea Brazil wears the infant's shirt with teddy bear (see detail).

Presser foot: fancy stitch foot #2
Dual feed: disengaged
Feed dogs: up
Tension: *top*, −3+; *bobbin*, normal
Fabric: infant's undershirt or onesie; 1″
    (2.5cm) square of woven fabric such as
    percale
Thread: machine embroidery thread, medium
    to light color
Accessories: embroidery scissors
Stabilizer: Wonder-Under fused to square of
    fabric and freezer wrap or tear-away

The program for the teddy bear is given in Figs. 11.28 and 11.29. Consult your instruction book for the method of entering this program if you are not already familiar with it.

I like to trim my grandchildren's undershirts, onesies and T-shirts into "designer" garments by stitching the bear on them. In order to make it look like a logo or trademark, I used to stitch it over felt, but the felt didn't stand up to laundering. Here is a better method.

Iron fusible web, preferably Wonder-Under, to the wrong side of a piece of woven fabric a bit larger than the bear embroidery. A 1″ (2.5cm) square is more than adequate. Position the fabric where you want to do the embroidery, but don't fuse it down yet. Pin it, slip some freezer wrap or tear-away underneath the shirt and, after you have it under the presser foot, remove the pin and stitch the bear.

With sharp-pointed embroidery scissors, carefully trim away the surplus fabric and remove the stabilizer from the back. A quick press with the steam iron secures the bear stitchery, and you have a cute little emblem on the shirt. Frankly, my grandchildren like the bear better than alligators.

If you have worked on the projects throughout this book, I am sure you have

176

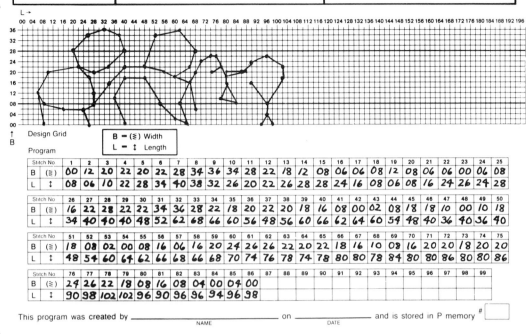

Stitch No	1	2	3	4	5	6	7	8	9	10	11	12	13	14	15	16	17	18	19	20	21	22	23	24	25
B (⋚)	00	12	20	22	20	22	28	34	36	34	28	22	18	12	08	06	06	08	12	08	06	06	00	06	08
L ↕	08	06	10	22	28	34	40	38	32	26	20	22	26	28	28	24	16	08	06	08	16	24	26	24	28

Stitch No	26	27	28	29	30	31	32	33	34	35	36	37	38	39	40	41	42	43	44	45	46	47	48	49	50
B (⋚)	16	22	28	22	22	34	36	28	22	18	20	22	20	18	16	08	00	02	08	18	18	10	00	10	18
L ↕	34	40	40	40	48	52	62	68	66	60	56	48	56	60	66	62	64	60	54	48	40	36	40	36	40

Stitch No	51	52	53	54	55	56	57	58	59	60	61	62	63	64	65	66	67	68	69	70	71	72	73	74	75
B (⋚)	18	08	02	00	08	16	06	16	20	24	26	26	22	20	22	18	16	10	08	16	20	20	18	20	20
L ↕	48	54	60	64	62	66	68	66	68	70	74	76	78	74	78	80	80	78	84	80	80	86	80	80	86

Stitch No	76	77	78	79	80	81	82	83	84	85	86	87	88	89	90	91	92	93	94	95	96	97	98	99
B (⋚)	24	26	22	18	08	16	08	04	00	04	00													
L ↕	90	98	102	102	96	90	96	96	94	96	98													

This program was created by _____ on _____ and is stored in P memory # [ ]
NAME   DATE

Fig. 11.28 Personal program for front of bear. Single pattern, needle down; stitch, pivot, bring up corresponding program (Fig. 11.29) to complete.

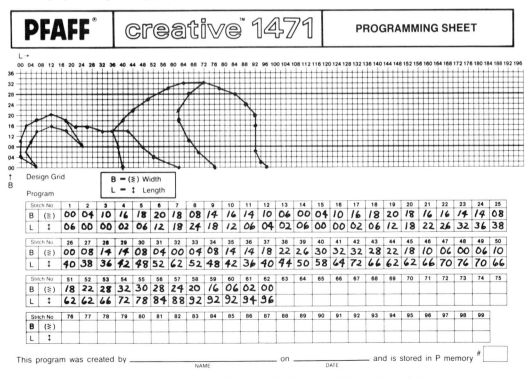

Stitch No	1	2	3	4	5	6	7	8	9	10	11	12	13	14	15	16	17	18	19	20	21	22	23	24	25
B (⋚)	00	04	10	16	18	20	18	08	14	16	14	10	06	00	04	10	16	18	20	18	16	16	14	14	08
L ↕	06	00	00	02	06	12	18	24	18	12	06	04	02	06	00	00	02	06	12	18	22	26	32	36	38

Stitch No	26	27	28	29	30	31	32	33	34	35	36	37	38	39	40	41	42	43	44	45	46	47	48	49	50
B (⋚)	00	08	14	14	08	04	00	04	08	14	14	18	22	26	30	32	32	28	22	18	10	06	00	06	10
L ↕	40	38	36	42	48	52	62	52	48	42	36	40	44	50	58	64	72	66	62	62	66	70	76	70	66

Stitch No	51	52	53	54	55	56	57	58	59	60	61	62	63	64	65	66	67	68	69	70	71	72	73	74	75
B (⋚)	18	22	28	32	30	28	24	20	16	06	02	00													
L ↕	62	62	66	72	78	84	88	92	92	92	94	96													

Stitch No	76	77	78	79	80	81	82	83	84	85	86	87	88	89	90	91	92	93	94	95	96	97	98	99
B (⋚)																								
L ↕																								

This program was created by _____ on _____ and is stored in P memory # [ ]
NAME   DATE

Fig. 11.29 Personal program for back of bear, with final stitching of both halves together.

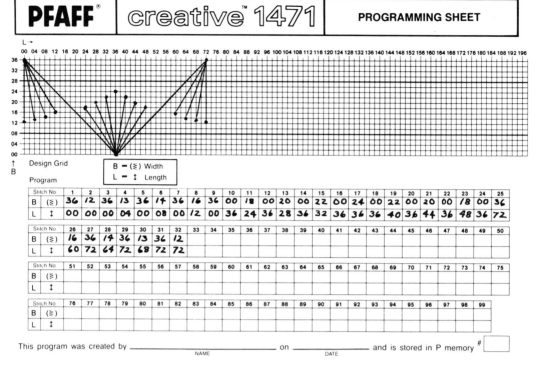

Design Grid   B = (≳) Width   L = ↕ Length

Program

Stitch No.	1	2	3	4	5	6	7	8	9	10	11	12	13	14	15	16	17	18	19	20	21	22	23	24	25
B (≳)	36	12	36	13	36	14	36	16	36	00	18	00	20	00	22	00	24	00	22	00	20	00	18	00	36
L ↕	00	00	00	04	00	08	00	12	00	36	24	36	28	36	32	36	36	36	40	36	44	36	48	36	72

Stitch No	26	27	28	29	30	31	32	33	34	35	36	37	38	39	40	41	42	43	44	45	46	47	48	49	50
B (≳)	16	36	14	36	13	36	12																		
L ↕	60	72	64	72	68	72	72																		

Stitch No	51	52	53	54	55	56	57	58	59	60	61	62	63	64	65	66	67	68	69	70	71	72	73	74	75
B (≳)																									
L ↕																									

Stitch No	76	77	78	79	80	81	82	83	84	85	86	87	88	89	90	91	92	93	94	95	96	97	98	99
B (≳)																								
L ↕																								

This program was created by _____ NAME ____ on _____ DATE _____ and is stored in P memory #[   ]

Fig. 11.30 Original program for fan stitch.

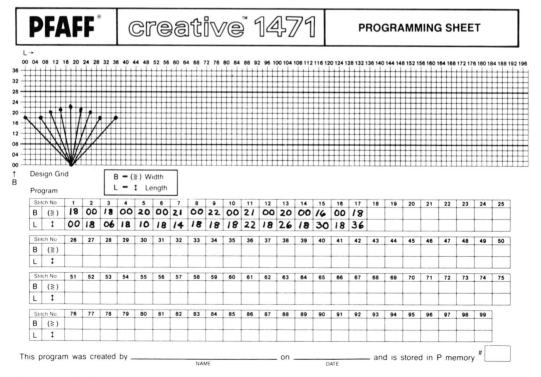

Design Grid   B = (≳) Width   L = ↕ Length

Program

Stitch No	1	2	3	4	5	6	7	8	9	10	11	12	13	14	15	16	17	18	19	20	21	22	23	24	25
B (≳)	18	00	18	00	20	00	21	00	22	00	21	00	20	00	16	00	18								
L ↕	00	18	06	18	10	18	14	18	18	18	22	18	26	18	30	18	36								

Stitch No	26	27	28	29	30	31	32	33	34	35	36	37	38	39	40	41	42	43	44	45	46	47	48	49	50
B (≳)																									
L ↕																									

Stitch No	51	52	53	54	55	56	57	58	59	60	61	62	63	64	65	66	67	68	69	70	71	72	73	74	75
B (≳)																									
L ↕																									

Stitch No	76	77	78	79	80	81	82	83	84	85	86	87	88	89	90	91	92	93	94	95	96	97	98	99
B (≳)																								
L ↕																								

This program was created by _____ NAME ____ on _____ DATE _____ and is stored in P memory #[   ]

Fig. 11.31 Redesigned program for fan stitch.

had plenty of experience in punching in the coordinates of many of the programs I have given you. What about creating your own?

Even if you are not artistic, you can come up with some nice stitches, I do not particularly care for some of the "cute" stitches, such as ducks and doggies. In fact, the teddy bear is one of very few little animals I have running around in my machine.

When creating new stitches for the P programs, keep them simple. My most successful programs have been those that take less than 40 coordinates, which means that I have more than enough available memory at all times.

If you are doing a repeat design, enter the design only to the point where it starts to do the repeat. This may seem like a stronger statement, but I have had many students who exhuberantly try to fill the entire graph strip at the top of the paper. So enter coordinates only to the point where the design starts to repeat, and let the machine do the work for you.

Sometimes a simple change in the design can reduce the number of coordinates by almost half, and the end results will be the same. For example, the fan design shown in Fig. 11.30 was my original sketch and would have taken 32 coordinates. After reworking it (Fig. 11.31), it required only 17 coordinates. By putting this P program into an M memory and mirroring the P program for the second entry, I have an al-most identical stitch to my first fan program.

Any of your P programs can be used as a regular program would. You can change the size as far as length and width, mirror it, use it as a single program, and/or combine it with any other P program or regular program by putting it in an M memory. You can put the P program into the M memory, but the M memory programs cannot be put in the P memory.

If you remove a P program that you have entered in another M memory, it will be removed from the M memory too.

Look for ideas for programming on your china, silverware, engraving on jewelry — anywhere. Do keep a scrapbook or clipping file for ideas. I like to keep them as simple as possible, because in the process of being shrunk down from a graph strip that is approximately 1⅜" (3.5cm) wide to the 6mm stitch width, details will either be lost or simply muddy up the design.

Your Pfaff dealer has inexpensive portfolios with new stitch designs in them, in addition to the designs in the back of your instruction book. Try them out, play with them, change them. Have fun with them.

I hope you have enjoyed this book and exploring all of the wonderful features on your Pfaff Creative. There would be no way to put everything in one volume. Every day, users like yourself are discovering more wonderful things about the machine. The more time you spend with your machine, the more you will discover.

CHAPTER 12

Making the Tote Bag

The year I became program chairman for an embroiderer's guild, I began to assess previous programs: Why was one a success, another a failure? I remembered the many needlework workshops I had taken, the many projects I had started in those classes and never finished because they were too big or demanded too much of my time. And I knew I wasn't the only one who felt this way, as other members also had boxes of half-finished needlework.

That's when I came up with the idea of the tote bag. I asked the teachers that year to gear their workshops toward making samples small enough to fit in a 6" (15.2cm) square frame. The fabric squares could then fit into the frames made by the handles on a tote bag I designed. Each new square could easily slip in and out. Not only were the class projects small enough to complete easily, but they were useful and decorative as well.

I'm using the same tote bag for this book (Fig. 12.1; see also cover). After you've made the tote bag, it can be used to show off the sample squares found in the lessons.

First, I'll explain how to finish the squares you made throughout the lessons in this book. Then I'll explain the tote bag.

Finishing the squares

Specific instructions for each square are included in the lessons. A brief recap: Start with a piece of fabric large enough to fit in a 7" (17.8cm) hoop, if you will be working with one. I suggest starting with a 9" (22.9cm) square, as it is better to have extra fabric than not enough. The finished square will be 6¾" (17.1cm). The area that will show in the frame will be 6" (15.2cm) square. Cut a piece of acetate or cardboard 6¾" (17.1cm) square to use as a template.

After completing the embroidery, quilting, appliqué—whatever the lesson calls

Fig. 12.1 The tote bag, with one of the squares in position on the pocket.

for—center the acetate pattern over the square. Draw a line at the edge of the acetate all the way around with a water-erasable marker or white chalk pencil.

Back the square with stiff fabric, fleece, or iron-on interfacing if it is not stiff enough for the pocket. Stitch along the line you've drawn and cut off the extra fabric to that line.

Slip typing paper or heavy tear-away stabilizer under the square. Finish by satin stitching at stitch width 4 around the edge. Dab the corners with Fray-Check to keep them from raveling.

Glue or stitch Velcro dots under the corner of each square to correspond to the ones in the pocket frame. (If the square is stiff enough, this will not be necessary.) An alternative to Velcro is an idea from Marilyn Tisol of Hinsdale, Illinois. She backs each square she makes by first cutting a piece of plastic canvas the size of the square; then she attaches the fabric square to it by whipping the edges together. The plastic is rigid enough to keep the square in the frame.

Tote bag construction

My tote bag is made of canvas, but it can be made of any heavy-duty fabric. I used canvas because I wanted a bag that would stand by itself. If the fabric you've chosen is not heavy enough, press a layer of fusible webbing between two layers of material. Whatever you choose, pre-wash and press all fabrics before you cut.

Supplies:
1½ yards (1.4m) of 36″ (0.9m) canvas (includes body of bag, handles, pockets, and bottom of bag)
3⅛ yards (2.9m) of 1″ (2.5cm) wide fusible webbing
Teflon pressing sheet
Four Velcro dots
Sewing thread to match canvas, or monofilament
Rotary cutter and board are timesavers

24″ × 6″ (61.0 × 15.2cm) plastic ruler
Water-erasable pen, pencil or sliver of soap
Ordinary sewing foot #0
Jeans needle

My tote (see color insert) is made up of many colors and looks as if Dr. Seuss invented it. It includes royal blue for the bottom, yellow pockets, green handles, and red for the body of the bag.

I chose those colors because the striped lining fabric included them all. I backed the lining with Pellon fleece and quilted down each stripe to give my bag even more body. I added pockets to the lining, too.

Lining is optional, but if you choose to include one, you will need another piece of fabric at least 34″ × 20″ (86.4cm × 50.8cm). Add 20″ × 20″ (50.8cm × 50.8cm) to this if you wish to make pockets for your lining.

The layout of the bag is provided in Fig. 12.2; note that the layout is predicated on cutting all pieces from a single length of cloth, rather than several different colors.

Body of bag:
34″ × 20″ (0.85m × 50.8cm)

1. Cut out fabric. Fold in half and notch bottom on both sides, 17″ (43.2cm) from top. Draw a line between the notches on the inside (Fig. 12.3).

2. Place a 1″ (2.5cm) strip of fusible webbing along both 20″ (50.8cm) edges on the right side of the bag and fuse in place using the Teflon pressing sheet. Fold at the top of the webbing to the backside. Press the fold, using the Teflon pressing sheet on top to protect your iron. Then fold over 1″ (2.5cm) again, using the pressing sheet *between* the fusible webbing and the body of the bag.

3. Mark a line down the length of this piece 6¼″ (15.8cm) from each side, as shown in Fig. 12.4 to use later as guidelines for construction of the bag.

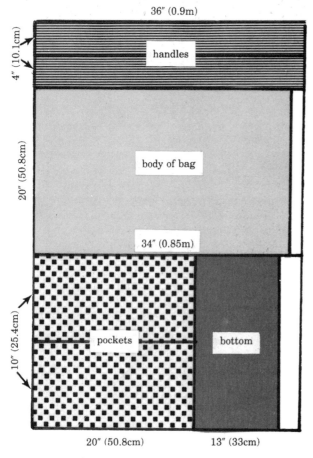

Fig. 12.2 Layout for the tote bag.

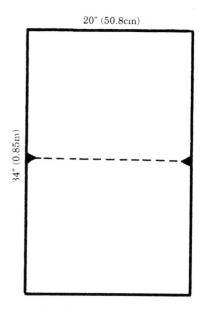

Fig. 12.3 Notch and mark the inside of the bag.

Fig. 12.4 Mark the outside of the bag.

Pockets: 10″ × 20″ (25.4cm × 50.8cm); cut 2

1. Use the ruler and marking pen to indicate stitching lines from top to bottom–6¼″ (15.8cm) from each side. Center area will be 7½″ (19.1cm).

2. Cut slits 1½″ (3.8cm) down from the top on these lines. Make a mark ¾″ (19.0mm) from the top and another ¾″ (19.0mm) down from the first. Draw lines through those marks across the top of the pockets (Fig. 12.5A). It is easier if you mark the middle section on the *back* of the fabric, so you'll be able to see the lines as

182

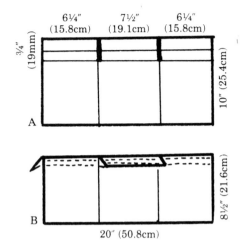

Fig. 12.5 Pocket construction.
A. Mark lines to indicate the
pockets. Then mark lines
across the pockets, ¾"
(19.0mm) and 1½" (3.8cm)
from the top. Cut down 1½"
(3.8cm) between the pockets. B.
Fold the tops of the side pockets
to the back, the top of the middle pocket to the front.

you fold. Fold on the lines as follows: Each
side should be folded twice toward the inside of the bag. The middle 7½" (19.1cm)
should be folded twice toward the front of
the fabric. This middle flap creates the top
of the frame.

3. Stitch across the top of all three pockets ⅛" (3.2mm) from the top edge. Do this
on both pocket pieces.

4. Then stitch across side pocket sections through all three layers of fabric at
⅛" (3.2mm) from each bottom fold. Finish
both side pockets on both pocket pieces
this way (Fig. 12.5B).

5. Open out the top of the middle sections on both pocket pieces to enable you to
stitch across the folds without stitching
them to the pockets. Stitch across the 7½"
(19.1cm) middle sections on both pocket
pieces at ⅛" (3.2mm) from each bottom

fold. This flap will create the top of the
frames in which you'll slip the 6" (15.2mm)
squares.

Handles: 4" × 36" (10.2cm × 0.9m); cut 2

1. Stitch down one long side 1" (2.5cm)
from edge. Fold. Do the same with the other side. (This stitching is used as a guide to
make folding the handles easier and more
accurate.) Bring folded edges together and
fold again, creating the 1" (2.5cm) wide
handles. Place strips of 1" (2.5cm) fusible
webbing inside the length of the handles
and press to fuse. The handle is four layers
(plus fusible webbing) thick (Fig. 12.6).

2. Topstitch both sides ⅛" (3.2mm) from

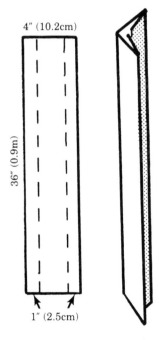

Fig. 12.6 Stitch down the length of the
handles 1" (2.5cm) from each side. Fold
down 1" (2.5cm) at each side, the length
of the handle. Then fold the handle in
half. Place strip of fusible webbing inside and press in place. Stitch the handles together.

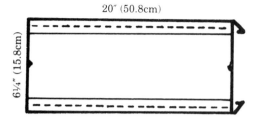

20" (50.8cm)

6¼" (15.8cm)

Fig. 12.7 Follow this diagram to
fold, mark and stitch the bottom
piece of the bag.

edge. Use Program 01 to move the needle
position if needed. Then sew ¼" (6.3mm)
in from those lines of stitches on both
sides.

Bottom: 12½" × 20"
(31.8cm × 50.8cm)

1. Fold over 1" (2.5cm) top and bottom
along the 20" (50.8cm) edges and topstitch
across ⅛" (3.2mm) from the fold. Draw a
line ¾" (19.0mm) from each fold.

2. Fold the bottom in half the long way
and notch on the fold on both sides, 6¼"
(15.9cm) from top and bottom (Fig. 12.7).

Assembly

1. First sew pockets to the bag. The
pockets will be 3" (7.5cm) from the top.
(Remember that the bag has been folded
over 2" (5.1cm) at the top. Measure from
the top of the last fold. Line up the markings, 6¼" (15.9cm) from each side on bag
and pockets and pin in place. Stitch on the
lines you've drawn to create pockets and,
using a ¼" (6.3mm) seam allowance, stitch
down each side and across the bottoms of
the pocket pieces.

2. Sew handles next. Find the center of
the bag by folding it double the long way.
Measure 3" (7.6cm) from the center to each
side of the bag and make a mark with the
water-erasable pen; 6" (15.2cm) will be
open in center. Using the 24" × 6" (60.9cm
× 15.2cm) ruler, draw guidelines through
these marks the length of the bag. Pin han-

dles in place outside those lines. Stitch
across the bottom of the handles and up,
⅛" (3.2mm) from the edge, on the existing
outside stitching. Extend your stitching all
the way to the top of the bag. Do this on
the next outside lines as well (you will often stitch on top of other lines of stitching). The top edge of the bag will not be
sewn down until later, but sew through
the folds as you attach the handles.

3. To make the open frame, stitch only
the top of the handles above the pockets on
both sides. Leave ¾" (19.0mm) around the
frame to insert workshop squares (Fig.
12.8).

4. Attach bottom next. Match notches
with those of the bag and pin the bottom in
place. Stitch over the ⅛" (3.2mm) stitching
line to ¾" (19.0mm) from each side of the
center pocket (see Fig. 12.8). *Do not* stitch
across the center pocket. Then stitch all
across the bottom piece on the ¾"
(19.0mm) mark. This will create the bottom of the frame. Double check. Is the
frame done correctly? Be sure you can slip
a fabric square inside.

5. Finish the side edges of the bag with a
zigzag stitch (Fig. 12.9). Then put it all together. Fold at center bottom notches with
right sides together. Check to see that
pockets and bottom meet at each side.
Stitch in a ⅝" (15.9mm) seam line from top
to bottom. Now refold the top edge of the
bag and press in place to fuse. Topstitch in
place at the top edge and bottom fold.

6. Bag corners should be finished this
way: On the inside, pinch the bottom by
matching the side seam with the line
drawn across the inside of the bottom of
the bag (Fig. 12.10). Measure, on the seam
line, 2" (5.1cm) from the point. Draw a line
across. Be sure it is exact on each side so
stitching is perpendicular to the side
seams. Stitch on drawn line for corners.
This forms the bottom of the bag. If you
wish to cut a piece of ⅛" (3.2mm) Masonite
or linoleum tile to fit the bottom, do so now
before you line your bag.

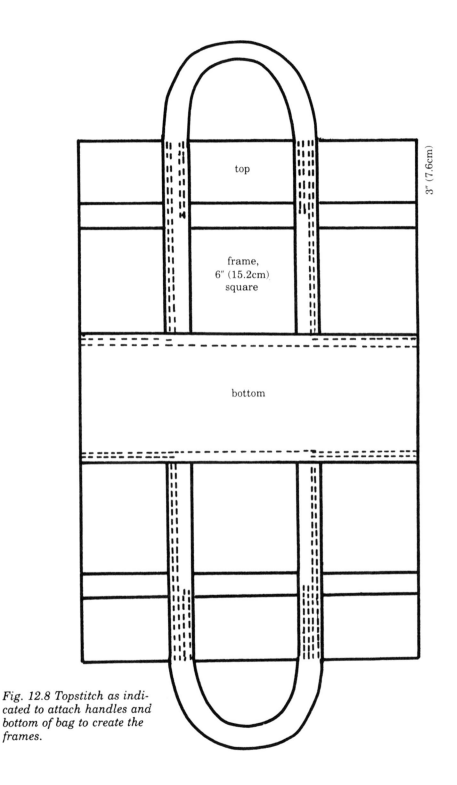

top

frame,
6″ (15.2cm)
square

bottom

3″ (7.6cm)

Fig. 12.8 Topstitch as indicated to attach handles and
bottom of bag to create the
frames.

185

Fig. 12.9 Finish the edges with zigzag stitches. With right sides together, stitch each side of the tote bag.

Fig. 12.10 Make the tote bag corners by stitching lines perpendicular to the side seams, 2" (5.1cm) up from the points.

7. Press one side of four adhesive-backed Velcro dots into the four corners of the frame.

Lining

If you line your bag, create the lining as if making another bag. Do not include bottom, pockets or handles. However, if you wish to add pockets to the lining, then cut out two pieces of 10" × 20" (25.4cm × 50.8cm) fabric, the same size as the bag pockets. At the top of each pocket piece, turn over 1" (2.5cm) two times and sew down at the top and at the fold. Press up 1" (2.5cm) at the bottom. Place the pocket pieces 3" (7.6cm) from the top of the lining and pin in place. Sew across the bottom of the pocket at the fold and ¾" (19.0mm) from the first stitching line. (The double line of stitching will add strength to the pockets.) Then attach the pockets to the sides of the lining by stitching down on each side with a ¼" (6.3mm) seam allowance. With a ruler and water-erasable marker, draw lines down the pocket pieces to indicate where you will divide the fabric for pockets. Stitch those in place.

Sew up the sides of the lining, using a ⅝" (15.9mm) seam allowance) and create the bottom corner. Fold over the top as you did for the bag. I use the double fold for stability.

Whip stitch invisibly by hand around the top to keep the lining and bag together. With heavy canvas, you may prefer to make the lining and then place wrong sides together (bag and lining) and machine stitch around the top.

AFTERWORD

Know Your Pfaff could go on forever, as there is no way to include, in one book, everything that can be accomplished by your machine.

I hope you're inspired to experiment, to fill your notebook with samples, and to take those long-cuts, choosing decorative over mundane.

A Brief History of Pfaff Sewing Machines

In the old minstrel country of Germany, the area of the Palatinate surrounding Kaiserslautern, instrument makers were much in demand. Johannes Pfaff (1776–1829) was a turner by trade, specializing in the manufacture of woodwind instruments. Six of his seven sons also became instrument makers or musicians: Franz carried on the woodwind tradition and one of his brothers, Georg Michael Pfaff (1823–1893), manufactured brass instruments. During a visit to the World Fair in London in 1850, where he exhibited his own instruments, Georg had the opportunity to study a new machine that was able to sew. He became fascinated with the possibilities of sewing machines.

In 1862, he built his first sewing machine in his own workshop: it was not made for sewing textiles, but for leathers. Georg recognized the potential of such a machine in the nearby area of Pirmasens, the center of the German shoe-manufacturing trade, so he changed his production entirely to sewing machines. His company, which grew from a very modest beginning, is today one of the largest sewing machine manufacturers in Europe and is represented in more than 130 countries of the world.

Between 1863 and 1871, Pfaff built long-shuttle sewing machines for the household and craft trades, but it was not until 1872 that Pfaff appeared as a brand name. Between the years 1882 and 1891, annual production exceeded 25,000 machines, necessitating a new factory. By 1910, Pfaff had built a million sewing machines.

The company began production of rotary hook sewing machines and introduced a high-speed zigzag machine in the 1920s. The demand for the household zigzag machines increased rapidly until 1941. During World War II, the factory at Kaiserslautern was destroyed. During the rebuilding, the factory was expanded and now included an investment foundry, enabling Pfaff to manufacture many of the small parts by means of investment castings. This eliminated the more expensive machining of small parts on the lathe, and is, in fact, much more consistent and accurate.

In 1951, the first aluminum household sewing machines were introduced, making possible a truly portable machine head.

Pfaff's takeover of the Gritzner-Kayser, AG, facility in Karlsruhe-Durlach in 1957 paved the way for an eventual separation of the industrial and household manufacturing plants in 1969–70. It was about this time that Pfaff introduced the 1200 series, the 1222 being the first electronically controlled push-button machine. It also had a unique feature in its dual-feed system, eliminating many problems when sewing newer synthetic fabrics. In 1982, the company introduced its first programmed machine with microprocessors. This was soon followed by a second version, the 1471 Creative, the most advanced sewing machine on the market today.

Pfaff Presser Feet and Attachments

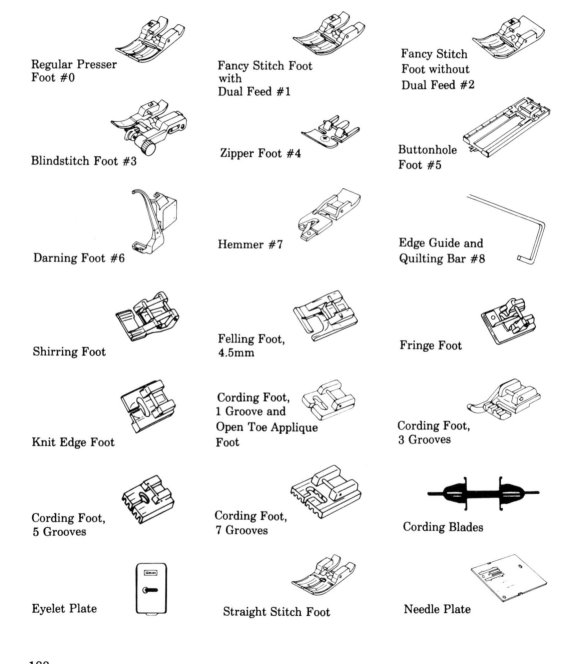

Regular Presser
Foot #0

Fancy Stitch Foot
with
Dual Feed #1

Fancy Stitch
Foot without
Dual Feed #2

Blindstitch Foot #3

Zipper Foot #4

Buttonhole
Foot #5

Darning Foot #6

Hemmer #7

Edge Guide and
Quilting Bar #8

Shirring Foot

Felling Foot,
4.5mm

Fringe Foot

Knit Edge Foot

Cording Foot,
1 Groove and
Open Toe Applique
Foot

Cording Foot,
3 Grooves

Cording Foot,
5 Grooves

Cording Foot,
7 Grooves

Cording Blades

Eyelet Plate

Straight Stitch Foot

Needle Plate

Sources of Supply

Pfaff Information

Pfaff American Sales Corp.
610 Winters Ave.
Paramus, NJ 07653
Owner's Manual, videocasettes, additional stitch programs, information on local dealers

(**Note**: The following listings were adapted with permission from *The Complete Book of Machine Embroidery* by Robbie and Tony Fanning [Chilton, 1986].)

Threads

Note: Ask your local retailer or send a pre-addressed stamped envelope to the companies below to find out where to buy their threads.

Extra-fine

Assorted threads
Robison-Anton Textile Co.
175 Bergen Blvd.
Fairview, NJ 07022

DMC 100% cotton, Sizes 30 and 50
The DMC Corporation
107 Trumbull Street
Elizabeth, NJ 07206

Dual-Duty Plus Extra-fine, cotton-wrapped polyester
J&PCoats/Coats & Clark
30 Patewood Dr., Ste. 351
Greenville, SC 29615

Iris 100% silk—see Zwicky

Madeira threads
Madeira threads
56 Primrose Drive
O'Shea Industrial Park
Laconia, NH 03246

Mettler Metrosene Fine Machine Embroidery cotton, Size 60/2
Swiss-Metrosene, Inc.
7780 Quincy Street
Willowbrook, IL 60521

Mez Alcazar 100% Viscose rayon
Pfaff American Sales Corp.
610 Winters Ave.
Paramus, NJ 07653

Natesh 100% rayon, lightweight
Aardvark Adventures
PO Box 2449
Livermore, CA 94550

Paradise 100% rayon
D&E Distributing
199 N. El Camino Real #F-242
Encinitas, CA 92024

Sulky 100% rayon, Sizes 30 and 40
Speed Stitch, Inc.
PO Box 3472
Port Charlotte, FL 33949

Zwicky 100% cotton, Size 30/2
White Sewing Machine Co.
11750 Berea Rd.
Cleveland, OH 44111

Ordinary

Dual Duty Plus, cotton-wrapped polyester— *see* Dual Duty Plus Extra-fine

Also Natesh heavyweight, Zwicky in cotton and polyester, Mettler Metrosene in 30/2, 40/3, 50/3, and 30/3, and Metrosene Plus

Metallic

YLI Corporation
45 West 300 North
Provo, UT 84601

Troy Thread & Textile Corp.
2300 W. Diversey Ave.
Chicago, IL 60647
Free catalog

Machine-Embroidery Supplies
(hoops, threads, patterns, books, etc.)

A–1 Sew Craft
12359 Cavell Avenue
Champlin, MN 55316
Pfaff videos, books, patterns

Aardvark Adventures
PO Box 2449
Livermore, CA 94550
　　　Also publishes "Aardvark Territorial
　　　Enterprise"

Clotilde Inc.
1909 SW First Ave.
Ft. Lauderdale, FL 33315

Craft Gallery Ltd.
PO Box 8319
Salem, MA 01971

D&E Distributing
199 N. El Camino Real #F-242
Encinitas, CA 92024

Verna Holt's Machine Stitchery
PO Box 236
Hurricane, UT 84734

Nancy's Notions
PO Box 683
Beaver Dam, WI 53916
　　　Catalog $.60 in stamps

Patty Lou Creations
Rt 2, Box 90-A
Elgin, OR 97827

Sew-Art International
PO Box 550
Bountiful, UT 84010
　　　Catalog $2

Speed Stitch, Inc.
PO Box 3472
Port Charlotte, FL 33952
　　　Catalog $2

SewCraft
Box 1869
Warsaw, IN 46580
　　　Also publishes newsletter/catalog

Treadleart
25834 Narbonne Ave., Ste. I
Lomita, CA 90717

Sewing Machine Supplies

The Button Shop
PO Box 1065
Oak Park, IL 60304
　　　Presser feet

Sewing Emporium
1087 Third Avenue
Chula Vista, CA 92010
　　　Presser feet, accessories

Singer Westbank Sewing Center
1800 Stumpf Blvd.
Gretna, LA 70056
　　　Mini-Serger attachment for any ma-
　　　chine

Miscellaneous

Applications
871 Fourth Ave.
Sacramento, CA 95818
　　　Release Paper for appliqué

Berman Leathercraft
145 South St.
Boston, MA 02111
　　　Leather

Boycan's Craft and Art Supplies
PO Box 897
Sharon, PA 16146
　　　Plastic needlepoint canvas

Cabin Fever Calicoes
PO Box 54
Center Sandwich, NH 03227

Clearbrook Woolen Shop
PO Box 8
Clearbrook, VA 22624
　　　Ultrasuede scraps

The Fabric Carr
170 State St.
Los Altos, CA 94022
　　　Sewing gadgets

Folkwear
Box 3798
San Rafael, CA 94912
　　　Timeless fashion patterns – $1 cata-
　　　log

The Green Pepper Inc.
941 Olive Street
Eugene, OR 97401
　　　Outdoor fabrics, patterns – $1 catalog

Home-Sew
Bethlehem, PA 18018
　　　Lace – $.25 catalog

Kwik-Sew
3000 Washington Ave. N
Minneapolis, MN 55411
　　　Knit and sweatshirt patterns

Libby's Creations
PO Box 16800 Ste. 180
Mesa, AZ 85202
　　　Horizontal spool holder

LJ Originals, Inc.
516 Sumac Pl.
DeSoto, TX 75115
    TransGraph

Lore Lingerie
3745 Overland Ave.
Los Angeles, CA 90034
    1 lb. of silk remnants, $9.45

Osage Country Quilt Factory
400 Walnut
Overbrook, KS 66524
    Washable fabric spray glue

The Pellon Company
119 West 40th St.
New York, NY 10018
    Machine appliqué supplies

The Perfect Notion
115 Maple St.
Toms River, NJ 08753
    Sewing supplies

Salem Industries, Inc.
PO Box 43027
Atlanta, GA 30336
    Olfa cutters, rulers

Sew Easy
2701 W. 1800 S
Logan, UT 84321
    Sweatshirt patterns

Solar-Kist Corp.
PO Box 273
LaGrange, IL 60525
    Teflon pressing sheet

Stacy Industries, Inc.
38 Passaic St.
Wood-Ridge, NJ 07075
    Teflon pressing sheet

Stretch & Sew
PO Box 185
Eugene, OR 97440
    Knit and sweatshirt patterns

Summa Design
Box 24404
Dayton, OH 45424
    Charted designs for knitting needle
    machine sewing

Susan of Newport
Box 3107
Newport Beach, CA 92663
    Ribbons and laces

Tandy Leather Co.
PO Box 791
Ft. Worth, TX 76101
    Leather

Taylor-Made Designs
PO Box 31024
Phoenix, AZ 85046
    Sweatshirt patterns

Theta's School of Sewing
2508 N.W. 39th Street
Oklahoma City, OK 73112
    Charted designs for knitting needle
    machine sewing, smocking directions
    and supplies for the machine

Magazines
(write for rates)

Aardvark Territorial Enterprise
PO Box 2449
Livermore, CA 94550
    Newspaper jammed with all kinds of
    information about all kinds of em-
    broidery, design, and things to order.
    I ordered the gold rings from them.

Creative Needle
1500 Jupiter Road
Lookout Mountain, GA 37350

disPatch
1042 E. Baseline
Tempe, AZ 85283
    Newspaper about quilting and ma-
    chine arts

Fiberarts
50 College St.
Asheville, NC 28801
    Gallery of the best fiber artists, in-
    cluding those who work in machine
    stitchery.

Needlecraft for Today
4949 Byers
Ft. Worth, TX 76109
    Creative uses of the sewing machine

SewCraft
Box 1869
Warsaw, IN 46580
    Newspaper and catalog combination
    containing machine embroidery arti-
    cles, designs and supplies.

Sew News
PO Box 1790
Peoria, IL 61656
 Monthly tabloid, mostly about gar-
 ment sewing

Threads
Box 355

Newton, CT 06470
 Magazine on all fiber crafts

Treadleart
25834 Narbonne Ave., Ste. 1
Lomita, CA 90717
 Bimonthly about machine embroidery

Bibliography

Alexander, Eugenie, *Fabric Pictures*, Mills and Boon Ltd., London, 1967.

Ashley, Clifford W., *The Ashley Book of Knots*, Doubleday & Co., 1944.

Bennet, dj, *Machine Embroidery with Style*, Madrona Publishers, 1980.

Brag, Rachel, *No-Sew Customized Sweatshirts* (Country Thread Designs, RR1, Box 27, Kindred, ND 58051), 1986.

Butler, Anne, *Machine Stitches*, BT Batsford, Ltd., 1976.

Clucas, Joy, *Your Machine for Embroidery*, G. Bell & Sons, 1975.

Coleman, Anne, *The Creative Sewing Machine*, BT Batsford, 1979.

Ericson, Lois, *Fabrics. . .Reconstructed* (Lois Ericson, Box 1680, Tahoe City, CA 95730), 1985.

———, *Belts. . .Waisted Sculpture*, 1984.

Fanning, Robbie and Tony, *The Complete Book of Machine Quilting*, Chilton Book Co., 1980.

———, *The Complete Book of Machine Embroidery*, Chilton Book Co., 1986.

Gray, Jennifer, *Machine Embroidery*, Van Nostrand Reinhold, 1973.

Hall, Carolyn, *The Sewing Machine Craft Book*, Van Nostrand Reinhold, 1980.

Harding, Valerie, *Textures in Embroidery*, Watson-Guptill, New York, 1977.

Hazen, Gale Grigg, *Sew Sane* (The Sewing Place, 100 W. Rincon Ave., Ste. 105, Campbell, CA 95008; $14.95 postpaid), 1985.

Hogue, Refa D., *Machine Edgings* (c/o Treadleart, 25834 Narbonne Avenue, Lomita, CA 90717).

Hoover, Doris and Nancy Welch, *Tassels* (out-of-print), 1978.

James, Irene, *Sewing Specialties*, I. M. James Enterprises, 1982.

Lawrence and Clotilde, *Sew Smart*, IBC Publishing Co., 1984.

———, Supplement, IBC Publishing Co., 1984.

Macor, Alida, *And Sew On*, Alida Macor, 1985.

McNeill, Moyra, *Machine Embroidery — Lace and See-Through Techniques*, BT Batsford, 1985.

Mulari, Mary, *Designer Sweatshirts* (Box 87, Aurora, MN 55705), 1986.

Nall, Mary Lou, *Mary Lou's Sewing Tchniques* (c/o *Treadleart*, 25834 Narbonne Avenue, Lomita, CA 90717).

Nicholas, Annwen, *Embroidery in Fashion*, Watson-Guptill, 1975.

Ota, Kimi, *Sashiko Quilting* (Kimi Ota, 10300 61st Ave. So., Seattle, Washington 98178), 1981.

Pullen, Martha, *French Hand Sewing by Machine* (518 Madison St., Huntsville, AL 35801), 1985.

Sewing Specialty Fabrics, Singer Sewing Reference Library, 1986.

Shaeffer, Claire B., *The Complete Book of Sewing Short Cuts*, Sterling Publishing Co., Inc., 1984.

Short, Eirian, *Quilting*, BT Batsford, London, 1983.

Skjerseth, Douglas Neil, *Stitchology*, Seth Publications (PO Box 1606, Novato, CA 94947), 1979.

Thompson, Sue, *Decorative Dressmaking*, Rodale Press, 1985.

Warren, Virena, *Landscape in Embroidery*, BT Batsford, 1986.

Wiechec, Philomena, *Celtic Quilt Designs*, Celtic Design Co., 1980.

Zieman, Nancy, *The Busy Woman's Sewing Book*, Nancy's Notions Ltd., 1984.

Index

196